This new series is de[...] history of the world's special forces. These [...] operate in small tea[...] and cause havoc out[...] Today's special forc[...] tacular success of th[...] embassy siege, the [...] countless actions thr[...] international terrorism. But they have their origins in the Second World War. This unique series traces their development.

Special Forces Library

D. I. HARRISON

These Men are Dangerous

The Special Air Service at War

GRAFTON BOOKS

A Division of the Collins Publishing Group

LONDON GLASGOW
TORONTO SYDNEY AUCKLAND

Grafton Books
A Division of the Collins Publishing Group
8 Grafton Street, London W1X 3LA

Published by Grafton Books 1990

First published in Great Britain by
Cassell & Company Ltd. 1957

A CIP catalogue record for this
book is available from the British Library

ISBN 0-586-20776-7

Printed and bound in Great Britain by
Collins, Glasgow

Set in Times

'. . . Captured SAS troops must be handed over at once to the nearest Gestapo unit . . . these men are very dangerous, and the presence of SAS troops in any area must be immediately reported . . . they must be ruthlessly exterminated.'

Adolf Hitler

Contents

MAPS

Introduction

Down the forest ride and into the clearing swept the drenching rain. The trees bowed and swayed in the wind. Tense, the little group huddled closer together. From the miniature radio the opening bars of *Sur le Pont d'Avignon* blared out, then faded, rising and falling with each swing of the improvised aerial slung above the rain-soaked parachute that served as a tent. There was a brief pause, then the calm, clear voice for which they had been waiting:

'Hello Sabu. Hello Sabu. Message for . . .'

From a secret, powerful BBC transmitter somewhere in England orders were going out to the men of Britain's Special Air Service hundreds of miles behind German front lines in France. Dotted about in small parties all over France, they listened intently to the apparently meaningless confusion of letters that poured over the ether. The little group in the forest . . . the man standing by his jeep, one hand on his machine-gun, waiting, watching the road for a German convoy . . . the men hiding in the cellar of the farmhouse while in the kitchen above their heads German officers sat down to eat . . .

'Hello Sabu. Hello Sabu . . .'

Code experts of the German Intelligence swore as they were handed the latest batch of messages intercepted by their monitor stations – and started once again on the impossible task of trying to break them down. Far into the night they sweated and worked, trying to wrest from them some meaning, some small clue; while men of the SAS were busy supplying the answers, blowing up this or that railway line, mining key roads along which German reinforcements were being rushed to the Normandy beach-heads.

These men, with the badge of a flying dagger and the motto *Who Dares Wins*, were only too well-known to the Germans. Started in September 1941 by Lieutenant-Colonel (then Lieutenant) David Stirling, DSO and Lieutenant Jock Lewes with seventy-five men of the Middle East Commando, the audacious exploits of the Special Air Service behind Rommel's lines in the desert soon became a byword among Germans and Italians.

Swooping swiftly and silently out of the desert they carried out their blitz raids and then, just as suddenly, vanished again into the uncharted regions south of the coast road. Axis convoys, driving along unsuspectingly in the safety of their own back areas, suddenly found themselves under withering fire from the machine-guns of SAS jeeps. Planes, dispersed on their aerodromes, burst into flames as SAS time-bombs exploded. In all, more than four hundred enemy planes were destroyed by these adventurous raiding-parties.

Men of the SAS came from every walk of civilian life. My own colleagues included a fish-and-chip shop owner, a poacher, a dock labourer, a fireman, a prison warder and a merchant banker. Their ages ranged from under twenty to over fifty. All were volunteers drawn from a score of different regiments, but 'tough guys' found no place in the organization. As David Stirling said: 'Most of the work is night work and all of it demands courage, fitness and determination in the highest degree; but also, and just as important, discipline, skill, intelligence and training.

'Many of these characteristics can be acquired. Training is designed to foster them. But this is only possible with really keen men. It is, therefore, no good men volunteering for this type of work for the novelty of it or for a change. We need the type of man who genuinely feels he has a special aptitude for work of this nature.'

Training was thorough. Every man was a parachutist, but to the men of the SAS parachuting was only one of many ways of getting to the area of operation. A thorough knowledge of explosives was required – and a well-developed flair for sabotage of all kinds. No matter how thorough his training, the expert saboteur must have that peculiar kind of kink, that instinct that tells him where a few grains of sand will do the most damage. Long marches with heavy loads developed stamina.

Everything possible was done to encourage individuality and initiative. Officers and men received the same training so that, in the event of only one man of a party surviving, he should be equipped to go ahead and finish the job himself. A new relationship was fostered between officers and men, based on mutual respect and real friendship. That, with the ability to live with one's fellows, was indispensable when small groups of men were required to live, sometimes for months at a stretch, in the heart of enemy territory. Never before were the opposites of individuality and team work so successfully wedded together.

The end of the desert campaign found David Stirling a prisoner of war. Jock Lewes had found a desert grave – killed by dive-bombing Stukas while returning from a raid.

1

'Who Dares Wins'

I had been hanging about too long at the training depot on the shores of Egypt's Bitter Lakes waiting to get back to my unit, now somewhere west of Alamein. I was desperate with boredom and ready to volunteer for anything.

'Why not go along and see David Stirling at Kabrit? If the SAS want anyone they just take them.'

The speaker was a chance acquaintance to whom I had been pouring out my heart. And now here I was, waiting outside the mess. My valise and suitcase lay forlornly on the sand where I had dumped them while I walked up and down impatient to be away. All goodbyes had been said. I wanted only to be away from the place where I had stagnated too long. I took the scrap of paper out of my pocket and read it again.

'To Lieutenant Harrison, Cheshire Regiment.

'You have been accepted for the 1st SAS Regiment and an immediate posting has been applied for. You will be collected at two o'clock this afternoon.'

A long, low, powerful-looking car shot off the road and tore over in a flurry of dust and sand to pull up beside me.

'Harrison?' The lieutenant at the wheel shot the question at me. 'OK. Sling your bags in and jump in. Hold tight.'

With a roar the car leaped forward to regain the road. Round went the needle . . . fifty, sixty, seventy. A three-tonner coming towards us grew rapidly from a pinpoint until it seemed to fill the road. With a crack like a whip it was gone. I glanced at the man next to me. He seemed blissfully unaware of everything: me, to whom he had spoken not a word since his first greeting; the rest of the traffic; even the road which we had already left twice, inadvertently or not I did not know. I told myself I would cheerfully throw myself out of aeroplanes for the rest of my life if only I got to Kabrit alive.

Rounding a corner at speed, I caught sight of rows of tents standing out dazzlingly against the fawn brown of the sand. Tall scaffolding structures towered above them looking for all the world like giant swings. I had a sudden empty feeling in the pit of my stomach as I gazed up at the rickety platform from which I would soon be hurling myself into space.

In the orderly room everyone was charming and delightfully vague.

'Harrison? Yes, that's right. I think you will be going to A Squadron. Did hear they are going up to Syria tomorrow. Ski-ing, or something . . .

'The mess sergeant will fix you up with a tent. You may find someone over there from A . . . give you some griff about tomorrow.' Then, as an afterthought, 'But I think you'll find they are all in Cairo today.'

Tea was a solitary meal. I do not know what I had expected but, for all that happened, I might just as well not have existed. I was delighted, therefore, when a voice hailed me from the bar. 'Just arrived? My name's Davis – Peter Davis.'

'A Squadron?' I asked, introducing myself.

He shook his head. 'No. I'm expecting to go up the blue to join B on Monday. 'Fraid I can't stay too long. Got to pack, and clean my gun.'

'Mind if I talk to you while you pack?'

'Not at all. Come on over.'

From the table in his tent he picked up an unusual-looking weapon. Unusual, that is, to me. 'German,' he explained briefly. 'Schmeisser machine pistol. Look at it. Lovely weapon.'

As he cleaned it Peter told me about Colonel Stirling who was 'up the blue' on operations; of Major 'Paddy' Mayne, tall, broad, young Irish leader of A Squadron; of daring raids hundreds of miles behind the enemy lines. Eagerly I drank it all in – and wondered what I had let myself in for.

Now, too, for the first time I was able to examine more closely the badge of my new unit. In the form of a dark blue cloth shield, it had embroidered on it a silver dagger with pale blue wings. Across the lower part of the blade, in a scroll, were the words *Who Dares Wins*. The parachute wings of the SAS, unlike those of the Parachute Regiment, had a straight top edge and were worked in light and dark blue silk with, in the centre and almost unnoticed, a small white parachute. Some of these wings, I had noticed, were worn on the arm and some on the left breast. Peter explained:

'You get them on the arm when you have qualified as a parachutist. We call them operational wings when they are worn on the breast. The CO awards them for three successful operations behind enemy lines. Believe me, the privilege of wearing op. wings is more sought-after than any medal.'

The following morning I found another friend. Like myself, Alec Muirhead had arrived the day before and had been posted to A Squadron. He, too, had heard that we might be going to Syria. We returned to our tents after breakfast in an almost deserted mess tent to find our kits had gone. Then we heard the noise of revving engines. By the road a line of three-ton trucks was drawn up.

Acting on instinct we raced over to them. 'A Squadron?' we chorused.

'That's right,' yelled back one of the drivers above the noise of the engines. 'Hop in. We're off to Syria.'

Behind and far below us the roof-tops of Tripoli still basked in the late afternoon sunshine. Beyond, the sea shimmered and flashed like tinsel. The trucks were making slow progress up the long road winding its way into the mountains of Lebanon.

Ahead, the purple and white of the furthest peaks melted away into the dull, leaden grey of the sky. Snow, the people at the last village had predicted. Plenty of snow. Every village was the same. There would be snow before nightfall. Already there had been much snow. The passes had been closed. True, a few cars had got through yesterday, but now . . . They shrugged their shoulders. There would be more snow.

Almost hermetically sealed in the cab of my truck, I could still feel the cold stealing over me as we climbed steadily out of the valley. The fragrant-smelling, sun-drenched orange groves of Palestine, through which we had driven only the day before, were no more than a memory. For over an hour we continued climbing, the road twisting and turning more and more as we drove on towards the heart of the range. Almost unnoticed the shadows lengthened while, overhead, the clouds heavy with snow billowed and curled round the mountain peaks.

Suddenly my heart went cold. The truck in front slithered and poised on the edge of what was now no more than a narrow track, while earth and stones went spinning madly into space. Then with a lurch it tipped over and came to an uneasy rest on its axle while the rear wheel screamed angrily over a drop of several hundred feet. Gingerly the men in the back clambered over the

tailboard to safety. The truck ahead of it, halted by the
urgent hooting of horns, backed up. While we all held our
breath it began slowly to tow the other from its precarious
roost.

As we moved off again the first snow-flakes fluttered
gently to the ground. Soon they were coming thick and
fast. Driving was doubly dangerous now. For the first
time for what seemed hours my driver spoke. 'A ruddy
blizzard, a goat-track with an almighty drop to perdition
just a few inches away, and darkness coming on. We'll
have to get a jilty move on.' He relapsed into silence
again and together we peered anxiously through the
falling snow. One slip . . .

Along the treacherous, crumbling track, over jagged
ravines and round icy bends the trucks rumbled on until,
in the fast-fading light, we arrived at the village of
Bercharre, five thousand feet above sea-level. Somewhere
above us among the snows nestled the famous ancient
Cedars of Lebanon – and the Middle East Ski School.

The column came to a halt. Frozen and aching with
cramp we stumbled out into the deep snow. All along the
column men were swinging their arms for warmth and
trying to rub the stiffness out of their legs. A figure
loomed up out of the darkness. It was Alec, muffled up
to the eyebrows.

'The people here say we can't get through,' he grunted.
'Snowed up. But we're having a shot at it.'

With that he disappeared into the darkness again. I
climbed back into the cab. By now it was as black as
pitch. Slowly the trucks passed through the village. The
snow, which had eased up while we had been halted, now
swept down on us with all the force of a gale. All we
could see were the wheel-marks of the leading vehicles:
on either side just inky blackness. It was like driving along
a tight-rope, and all the time the wind howled furiously

round us as though threatening to hurl us to the rocks below. For an hour and a half the nightmare ride continued, then we halted again. Above the shrieking of the wind I could hear the voices of men shouting, and the angry revving of engines.

A figure staggered up, leaning against the wind. 'Taken the wrong road,' he bawled across. 'Got to turn round and go back to Bercharre. They've got one helluva job down there' – he thumbed in the direction of the head of the convoy – 'turning on a hairpin bend. Just as likely to slide over the edge.'

Two hours later we were back in the village. Somewhere above us a door must have been opened. For a moment a shaft of yellow light cut through the falling snow, and was gone. We waited. Down the line came the word: 'Leave the trucks where they are and fall in by the side of the road. We're spending the night at the monastery.'

The head of the monastery was kindly-faced and courteous. The snow-plough, he explained, would be down from the Ski School in the morning. Till then we were to be his guests. Soon, from the cloisters, came the roaring of the petrol cookers, the shuffling of feet and the clanking of mess tins. Supper was nearly ready.

2

School for Ski Troops

Leaping out of bed, I strode quickly over to the window and flung open the casements. Outside, the sun shone brilliantly on the white even crispness of the snow. Of the previous night's storm nothing remained except that deep untrodden snow. From a distance, I heard the familiar sound of the petrol cookers roaring away down below. I opened the door of the tiny cell and the smell of bacon, wafted up the stairs and along the cold stone passages, reminded me that I was hungry. Over breakfast we heard that the snow-plough was already on its way down from the Ski School.

It was nearly eleven o'clock, however, before we got away. We had a last view of the monastery as the trucks pulled themselves with a good deal of groaning up the steep hill above the village. Then we were alone with the sky, the sun and the snow-covered mountain-slopes. Wherever we looked there was nothing to break the monotony of the dazzling white of the scenery except our trucks in their dark brown desert camouflage.

For over an hour we struggled up the hills, till Bercharre was little more than a grey smudge of streets far below. We had negotiated the first of a series of wicked hairpin bends, with nothing but a low stone wall between us and destruction, when there came a cheery shout from somewhere above us. Although we craned our necks, there was nothing to be seen but the brilliant white of snow-bound mountain-sides.

Then, about thirty yards away, something – or someone – moved. Slowly, like some spirit of the snows, the figure

drew nearer, gliding silently along. He was dressed from
head to foot in loose-fitting white garments which had
accounted for his earlier invisibility. The polished brown
of his skis was hidden beneath two inches or so of still-
virgin snow. Only now, as he came gliding along the ledge
above us, did the tips of his skis break the surface like
twin periscopes.

'You've got about another half-mile,' he called out.
'Mind if I hook on to the back of your truck? It's much
easier.' He grinned. 'I'm one of the instructors. Saw your
trucks from up there.' He waved vaguely in the air with
one of his sticks.

We started firing eager questions at him, and he was
still talking when the trucks pulled up in front of a bleak,
grey stone building. In peace-time a hotel catering for the
hundreds of ski-ing enthusiasts who yearly made the
pilgrimage to the Cedars, it looked now more like a
barracks. There were Nissen huts on the flat roof and,
above the door, the plain, painted legend *Middle East Ski
School*.

As I passed through the door into the dimly lit interior,
the chill of damp, cold stone hit me with a shock. After
the cold of the journey I had expected roaring fires and
blistering radiators. I had not stopped to think of the
difficulties of supplying such a place, 6,700 feet up in the
Lebanese mountains.

After lunch Major Riddell, the chief instructor, offered
to take a few of us out and show us around. His eyes
glinted keenly from a lean, weather-beaten face as he
explained: 'Of course, work does not really start until
tomorrow, but if you would like to go out on one of the
slopes . . . ?'

We had drawn skis and clothing from the store and
been shown how to put them on. Now, sweating profusely
and slipping and sliding all over the place, we made our

way painstakingly up the road to the top of Chapel Hill – a hundred and fifty yards of sheer agony. By the time I reached the top the lesson had started.

'Now when doing the kick turn,' Major Riddell was saying, 'you kick one ski up, like this.' He demonstrated, digging the back of one of his skis into the snow, tip pointing to the sky.

'We'll take it stage by stage. Now all do just as I have done. Ready? All together. Up!'

I gritted my teeth, steadied myself on my sticks, took a deep breath, then – up! I swung the ski skywards, followed it, describing a far from graceful arc through the air, and with a thud was down, snow in my eyes, my ears, everywhere. All around me was a struggling mass of bodies, sticks and skis. We struggled to our feet and started again, practising it again and again until we could do it and still stand up.

'All right now. We'll just have a shot at going down this slope.'

During the next six weeks we were to go down that slope many times, in gentle traverses from side to side. Now Major Riddell pointed his skis straight at the bottom and pushed off. In a flurry of snow he arrived safely in the valley below. Grinning broadly, he called up to us. 'Come along. Nothing to be frightened of.'

Somewhat dubiously we pointed our skis, and pushed off. Immediately the chapel vanished, the trees in the valley vanished. Everything vanished in a mad swirl of white.

Next morning the course started in earnest. We learned to walk and turn. Like pompous penguins we 'herringboned' up hills. We learned the easy way of traversing up hills, and still lost pints of good honest sweat. Back in the hotel we had to wear greatcoats and mufflers to keep warm. In the mornings we woke to find our wet ski clothes, even our boots, frozen stiff.

With snow all round us we soon began to forget the desert with its heat, dust and flies. And sometimes as we sat in our rooms huddled round the cold radiators we wondered why we were there. The official story was that it was a reward for good work done in the desert, but as the days passed, there came a spate of rumours.

The Germans were pressing hard through the Caucasus towards the Russian oilfields at Baku. We, so the rumour had it, were to be taken through the Black Sea by submarine and landed behind the German lines, here to carry on our work of harassing their communications. Sweeping down from above the snow-line we were to ambush his troops, blow up his supplies and report on his movements. We could get no confirmation of this, but neither were there any denials. From then on there was an edge to our training.

After two and a half weeks we could climb a hill with moderate ease, and glide down again with a fair measure of confidence. For six and a half days a week we slaved at it, gliding, falling, picking ourselves up again. Cursing and sweating up the hills – an hour to get up and five minutes to come down. There were no cable railways. It was hard, uphill work with an occasional brief but exhilarating dash across the snow into the peace of the valley. For six and a half days, for on Wednesday afternoons we were free. And on Wednesday afternoons, immediately after lunch, in twos and threes we drifted down to the locker rooms. For a while bedlam reigned and the rooms echoed and re-echoed to the sounds of laughter: strong, hearty, good-natured laughter, the chatter of small talk and the shouts of men in high spirits. Gradually silence came again as, still in our twos and threes, we glided away to spend the afternoon on the nursery slopes, or to attempt that run we had noticed the other day but had not been allowed to try. The snow was in our blood.

On the third Wednesday after our arrival I found myself trudging along by Alec Muirhead's side, rucksack on my back and a good deal of foreboding in my heart. Behind and below us lay the water tower that served the school and the village, looking for all the world like a small pebble. To the right, a small dark smudge – the sacred Cedars of Lebanon. Immediately behind us our zigzag tracks showed black where they had trapped the only shadows among that vast expanse of white.

Ahead of us the edge of the snow seemed to cut a black line across the sky. It had been aptly named False Crest. From where we stood it seemed we could go no further. It was the edge of the world. For another five minutes we trudged on in silence. At the crest we would rest.

Standing squarely across the slope we removed our skis. Many a man has come to grief by neglecting that precaution; has slipped his foot from the trap, only to see his ski go hurtling away by itself down the slippery mountainside.

'How far now?' I was sweating freely.

'We've come about a thousand. That leaves us something over two thousand feet to go.' Alec looked towards the far ridge. 'A bit windy up there, by the looks of it.'

'Yes, and cold,' I added bitterly, 'with the last five hundred feet sheer ice. And what do we get when we get there?'

'The view, old boy, the view from ten thousand feet.'

Two days later we had to pass the elementary test. The sun shone vividly from an ice-blue sky. Three thousand feet above us, wisps of white cloud trailed across the surrounding peaks. Wearing goggles to protect our eyes from the dangerous glare we winged our way down Chapel Hill, through the clump of sturdy cedars towards the examination ground. All morning we climbed, executed kick turns, snow-plough turns. We glided, halted, ran along balancing first on one ski then on the other, till we were passed OK. Now I was lined up with about twenty others for the climax of the test – a three hundred-foot climb followed by a speed descent.

A whistle shrilled and we were off. Some took it the hard way, by direct ascent. Most, like myself, preferred the long easy traverses across the slope. Ten minutes later I was at the top, breathless but happy to know I had done it under time. Only the descent remained. I had studied that run down. I could go at it like a bull at a gate. That did not appeal. The alternative was a wide sweep round the hill, coming in to the finishing line almost at right angles to the course. But it meant steady judgement round the curves.

The whistle shrilled again. The starter's thumb jabbed at his stop-watch. Away we went. Gently, gently. Round the first curve all right. It was too easy. In front someone stumbled. Too late I swerved. I was over. Head first I ploughed into the soft snow, rolling over and over. One ski was wrenched from my foot and I had a brief glimpse of it careering down to the bottom, skimming lightly round the second curve. Sliding, rolling, I followed it at great speed, up the banking of the curve, and over the top.

That evening a short note was posted up to say that those who had failed in either the ascent or descent would be re-examined the following day. I breathed again.

Three weeks remained of the course. Under Captain Pugh, doctor as well as expert skier, and later to be a member of the successful Everest expedition, we learned what real climbing was. We came to appreciate the value of 'ropes', a network of cords pulled tight over the skis to prevent them slipping as we climbed. We were initiated into the secrets of navigation through fog and blizzard by the use of compass, map and altimeter, and into the hazards of cornice jumping. We learned to ski easily and comfortably over twenty-foot drops. Each night we returned to the school, ready to drop.

But worse was to come. We were called into the lecture-room. Captain Pugh wasted no time.

'Tomorrow the first section are going to climb here.' He pointed to a spot on the map. 'It is over ten thousand feet. They will take with them shovels, picks and tents, and will begin to build a camp. It will be known as Summit Camp and they will stay there overnight, returning the next day when the second section will go up and complete the work. It is to be a permanent camp and the other sections in turn will each spend a night there. In that way you will all get some idea of the problems involved in living high above the snow-line.'

He gave us the details – how the camp was to be built, what precautions to take to prevent ourselves freezing to death. 'Remember,' he said, 'these tents may be small but they take two men – just. In that way you will create a fug, and warmth. Do not on any account take the slightest bit of snow into the tent with you.' He demonstrated how, head first, we were to enter the tents through a small hole just big enough to take a man, brushing off the snow outside as we wriggled through, and not forgetting to clean our boots of snow.

'And when you get into your sleeping-bag, you take your boots to bed with you. If you don't they'll be frozen solid in the morning.'

The first party left laden like pack-horses, with Alec in charge. It was a wicked route, needing all our acquired knowledge of navigation and ski-ing. As soon as Alec returned I buttonholed him. Oh, it had been all right, he said. He had woken during the night to find it snowing inside the tent. The heat of their bodies had caused condensation on the roof of the tent, and the cold outside had turned it to snow. That seemed to be his main impression.

Next day I set out with my own section. The camp had been built at the bottom of a thirty-foot wall of snow. Before leaving I checked and re-checked my route, carefully measuring off the compass bearings from the map. There was no room for a mistake in navigation because there were no landmarks near the camp.

The first part of the route was straightforward. Shortly after noon we left False Crest behind on the second stage of the trip. Clouds were beginning to gather round the peaks, and soon the ridge that marked the ten-thousand-foot line was shrouded from view. An icy wind began to blow down the mountain-side, and the sky grew darker. It was tiring work climbing into the wind, and rests were more frequent now. The first snow-flakes began to fall. Blizzard! I remembered the stories I had heard of men, lashed almost into insensibility by wind and snow, dropping through exhaustion and being buried by the hurtling snow.

Huddled together under a ledge where there was some little protection we talked it over, shouting to make ourselves heard above the whistling of the wind. We decided to go on. It was all compass work now. Every twenty yards or so we stopped while I checked our bearings. There was an eerie feeling of going round and round in circles but we knew our only hope lay in trusting the compass.

Our ears were singing with exertion, sweat poured from our bodies, but our hands were numbed with cold. Every time we stopped we swung our arms vigorously, banging our hands savagely against our bodies to ward off frost-bite. Gradually the skies began to lighten, the wind lessened, and the snow began to clear. Half an hour later the blizzard had all but blown itself out. But the treacherous ice near the top of the ridge was now covered with a thin film of soft, sliding snow, deceptive and dangerous.

By the time we reached the top of the ridge the light was failing. Soon it would be dark, but we had five miles to go and only three hundred feet to climb, so we made good time. With one mile to go snow began to fall again but not, this time, with blizzard force. It was difficult to see where we were going. The curtain of falling snow blended with the surrounding white, making it almost impossible to pick out the configuration of the ground, but at last we reached the area of the camp. Systematically we began to search for the tents.

There was a shout from one of the section. We ski-ed over to where he was standing. There was the thirty-foot wall of snow but, search as we might, no sign of tents. We began again. Another shout. Another search, and again no tents. Then the truth dawned. There were dozens of these walls of snow, not one. Round and round we went from one to another, becoming more and more confused. And round us swirled the snow, thicker and thicker through the gathering darkness.

For the second time we huddled round in conference, a small group of white-robed figures. The prospect ahead of us was depressing. We could stay where we were for the night, after digging a cave in one of the snow walls, or we could attempt the journey back in darkness and snow. We decided on action.

It was completely dark, and the snow was still falling steadily as we slipped over the edge of the ridge on to the snow-covered ice and glided away. Unable to see a thing, we had no way of telling whether we were moving or still. Only when we were travelling over bumpy ground did the jolting sensation tell us we were on the move. I soon learned to prod forward with one of my sticks, and the speed with which it was whipped to the rear gave me an idea of my own speed. But nothing could banish the uncanny feeling of ski-ing into nothingness. The snow and darkness made a baffling wall through which we could see nothing.

We seemed to have been travelling for an eternity before the snow eased off a little. We could now see a matter of perhaps fifty or a hundred yards. To the right and left of us were steep walls of snow. Immediately ahead the ground sloped sharply away and twisted out of sight to the left. Only then did I realize what had happened. In the darkness and snow we had come down Devil's Gorge – in daylight scrupulously avoided by all but expert skiers. A few minutes later the lights of the school could be seen gleaming through the trees.

The sequel came two days later when the next section returned from Summit Camp. They had found our tracks, not quite obliterated, and at one point we had been standing within twenty-five yards of the tents. The tents themselves had been buried by the heavy fall of snow. Perhaps it was just as well we did not find them.

The rest of the course was given over mainly to lectures on first aid under snow conditions, military tactics, and innumerable competitions. These competitions gave us a great deal of fun but, at the back of our minds, was the thought of the approaching advanced test, finale of the course – a three-thousand-foot climb against time without the help of ropes, and a speed descent.

Yet when it was all over, here we were on the balcony of the school, watching students of the next course gathering for morning parade. Alec pulled a wry face. 'We just got away in time. Look at them, falling in in threes.'

Across the snow came the shouted commands: 'Shoulder skis.' 'Put on skis.' 'Forward march!' In their threes the sections clumped stolidly away, climbing gradually out of sight, instructors at their head.

We turned our backs on the snow. In the room beyond, our bags were packed and waiting. Down below in the forecourt, the trucks awoke from their six weeks' sleep and roared into life. It was good-bye to the cold and the crisp sunlight, and back to the dusty heat and smells of Egypt.

We had travelled up to the Ski School thrilled by the ease with which we stepped from blazing summer into the depths of winter, but it was nothing to the suppressed excitement that gripped everyone on the way back. It was a quiet, ever-present undercurrent. No one talked very much about it, but you could sense it.

Rumours of David Stirling's capture had reached us in the heart of the Lebanese mountains. We knew that Paddy Mayne, our squadron commander, had been called to GHQ, Cairo – but beyond that, nothing. The war in the Middle East was over. In the Caucasus the Germans were being pushed back. What was there left for the SAS? What was there left for me? Several times on the trip back to Egypt, Alec and I had reviewed the facts with gloomy foreboding, unable to catch even a glimmer of hope.

It was thus with some trepidation that we heard, on our return to Kabrit, that Paddy was going to speak to everyone in the big marquee at eleven o'clock. Promptly at five to eleven, Alec and I wandered over to the marquee and took our seats. Peter Davis was there. He had not gone to join B Squadron after all. Everyone was there, sitting on hard benches or perched on wooden tables. Those who could not find room to sit were standing about or leaning against the tent poles.

Major Mayne wasted no time with preliminaries. 'As some of you no doubt know, I have been up in Cairo during the past week, at GHQ.' He paused. 'The war in the desert is over. When I first went to GHQ I was told that there was no more useful work for the SAS. I did not agree. I said as much. It has been a hard fight and a long one. Now I have been given the choice of disbanding or carrying on in a new role – but with a reduction in establishment.'

There was a murmur of disappointment. The wind chased across the floor, swirling the sand along. The canvas billowed and flapped. This, I thought, is it.

'I have agreed to the formation of a Special Raiding Squadron to undertake special assault tasks for the army. I shall be in command for, as I think you know, Colonel Stirling is now a prisoner of war.

'Our strength will be reduced to about three hundred or three hundred and fifty, and we will be organized into a squadron headquarters, with three troops each of three sections consisting of an officer and twenty men. We will also carry a small reserve of officers and men.

'The RSM will now read out the names of the officers and NCOs of the Special Raiding Squadron, and I will leave it to section commanders to pick the men they want with them.'

The RSM picked up a sheaf of papers from the table and started to read. 'Number One Troop . . .' Quickly he ran through the names. I looked around unhappily. At the thought of returning to the soul-destroying routine of the training depot I could have cried with disappointment. The RSM's voice broke in on my thoughts.

'. . . Two Troop, A Section, Captain Marsh. B Section, Lieutenant Davis. C Section, Lieutenant Harrison.' Hardly able to believe my ears I stepped forward with Peter to join the other fortunate ones.

'. . . in reserve, Lieutenant Muirhead.'

I was delighted. With thoughts of the training depot banished from my mind, and with two good friends, I felt at that moment like a modern D'Artagnan. The Afrika Korps was defeated. Europe remained. Where would the attack go in? The Balkans? Italy? Southern France? I did not care where it would be now I knew I would be there.

A week later I was in Palestine, just south of the Syrian border at a little place called Az-zib. On a rough, rising piece of ground a new tented encampment had risen. With a few men I had gone ahead to help prepare it. Now it awaited only the men to occupy it, the men of the newly-formed Special Raiding Squadron. Half a mile from the sea, the hills of Galilee rose grey and rugged behind it. To the north the hills of Syria frowned down from beyond the border. Here it was that the men of the SRS were to train for their part in blasting open the fortress of Europe.

They arrived one night by train from Eygpt, and only the bullfrogs heard them come, croaking their welcome from a thousand throats as they lurked in the ditches. At the camp, hot stew simmered and boiled on the flaring cookers. Buckets of tea stood waiting. In the glare of headlights the stacks of kit-bags, packs and valises were tumbled on to the rough ground from the three-tonners. Over them swarmed officers and men, searching, pulling and tugging. Among the rows of tents jeeps plied to and fro, roaring along in booster, stopping here and there to throw off a couple of kit-bags or a valise.

As dawn broke, the croaking of the bullfrogs died away. From the tents came the sounds of heavy breathing and the snoring of tired men. From somewhere on the road below came the shouts of Arab herdsmen. And on the warm morning breeze the scent of the orange groves was wafted through the camp.

3

Raiding Squadron

Somewhere a bugle was blowing. Sleepily I opened my
eyes. The bugle blared again. I grinned. Whose idea it
was to adopt the opening bars of *Bugle Call Rag* as the
squadron call I did not know, but it suited perfectly the
spirit of the unit. During our first week in camp, whenever
it was played, there always came an answering roar from
all the tents. We cherished the fond hope that the call
would be used someday during an official inspection, with
the vision it conjured up of the visiting general 'trucking'
across the parade ground.

I looked at my watch. Five past six. Quickly pulling on
a pair of shorts and tugging on my boots, I dashed out of
the tent. The sun lingered below the Galilean hills, and
there was still a bit of a chill in the air. I sprinted over to
where the rest of the squadron were falling in, with the
eyes of the PT sergeant-major on me.

'Come along, sir, come along. Everybody's waiting.
Right turn. Double march!' He snapped out the order
and we moved off at a steady lope. All the way down to
the field behind the camp he shouted friendly abuse at us,
urging us on, telling us off.

'What have you stopped running for? I haven't told you
to stop. Right! Round me in a circle. When I shout "go",
try and jump on the back of the man in front of you . . .
Go!'

We ran here, we ran there, we sweated, we swore – but
discreetly. 'What's that? You're cold? Right! Double over
to that tree and back.'

And away we went. No one was free from his biting

witticisms, from the newest parachutist to the most senior officers.

'Come on, Mr Harrison, sir. Come on. Put more work into it. You can't say "Carry on, sergeant" on this parade, you know.

'Too much hooch last night, eh? I'll sweat it out of you, I will. Up, down, up, down, up . . .' Sweating and straining, we heaved our bodies up, down, up, down, up . . . Trembling arms threatened to give way.

'All right. Just one more.' We sighed with relief and managed to pull just one more out of the bag.

'And now one for the colonel.' We groaned.

'And one for the unit. All right. Up on your feet.'

After breakfast we went down to the training field. There we learned to hold and fire a rifle. Just that, though there was not one man in the unit who could by the greatest stretch of imagination be called a recruit. It was typical of the training. Nothing was taken for granted. What can be learned can be forgotten, so we started from scratch.

It was this thoroughness that accounted in great measure for the success of our undertakings and our remarkably low casualty rate in the operations to come. We learned again how to read a map, to use a compass, and many more of the elementary things a soldier has to know. Only when every man had passed his elementary tests was the more interesting training reached. We stripped and reassembled our weapons till we knew them better than we knew our own faces. We learned to handle them blindfold with equal ease.

After lunch each day, in shorts and boots again, we trotted down through the orange groves to the beach. There, at the water's edge, with the Mediterranean sun beating down, we ran, jumped, stretched, and heaved again for twenty minutes while the sweat poured down our bodies.

'Hands on hips. Deep breathing.' We breathed deeply and calmed the thumping of our hearts.

'Left turn! Double – march!' Straight into the sea we splashed. Within a week there was not a man who could not swim.

Soon we were doing long, gruelling marches through the wild grey hills, in the sweltering heat of an early summer. We were taken out one morning in trucks and dropped on the shores of Lake Tiberias – the biblical Sea of Galilee – with rifles, equipment and potted rations. There we were left to make our own way back to the coast. Somewhere on the route we were to be ambushed. That meant keeping on the alert all the time, and making use of every scrap of cover. As the crow flies, the distance was about forty miles. When you threw in for good measure innumerable streams, towering jagged peaks of stone to be climbed or by-passed, and the thick and at times almost impenetrable scrub, you began to wonder whether you would make it. Add to this the overpowering heat, without a breath of wind, and a twenty-four-hour time limit.

We set off at about eleven in the morning, moving on a compass bearing. Maps were a snare for the unwary. They were apt to show tracks that had long since fallen into disuse and disappeared. New, well-worn tracks were not marked. Whole Arab villages, marked quite plainly, were found to have disappeared too. Of some, only a few lumps of stone remained peeping through the long grass and tough thorns. In their stead new villages had sprung up, perhaps a few miles away, each with its attendant network of tracks. So we stuck to our compasses and trudged on.

Shortly after noon a whistle shrilled. Our small column

halted. A man had fainted. Another, going to his assistance, passed clean out. From a sky that hurt to look at,
the sun glared malevolently down. By two o'clock five
more men had been struck down by the sun. The whistle
shrilled again. There was nothing for it but to lie up till
sunset. Like animals we crawled with our remaining
strength into holes in the rocks, under ledges, anywhere
where there was the slightest bit of shade. I worked my
way into the heart of a thick, sturdy thorn bush. There
for the next few hours I dozed fitfully, curled up among
its twisted and gnarled branches.

I had hardly closed my eyes, it seemed, when the
whistle blew again. By now the sun was dipping down
towards the western peaks. We pushed on. Just before
dark we refilled our water-bottles at a stream that rushed
in a torrent down the side of the hill, and bathed our feet.
Then, through the darkness we struggled on, climbing out
of one valley, dipping down into the next.

About two o'clock in the morning it started to rain. We
opened our shirts at the neck and let it pour over us.
After half an hour it stopped and a cold breeze sprang up,
drying it on our bodies.

The purple of the hills merged into grey. Dawn was
near. Ahead was the last big ridge. Bending low we forced
ourselves on, spurred by the thought of a ten minutes'
rest at the top. As we reached it the hills became bathed
in gold as, behind us, the sun rose over Galilee. We lay
down where we were and slept.

For ten glorious minutes we slept. When we awoke it
was quite light. Down below us in the valley the morning
mists were rising. We marched into them. The Arabs in
the village stared as we passed. We did not care. From
somewhere ahead of us came the sound of rushing water.
Coursing down beneath frowning cliffs was the stream
that rushed torrent-like into the sea at Az-zib. Boldly we

strode into mid-stream and marched towards the sea. By half past ten we were in camp, twenty-three and a half hours after leaving the Sea of Galilee.

Marches like this played an invaluable part in fitting us for our task in Europe. They made us fit, and they showed us what we could do when necessary. Much of our training was done at night to accustom our eyes to the dark and to give us a confidence of movement bred out of us by civilization.

After six weeks in Palestine we were fit to tackle anything that might come along. There were few German or Italian weapons we had not learned to fire. In any prolonged action behind the enemy lines, when ammunition might run low, we could always rely on captured enemy weapons to enable us to carry on the fight. The mysteries of explosives were mysteries no longer. Just over the border in Syria we practised cliff climbing, with and without ropes, in daylight and in darkness. We evolved our own system of tactics, which we considered more suitable to our specialized work. All we wanted now was something to tackle.

In our camp was a small wooden hut that had once served as a cinema to the nearby community at Naharhia. To this hut one April afternoon came Lieutenant-General Dempsey, then commanding 13 Corps. While guards paraded round outside, he told us we had been put under his command for the forthcoming attack on Europe. Our task would be to put out of action a certain coastal defence battery commanding the approaches to the invasion coast. 'I know I need not impress on you the importance of succeeding in this task. I am confident you will succeed,' he concluded.

The rest of the day we spent staging a training demonstration for him. It was at least a genuine sample of the kind of training we had been doing. Down on the beach men were wriggling on their stomachs across the sand with machine-gun bullets zipping a few inches above them. That evening our troop carried out a full-scale attack on a pill-box position in the border hills. Starting from the water's edge, we scrambled to the top of the cliff then, swarming hand over hand down ropes, dropped down a fifty-foot embankment. Laboriously we wormed our way forward up the steep hillside, justly proud of our skill and fitness. It was not till later that we learned that General Dempsey had been with us all the way.

Next day the real training started in earnest. On the blackboard a piece of coastline was drawn. Somewhere in Europe that chalk line had an existence in reality, but it was too small a fragment ever to be identified. A cross represented the coastal battery. Somewhere in Europe enemy gunners were walking on that cross, cleaning their guns, looking out to sea, unaware that on a blackboard in Palestine the ground on which they stood was being carefully studied . . .

For days we worked out tactics and methods of attack on that blackboard. Then the problems got too big for the board. Across the fields behind the camp a scale model of the battery position was marked out with picks and heaps of stones. Every hedge, every stone wall was there. The battery itself was represented by a barbed-wire enclosure.

It was about this time that a 3-inch mortar team was sent to join us. Alec was made mortar officer, although he had never fired one in his life, and soon showed that he had a natural flair for the work. His estimation of ranges was phenomenally accurate even if his methods of fire control were a little unorthodox, and he produced results.

Under covering fire from his mortars we attacked again and again across the fields towards the dummy battery. We did it by day and, later, by night. By the time we had finished we knew our way around it far better than the men who manned it. But it was one thing knowing how to attack the battery and another thing getting there.

At the beginning of May a small naval party arrived in camp. It was their job to show us how to get there. They took us down to Haifa harbour. Tied up alongside the quay was an antiquated motor boat that someone, somewhere, had decided was an assault craft. On its bows it bore proudly the letters LCA(L) – Landing Craft, Assault (Light).

The Navy were apologetic. These were all they had been able to get hold of. I looked round for the rest of them. Bobbing up and down, and looking for all the world like barges, they were in fact replicas of the first craft, minus engines. Piling a section into each of the three 'assault craft', we put to sea, the motor boat gallantly and somewhat miraculously towing the others. We turned and headed for a distant strip of yellow sand. The naval officer in my craft explained. We would go flat out – about ten knots – and when we were close enough to the beach the two engineless craft would cast off and carry on under their own momentum. Perhaps it was not perfect, but we would get the idea of how to make an assault landing.

We spent many a day down at the harbour, bobbing about in the boats, splashing through the shallows on to an 'enemy' beach, returning to camp wet through. Then the Navy broke the news. A real assault craft had arrived. True, it was one of the earlier types, but it was an assault boat, a landing craft, personnel (ramp). The ramp was the thing. No longer would we have to climb out precariously over the bows.

The very next morning we went far out into the bay in our new grey-painted monster. Then began the long run-in to the beach. A hundred yards from the shore the craft cut its engines. Down went the ramp in the bows. The naval officer in charge leaned forward and studied the water intently for a few seconds. 'OK. There's only eighteen inches.'

Waving the rest of the section on, I charged down the ramp. I came up spluttering and gasping. Frantically treading water, I saw the section were still in the boat, exploding with mirth.

When we were not taking a trip round the bay we were touring coastal defence batteries. We studied typical lay-outs and vulnerable spots. Back in camp we discussed the best way of laying our explosives, for guns captured had to be destroyed. By this time there was little we did not know about the operation except the *when* and the *where*. Then came the news that we were leaving Palestine for Suez and – so rumour had it – going straight on board ship.

4
Curtain Up

The docks at Suez were coming to life as our train pulled in. From the harbour came the mournful hooting of sirens. Down the filthy streets the trams clanged their way noisily into the town, crowded with Arabs of all ages, many of them clinging to the sides or perched precariously on the roofs. On the quayside a sleepy-eyed NAAFI manager stared aghast at the horde of weary, unshaven, khaki-clad figures who besieged his canteen for the inevitable 'char'.

Three hours later Alec, with his mortars and 3 Troop, was bound for the *Dunera*. The rest of us headed out in tenders towards the *Ulster Monarch* riding proudly at anchor, smart as a new pin in her light grey war-paint. From her davits swung the low-built, trim-looking assault craft. Eagerly we tumbled aboard, but excitement was shortlived. In the ward-room had been posted up, of all things, a training programme.

We trained for another month, embarking on and disembarking from the LCAs until every movement was perfect. For hours we were towed behind the *Monarch* in the assault craft to get us used to rough seas. We carried out mock attacks on shore batteries guarding the port of Suez, went for long marches at night, going ashore at dusk and returning to the ship at first light.

The climax of our training came when, with other ships of the assault force, we sailed down the Gulf of Suez, round the southern tip of Sinai, and up the Gulf of Akaba, with the barren sandy mountains of Sinai on our left and the equally barren hills of Arabia on our right. This was the dress rehearsal for invasion.

Everything went off as planned, although we managed to distinguish ourselves on our first evening by going for a fishing trip in the LCAs. Nothing might have been said had we not used explosive charges for bait. Although unorthodox it was highly successful. Immediately after each explosion we splashed over the side, swimming to where the stunned fish were floating on the water. The catch was good, and colourful, but hopes of a fish breakfast were dashed by the ship's cat.

There was also a polite note next morning from the naval officer commanding the force to the effect that our charges *did* sound rather like depth charges, and would we please desist and thereby spare the nerves of everyone concerned?

We made many friends aboard the *Monarch* that first month. It was a grand ship with a grand crew. The high standard of inter-service co-operation between ourselves and the crew of the *Monarch* and the crews of the LCA flotilla was a good augury for the future.

Back at Suez, the rehearsal over, General Montgomery came aboard to speak to us. Two days later we sailed up the Canal to Port Said for our final rendezvous. On 4 July 1943, we sailed into the Mediterranean. The adventure had begun.

That afternoon each officer was handed a pile of small blue booklets, one for each man, entitled *A Soldier's Guide to Sicily*. In that fashion we learned where the blow was to fall.

'All officers to report to the briefing room.' The long-awaited summons came over the ship's loud hailer. While the ship rolled and groaned in the heavy swell, maps and aerial photographs were issued. On the large wall map in the squadron commander's cabin we studied the dispositions of all the German and Italian forces on the island. We asked questions and got our answers. Nothing had been overlooked.

Later that evening Harry Poat, our troop commander, explained our particular role. 'This farm, here, will be contained by 3 troop; 1 Troop will attack from the left flank. We will go between the battery and farm, turn around and attack from inland. Tony's section will lead, with Peter following. You, Harry, will take the Engineers with you. It's your responsibility to see that they get safely on to the gun positions and are not molested while they fix their charges. Now make sure your chaps know those photos thoroughly, and that they understand what they have to do.'

During the following days the sun shone down on the perfect calm of a blue Mediterranean as the convoy sailed serenely on. I got down to details with my section. We knew exactly where we were to land, what kind of ground we had to cross, and we decided finally on our route. We were all set. If there were any last-minute changes a destroyer was to come out from a North African port to meet us.

As we came within range of Crete with its large German airfields there was a certain air of expectancy. We scanned the skies for that first German reconnaissance plane. Once spotted it would be but a very short time before we would be in the thick of it. But, over in Crete, a small force of men of the Special Boating Squadron – like ourselves, descended from the SAS – under the command of Major Lord Jellicoe, were busy keeping the German aircraft on the ground. How successful they were can be judged from the fact that not one enemy aircraft was seen during the whole approach to Sicily, although the huge convoy sailed under the very noses of the Germans.

The morning of 9 July opened as had all the preceding mornings – sunshine and a dead calm sea. As midday approached, however, the White Ensign at our stern, till then listlessly flapping round its mast, bestirred itself as the freshening breeze jerked it into life. Before long a half gale was blowing and towering waves, white-crested with spume, gave way to sickening troughs into which the ship lurched and twisted dizzily.

All that afternoon the rising wind lashed the seas into an angry maelstrom. Things looked bad, but the ship's officers were confident that the storm would blow itself out before zero hour. As if to lend persuasion to their prophecy, with the late afternoon the white crests vanished from the waves.

Just before dark we were called to attention by the loud hailer. 'Mount Etna can now be seen off the port bow.' Despite my sea-sickness I staggered up on deck. There, dimly outlined against a dull grey sky, was Etna's summit. I felt it was all rather like a Cook's tour as I thought: so there lies the enemy.

As we drew nearer our destination the moon came up, silhouetting the other ships in the convoy. Silently and fiercely they butted their way through the still-mountainous waves. In the ward-room a meal of bacon and eggs was being served, but my stomach, already sorely tried by the storm, jibbed at it. I went below to get my equipment on before the ship switched to invasion lighting, and then went back on deck.

Zero hour was at hand and the moon was already setting off the port beam. Gun crews were standing-to, 'just in case'. In the darkness I had a feeling they were eyeing me curiously, and perhaps a little morbidly.

My eyes now grew more accustomed to the dark. I could dimly make out the outline of the Sicilian coast. For a while the excitement took my mind off my stomach.

Ashore two fires were burning fiercely. The flashes of bursting bombs and the endless streams of red flak showed only too well that, ahead of us, the RAF were doing their stuff. There was a lull, then a roar getting deeper and louder as squadron after squadron of bombers droned towards the coast.

The wind was still high – too high for the paratroops, I thought, and no picnic either for the glider boys. This was to be their first big show, and they were not getting much of a break.

We were very close to the coast now, and my mind began toying with the idea of what would happen if we were spotted. But the realization that, for miles along the coast, invasion fleets were drawing nearer gave me an immense feeling of power. Confident in our strength, we were poised to strike.

To our right a searchlight from the shore spluttered into life, probing the night sky for raiders, anxiously, uncertainly. Then, in one terrible moment, all seemed lost. Without warning the light plunged and slowly, methodically, began to sweep the sea. Closer and closer it crept. The gun crews tensed, swung their guns quietly round, and waited. In the space of a few seconds we would be limned in the dazzling glare of its arcs. Then, as suddenly as it had swooped, it rose again into the night, and swept on over our heads.

Above the roar of the sea came a quiet voice over the loud hailer:

'SRS stand by.'

Instantly all speculation was banished. I made my way quickly to my station on the troop deck. Down there the scene was satanic. In the light of the red invasion lamps everything seemed to glow with fire, while long shadows darted and danced across the mess decks where we were assembled. Outside, the landing craft bumped and crashed against the sides of the ship as she tossed and lurched while, every few minutes, a wave higher than its fellows poured through the open oiling doors through which we were to embark.

The quiet voice spoke again:

'SRS embark.'

Slowly the head of the column moved forward to where the craft were swinging madly to and fro. From behind it was impossible to see what was happening but I could guess only too easily: the long wait while you judged the swing of the craft aright, the summoning of sufficient nerve to make a leap, the knowledge that one mistake would plunge you, weighted with equipment, into the boiling seas.

Less than half my section were embarked when that quiet voice spoke again:

'Lower and cast off.'

The risk of damage to our craft, pounded mercilessly by the heavy seas, had been too great. Freed now, it disappeared into the darkness, to reappear in a very short time on the other side of the ship where, sheltered from the worst of the storm, the rest of us quickly embarked. Leaving the shelter of the ship, we headed into the storm.

Up and down and round about we went. Giddily the stars whirled by as we were tossed to and fro by wind and sea. With monotonous regularity wave after wave crashed over us. Squatting in the bows, I was soaked to the skin. Over most of the craft was stretched a long awning, but it availed us little. Water swirled round our feet, but the motor pump chugging away gave us a certain amount of comfort.

Unmoved by the tempest, the flotilla leader stood peering into the blackness. He spoke without turning his head and the wind whipped his words back to us.

'Rotary pump, please.'

We were taking in too much water, too fast. What we did not know then was that our bows had been holed by the crashing of our craft against the side of the parent ship. But all thought of drowning was quickly forgotten in the face of a new peril. In sudden panic I groped on the floor for the all-too-inadequate cardboard basin provided by a thoughtful Navy against such an emergency. I found it, sodden and useless. Next thing, I was leaning over the side wedged between the guns we had mounted for'ard, my stomach writhing, my face convulsed with pain. Waves dashed against my head as it hung within a few inches of the water. They threatened to tear me from my precarious perch in the bows. I felt utterly miserable. The invasion was forgotten; but one trivial thing forced its attention on me. As each wave broke over me, tiny specks of phosphorescent light were left behind to glow and fade.

Gradually I began to take more notice of my surroundings. We were coming now within the lee of the land and the sea was calmer. Ahead of us an aircraft, friend or foe we could not tell, dropped a cluster of flares. At once everything was as bright as day. Our hearts sank. We were bound to be seen. But eyes ashore, peering through the darkness, were unable to pierce the sudden glare of the flares. Revealing as they were, they yet formed a curtain between us and our enemies. One by one they died out, leaving the night blacker than before.

Ahead and to starboard a British submarine rode on the surface, a small blue lamp pointing seaward to guide in the assault craft. In a matter of minutes we had left her astern. Suddenly over the water came the cries of men. Hearts in mouths, we strained eyes and ears. German E-boats? Out of the darkness floated a dim shape and with it came the voices again.

'Have a heart, lads. Have a heart.'

'Bury the hatchet . . .'

Someone in our craft yelled back, 'Shut up, you bloody fools! Shut up!'

In answer a torch flashed frantically through the darkness. We groaned. Someone shouted again, 'Put that bloody light out!' It seemed impossible that the enemy sentries could fail to hear the shouting and see the light.

Now we could recognize the outlines of the wrecked, three-parts submerged glider. Clinging to the wing were five lads, one of them with just his fingers twined into the torn fabric, the heavy seas threatening to tear him away. With each wave he sank lower and lower in the water. As we came up alongside I could see the dull despair in his eyes. He knew help was at hand but, battered almost insensible by the waves, doubted his ability to hang on. The others dared not go to his help lest they capsize their frail support. All they could do was shout to us to get him first.

Time had no more meaning till at last we had them in the stern of the LCA, shivering with exposure and shock. We had been drifting with our engines cut. Now, as they came to life again with a muffled roar, we saw we were not more than half a mile from the shore.

Skilfully riding the surf at the foot of the cliffs, the LCA commander kept her nose on to the jagged black rocks that threatened to smash us to matchwood, while the ramp was lowered.

'Jove! That's a bit of luck. The right spot. Well, good luck, chaps.'

We clambered ashore, slipping and sliding in our rubber-soled boots on the spray-drenched boulders. I tried to recall the photos of the area. There seemed little doubt that this was the right place.

In single file we began to scale the cliff. I could see neither foothold nor handhold. I felt for them instinctively, hauling myself up inch by inch. My dread of heights

had gone. Only once during the climb did it threaten to return. We had been edging our way along a ledge of rock for some minutes when . . . the ledge was not there any more. I remember thinking only that I must try another way. I could see nothing. It was as if someone else were guiding my hands and feet. I stretched up above me. The rock was broken but firm. I scrambled up.

How long that climb took I do not know. It could have been ten minutes or ten years. At the top I lay down among the rocks and boulders strewn around, and took out my .45 revolver. I had brought that and twelve hand grenades with me.

A moment later I was joined by my signaller with his small 38 set. 'Any news of the others?' I asked.

He shook his head. 'There's some dame singing on my frequency,' he whispered.

We lay there watching and listening while the rest of the section clambered up over the cliff-top and took up their positions one by one among the rocks on either side.

So far there had been neither sight nor sound of the enemy. The unexpected silence was unnerving. My imagination began to run riot. Somewhere above us, and unseen, they were preparing to open fire. A stone rattled loose and clattered down to the cliff-edge. From in front came the sudden, excited shouts of Italians. My finger tightened on the trigger. Then the shouts died away into the distance.

'Half right till we meet the wall . . .'

As we rose from the cover of the rocks and moved forward in open formation, I ran over in my mind the route we were to take. Soon we should reach the junction and . . . There was a sharp swishing sound through the air. As one man we fell flat. Above us and not more than thirty yards away there came a blinding flash and a deafening roar. Mortars! A bright red glow stained the night and I tried to sink into the flickering uncertain shadows that darted among the rocks. I felt as naked as a floodlit monument.

Cautiously I raised my head. Where the bomb had fallen a shed was burning. In the flare of the flames I could see, only a few feet away, a tangle of wire and beyond that the menacing muzzle of a big gun. We had been advancing right into the enemy battery, and into our own mortar fire. For a moment I was tempted to rush the battery from where we were. The defenders were obviously unaware of our presence but, if we attacked frontally, we would meet Tony and Peter with their sections coming in from the opposite direction. And my job was to get the Engineers safely on to the gun positions.

There was only one thing to be done. Retrace our steps and carry on with the original plan. It was obvious now that we had not landed at the right place but had scaled the cliff almost beneath the battery. We had lost a good deal of time so set off at a good pace, dropping to the ground every so often to avoid being spotted in the flash of bursting mortar bombs.

From somewhere on the right a light machine-gun opened up on us as we scurried across the open ground between the battery and the farm. Bending low, we made for the wall ahead as fast as we could. Once on the other side we were safe for the time being.

We were behind the battery now. Most of the buildings appeared to be blazing, and in the light of the flames we could see the guns. So far there had been no sign of the other two sections, so I guessed they must already have reached the gun positions. I had to get those Engineers there, fast.

From behind came a sharp rattle of machine-gun fire. Streams of green tracer cut through our ranks. As we dived for cover our two Bren gunners swung round, firing from the hip in the direction from which the tracer had come. No more firing came from the mystery gunner. His one burst had mercifully done no damage.

We were about to step over the one remaining wall between ourselves and our objective when, from our right front, came a stream of red tracer. Lying full length in the nettles behind the wall – it was no more than a foot high – I yelled the challenge at the top of my voice: 'Desert Rats!'

Back came the answer: 'Kill the Italians.' We breathed again. Tony and Peter. Somewhere we must have passed them in the dark. We scrambled to our feet. At once there came another burst of fire from their direction, and once more we fell flat. This time we lay there hugging the earth as bullets chipped the top of the wall. It was good shooting but we did not appreciate it.

I shouted again. Once more came the reply: 'Kill the Italians.' The firing continued. I crawled to the end of the section to have a look from higher ground. The last man peered through the darkness.

'Mr Harrison? They're our chaps. They keep shouting the challenge and I've answered right each time but I don't think they can hear me.'

I stared back, beginning to understand. 'That was me challenging. We've been shouting to each other. Come on, let's all shout together. Pass the word down.' We yelled at the top of our voices. Faintly came the answer. Tony stepped forward out of the night.

Together now, Tony leading, we stormed into the gun positions. The noise of battle was already dying down. Here and there an occasional shot was fired but, in the main, the fight was over. Then, out of the corner of my eye, I caught a slight movement three or four yards away, at ground-level. Something froze inside me as the light gleamed on the barrel of a machine-gun pointing straight at us. They could not miss.

I was too close to use a grenade and could pick off only one man at a time with my revolver. If only I could attract the attention of one of the tommy-gunners. All these thoughts passed through my mind in the fraction of a second before three very frightened Italians crawled out of their hole, hands high in the air. Taking them with us we crossed the wire and headed for the first gun.

While the engineers prepared the guns for the big bang

we started to round up the prisoners and wounded. If they could walk we herded them over against one of the huts where they stood dejectedly, a dazed look on their faces. They were dirty and unshaven, and had that unkempt look about them that men who have fought long and hard in impossible conditions might have – but without that excuse. A little way off, under separate guard, was a second group of prisoners, about twenty women and children. They had fled to the safety of the shelters on the battery position thinking it was yet another RAF raid. They were numb with fear. Italian home propaganda was nothing if not thorough.

On the whole battery position we found only one officer, and he claimed to be a doctor. He was lying in one of the gun-pits, his legs lacerated by mortar fragments that had embedded themselves deeply. As we carried him across the battery to the rest of the prisoners he waved his arms wildly, insisting loudly, '*Dottore, dottore, dottore!*' He calmed down a bit when we started to dress his legs, and watched our efforts with professional interest. Among his papers were visiting-cards describing him as 'obstetrician and gynaecologist'.

He confirmed that he was the only officer but that he was the doctor. There had been some German officers, however. He waved his hand vaguely in the direction of the high ground. He had sent them word that the British were landing but they would not believe him. No one, they told him, could land on a night like this. They would not come. Now, no doubt, they had fled.

By this time the Engineers had laid all their charges. From the pits came the warning, 'Stand clear.' The guns were ready to blow. Prisoners were shepherded to safety behind a rise in the ground. The wounded were carried there. We lay down and waited. There was a sharp concussion and flying pieces of metal whined eerily above our heads. As the sound of the explosion rolled away, from the signaller's wireless set came the strains of *Land of Hope and Glory*, as a broadcasting station crashed in on our frequency.

All that remained to be done was to send up the signal rockets to tell the invasion ships waiting off shore that the guns had been spiked. Then, and only then, did we discover that, although we had the rockets, someone had forgotten the sticks. The first one we stood up on a stone, whereupon it fell over and fizzled out. The second and third we flung into the air where they cavorted about like drunken aerial torpedoes on the Fifth of November. We need not have worried. Keen-eyed watchers on the convoy had seen the guns go up. The great fleet started to move in as the first light streaked the distant horizon.

We moved off by sections to take up our positions on the surrounding high ground, ready to meet the expected counter-attack. Out at sea, the dark smudges that were ships grew nearer. The bay itself seemed still and unreal, like a deserted stage after the audience has left the theatre. Only those sinister black shapes drifting heavily and listlessly in the morning swell remained to remind us of the drama of the previous night. Thirteen gliders had failed to reach the coast. And from all those we had picked up only five survivors. How many more had we passed by unheeding last night as we made for the shore? How many of them had watched our LCAs approach, with new hope in their hearts? Who can measure the despair with which they saw us glide by to be swallowed up again by the night? And after we had gone, the hungry sea, so peaceful now, had sucked them from their flimsy rafts, their fingers clawing feebly for a hold.

Across the dusty track in front of us stretched the body of a solitary Italian. In death his face had taken on the grey-green colour of his drab uniform. Only the dark blotch of red across his throat showed how he had died. I remembered the blackboard in Palestine.

At the crest of the rise was a low stone wall. I showed the section their positions and posted sentries. The rest relaxed. Only the tommy-guns of the sentries, poking aggressively over the wall, served to remind us that we were in enemy territory. It was hard now not to believe that we were on just another scheme back home. Yet, thirty miles down the coast, the main forces were landing on the beaches. Soon they would be pushing towards us. We were back in Europe.

Now we had time to take stock. We had landed at three fifteen in the morning, two hundred and eighty-seven strong. By five o'clock the battery had fallen, without the loss of a man.

Somewhere overhead planes wheeled and dived like birds. Faintly to us came the sound of their guns as they closed in combat. Then, shortly before six o'clock, the ground shook as heavy guns roared out. We tensed and waited for the crump and whine of the shells. Out at sea, far over to the left, a fountain of water shot into the air. Another battery somewhere inland was going into action against the right flank of the convoy.

We concentrated immediately at the farm. Harry Poat explained quickly. 'The battery seems to be there, just the other side of those trees.' He pointed. 'Get down to the trees and I'll give you further orders there.' He turned to me. 'Harry, you'll lead with your section.'

From the farmhouse we picked our way down the slope, across the fields. With the exception of a few grey stone walls the ground was quite open. From beyond the belt of trees came the boom and crash of the guns. We had gone about a quarter of a mile when the sergeant's hand fell on my shoulder. 'Careful, sir. Someone's firing at us.' I had heard nothing, but followed his pointing finger. A rifle cautiously slid over the top of a wall not forty yards away, followed by a helmet. I did not wait to wonder why I had not heard his first shot. We were down behind our own little wall slinging shots at that tin hat. Then we were over and after him. He bolted to cover but a grenade soon brought him out. Minus rifle he started the walk back to our HQ at the farm.

Behind us the Brens of another section chattered into action. Someone was sniping from a hut in the middle of a field. We had hit the outer ring of defences hastily thrown round the battery when news of our landing reached them: Another burst from the Brens and tracer whipped into the wooden hut. Four or five Italians dashed out, hands in the air. Then, thinking better of it, dashed back again into the now-blazing hut. All that I took in, in the space of a few seconds. We had our own troubles.

From a tree-shrouded farmhouse on our left came a ragged volley of rifle fire. Lying in the open across the farm track we returned the fire. As we jumped to our feet to rush the place, a white handkerchief tied to a rifle muzzle was waved to and fro among the trees. Our 'prisoners' were some of the glider boys who, landed in the wrong place during the night, had decided to try and hold the farm till our arrival. We had come ashore in khaki drill trousers and blue-grey shirts. Not unnaturally, they had taken us for Italians.

Things had moved so rapidly that we were now completely out of touch with our HQ. From the sounds of firing that came to us we could tell that the whole squadron was closing in on the battery in a wide arc. But exactly where the other sections were it was impossible to tell.

We now came under fire from yet another farmhouse further over to the left. It was a little off what I imagined was the direct route to the battery, but I could not afford to leave a strong point behind us. I split my section. The sergeant, with nine men, headed straight for the sound of the big guns which were still firing away. With the other nine I started off across the open ground towards the farmhouse.

We had advanced not more than twenty or thirty yards when the firing stopped and seven figures stood up. They were about a hundred and fifty yards away and, although they had not got their hands up, none of them carried weapons. Holding our fire we advanced in open formation across the dry, sun-scorched fields. We were about thirty yards away from them when, without warning, they dropped from sight behind a concealed bank. At the same time a light machine-gun opened up on us from a flank at less than a hundred yards' range – and missed.

Shouting to the others to get back to the cover of some broken ground behind us, I hurled a couple of grenades to cover our withdrawal. The first one had just burst when, over the top of the bank, came two Italian 'money-box' grenades. They landed about two yards from where my signaller and I were crouching, but succeeded only in blowing us off our feet. Had they been British or German grenades . . .

It was deadlock. We could neither advance nor retreat without making ourselves sitting targets. Neither could the Italians. I cursed myself for falling into such a trap. It was too far to throw a grenade but one of the men had a discharger cup on his rifle which could hurl a grenade the distance. I shouted at him to put over about six grenades, then learned that he had damaged the cup in the landing.

As a last resort I pulled out a German signalling pistol I was carrying and fired straight at the bank behind which the Italians were lying, hoping another section might see our plight and work round them. It was a forlorn hope, but successful in a way I had not dreamed. Landing in the long, parched grass the signal cartridge set it alight. Threatened by the flames, the Italians retreated into the nearby house under cover of thick smoke. As quickly as I could reload, I sent three more cartridges into the house. There was a flicker of flame, and smoke began wreathing its way out of the cracks in the windows. In five minutes the house was well alight. We watched for the trapped men to make a break for it, but they apparently preferred to take their chance with the flames.

There was nothing now to prevent us from joining in the attack on the battery itself. Skirmishing round, we arrived in time to go in with the second assault on the battery. The first attack had been so successful that they had carried the position before the supporting mortars had had time to come into action. The first men reached the guns as the first mortar bomb fell, so they withdrew to let the mortars get on with it. As we went in, an Italian mortar team, crouching in their emplacement, fell to our bayonets. We discovered later when we inspected their shining new mortars that they had not had one round of ammunition between them.

We were now overlooking Syracuse, and it was suggested that we might turn the captured guns on the town. But we were in the dark as to the position of our own troops. For all we knew they might have reached Syracuse already. Reluctantly we destroyed the guns and settled down to eat our meagre rations, our first meal since leaving the *Ulster Monarch*. Meanwhile 1 Troop and the mortars were still busy and, by the time we had finished our meal, two neighbouring gun positions had fallen to them.

After a short rest we pushed on, intending to link up as soon as possible with the British division pushing up the coast towards Syracuse. All afternoon we tramped down the narrow Sicilian lanes, churning up clouds of fine white dust that smothered us from head to foot, mingling with the sweat on our arms and faces, blinding and nearly choking us.

The little church blazed white in the brilliant sunlight. Outside the church doors stood the elderly priest. There were inside, he explained, only old men, and women and children who had sought sanctuary. He thanked us for sparing the church. He had been afraid for it when he heard the guns and the explosions. 'You see, we only finished building it last month. I hope later you will come back so that I may show you our church.' Then, wistfully, 'Tell me. When will the *biscotte* – biscuits – arrive? Our women and children are so hungry. No food, you realize. The Germans . . . all . . .' He shrugged his shoulders.

Here and there we struck opposition. We deployed, attacked, and took more prisoners. By this time they stretched in a long column, guarded by one corporal with a tommy-gun.

By evening we still had not made contact with our own main forces, so we stopped for the night by a cluster of farm buildings. After a wash at the well, and a brew of tea, we settled down to sleep along the edge of the track. For warmth we pulled bundles of hay from the fields and snuggled down. The fires flickered and died.

Next morning we contacted the 5th Division on the road to Syracuse. Their forward elements had reached it the evening before. To them we handed over our five hundred prisoners. Altogether we felt pleased with our work. We had landed less than three hundred strong and, in one day, had captured three batteries and completely cleared the whole of Capo Murro di Porco, at a loss to the enemy of seven hundred men killed, wounded and prisoners of war. Our own losses were one killed and two wounded. The enemy had lost in equipment eighteen big guns of all types, besides innumerable machine-guns, mortars, rifles and several range-finders. We had lost one water-bottle and two berets.

On the morning of 12 July we marched into Syracuse. By the same afternoon the whole squadron had been ferried back to the *Ulster Monarch*.

5

'Night of Terror'

Back on the *Monarch* everyone was talking at once. I realized then the truth of the saying that the man in the front line sees least of the battle. No one had a very clear idea as yet of the overall picture of the operation. But every man had his own story to tell, his own personal glimpse of the fighting to recount. Among the laughter and banter, fragments of humour and drama came to the surface.

'. . . leapt about two feet in the air, 'e did. Just folded up like a knife, with my tracer coming out of 'is back. And the . . .'

'Did you see yon puir laddie on the bridge outside Syracuse? Och! 'Twas horrible. Must have been caught by a flame-thrower or something . . .'

'Near shot ol' Tommo 'ere,' chirped up a Cockney voice from under the steaming shower at the far end of the mess deck. 'Thought he was a Wop.' He roared with laughter.

'Did you hear what the sappers found on that second battery? Fuses laid to all the ammo. If one of them Wops had had the guts to set them off, we wouldn't be here now. The whole blooming lot would have gone sky-high. Like what . . .'

'. . . keeping my eye on the last Wop in the column. So many of them it was the only way of seeing none of 'em gave me the slip. Suddenly I looks round. Can't see 'im anywhere. Took me near five minutes afore I found 'im. Eight more of the blighters 'ad popped up from somewhere and tacked on to the end of the column. I dunno . . .'

'If I never sees another tomato again it'll be too soon. Field after field of 'em. Blimey. If the folks back home could've seen them. Just pulling them off as we walked along, suckin' the juice and throwing the skins away . . .'

So it went on. Everyone wanted to talk. No one wanted to listen. My own stories were bursting to be told, and I promptly unburdened them on Alec as we climbed out of our dirty clothes and washed off all the filth we had collected. Afterwards, up on deck, it was his turn. Out in the bay the hulk of an ammunition ship, hit squarely by a German dive bomber, burned fiercely. The crackle of exploding ammunition came faintly to our ears, punctuated by an occasional dull boom as cases of high explosive went sky-high.

Shortly after the fall of the first battery Alec had noticed, down towards the lighthouse, what looked like a gun position in the middle of a field. Through his binoculars he could see figures moving around. Getting his mortars quickly into position he sent over just one bomb. It burst in the field not far from the gun-pit. Immediately, three Italians appeared and made a dash for it across the open field, one of them wheeling a bicycle.

Alec sent over a second bomb. The Italians heard it coming, stopped, and hared back as fast as they could to the shelter of their pit. There they stayed for several minutes, peeping over the sandbags. Obviously they had not the slightest idea where the bombs were coming from. Again, cautiously looking all round them, they started to steal across the open field. A third bomb sailed over. This time Italian number three dashed back to cover abandoning his bicycle, which lay with wheels spinning gaily. A few minutes later all three walked out, hands in the air, and submitted to being taken prisoner.

Below decks there was a queue of men waiting in the steam and soapy water for their turn under the showers.

Others were busy removing detonators from grenades, cleaning pistols or rifles, or putting equipment in order. Everyone was waiting longingly for the order to stand down and that long, long sleep they had been promising themselves for the past three days. My own thoughts were turning that way when a voice at my shoulder broke in. 'Wanted in Captain Poat's cabin, sir.'

I was the last to arrive. Peter was propped up against the wash-basin. Rolls of maps lay on the bottom bunk.

'We're going ashore again this evening.' Harry Poat pointed at the map he was holding, at a spot just up the coast from Syracuse. 'This is the place here – the Italian naval base at Augusta. It will be daylight when we land.'

Gone were all hopes of that nice long sleep. I do not think any of us fancied breaking the news to the men, but we need not have worried. The bush telegraph had been at work. They were waiting with a 'Tell us the worst' look on their faces.

'Just a little job before we go to bed,' I announced brightly. Miraculously they all cheered up. Till then only a rumour had threatened their plans for sleep. Now they were committed they were ready, even eager, for the details.

'We are going ashore at seven-thirty to occupy the naval base at Augusta. It will still be daylight, but opposition should be nil.

'Our information is that the army have by-passed it on their way up the coast. All we have to do is land, mop up and link up with them. So we need only take half our ammunition scale.

'Now that the whole squadron is on board the *Monarch* we shall have to go ashore in two flights. We'll be going in the second flight. We land here . . .' They crowded round the map.

It was a perfect summer evening. The sun was dipping

towards the land, and the air was still. From the Sicilian coastline to the eastern horizon there was nothing to disturb the tranquillity. The *Ulster Monarch* sailed on like a cruise liner.

As we turned in towards Augusta the enchantment faded. Scanning the water-front through my glasses I found it strangely deserted. It was like a town that had died. Without much difficulty I picked out the spot where we were to land. It did not look too bad. Twenty or thirty feet of rock and grass to scramble up, then straight back into the town. Plenty of broken cover while landing, thank goodness. The place might be deserted, or it might be a trap.

We were so busy watching the coast that few of us noticed the approach of a British cruiser and attendant destroyers from the north. But the cruiser had seen us. There was a short, sharp exchange of signals.

Cruiser: *Where the hell do you think you are going?*

Monarch: Am going in.

Cruiser: *Proceed south immediately.*

Monarch: Am going in to land troops.

Cruiser: *In that case what support do you want?*

Monarch: All you've got.

By this time the *Monarch* had sailed into the middle of the outer bay and lay hove-to. I watched from the upper deck as the first flight of LCAs was lowered into the water. Then: 'Wumff – wumff, wumff.' Just beyond the *Monarch* three puffs of black smoke blossomed in the air. All of a sudden I felt very naked standing on the deck. Wherever the army might be, it certainly was not manning the guns of that cliff-top battery. At fifteen hundred yards the enemy gunners pumped shells over as fast as they could.

There came a high-pitched whine and crash as the cruiser's guns went into action. Half-way up the cliff little puffs of white appeared where the shells struck home. Up in the stern, the crew of the *Monarch*'s little 12-pounder bustled round excitedly. With their third shot part of the control building behind the Italian guns disappeared in a cloud of smoke and rubble. When the smoke cleared there was an ominous gap in its outline. But the enemy guns were still in action. Their shells were landing beyond the *Monarch*, but it did not seem possible that they could long miss us at that range.

At full speed and with all her guns firing, one of the tiny escort destroyers dashed across our bows and headed straight for the battery. It was magnificent. She was asking to be blown right out of the water but she kept right on, guns still firing until she was close inshore. Then, turning broadside-on to the battery, she swung away to try again. The God of brave men sailed with all the men in that destroyer.

The first flight of LCAs was close inshore now. Invisible hands picked out cigar-shaped patterns on the water. From somewhere ashore machine-guns were going into action. There was now an unholy din going on. The whine and crash of shells from the cruiser, the agitated thumping of the destroyers' pom-poms, the dull boom of the little 12-pounder. And now the *Monarch*'s 20 mm cannon crackled into action. Streams of red tracer streaked across the bay, searching out those machine-guns, to whine and sing into the air as they ricocheted off the rocks.

As the ramps of the first landing craft clattered down, the machine-guns mounted in the bows came to life, raking the houses along the sea-front with a murderous fire. Then the blue- and khaki-clad figures were out, scrambling quickly up the rocky slope.

I have no recollection of the return of the LCAs or of going aboard them. I can remember crouching low for protection as we approached the landing area, listening to the peculiar whistle of the bullets as they whined over our heads. Then the ramp was down. The water lapped round the slimy boulders that formed a precarious causeway to the shore. I quickly weighed the pros and cons of wading ashore in comparative safety, or running the gauntlet across the boulders. Calling myself a fool every inch of the way, I plumped for keeping dry.

The houses ahead seemed deserted. In a grassy hollow to my right lay two huddled forms. One of the RAMC men was bending over them, but there was nothing he could do. They had been caught in the cross-fire of those hidden machine-guns.

Silently we padded through the streets in our rubber-soled boots, keeping a wary eye on the upper windows of the houses, taking elaborate precautions at every corner. It was obvious now that the port was not being held in any strength, but it is as easy to die at the hands of a sniper as facing a battalion.

The sound of sporadic rifle-fire and the occasional chatter of a tommy-gun came to us as we worked our way slowly forward. Apart from that, the place seemed like a cemetery. It jangled the nerves. Every window, every doorway, held a possible enemy. It was impossible to search every house. We advanced up both sides of the street, the last three men of each subsection walking backwards, watching warily for a hidden enemy to rise up behind us. We could not relax our attention for an instant. The Germans were either watching and waiting, or had left booby-traps behind.

Somewhere ahead the red, hungry glow of a burning building lit up the dusk. I dragged out my compass and checked. That was where I was heading. Half an hour later we arrived at our objective. It was quite dark now and the house was blazing furiously. In the square beyond, the other sections were waiting. All except 3 Troop. They had pushed on ahead to test the cross-roads where we were supposed to link up with 17 Brigade. Beyond that no one seemed to have a very clear idea of what was to happen next. Some of the sections had met with sniping on their way through the town. One of the sergeants had been shot through the throat but had refused to be evacuated.

One section had been resting in a street when a stream of green tracer shot up the centre of the road. All heads turned to watch it. Next moment the street was empty as men dived head first through the nearest windows and doors. We laughed about that, and fell to wondering again what was happening up front.

Carefully, 3 Troop had pushed ahead. They first knew that something had definitely gone wrong when they came to the bridge that joins Augusta – built on an island – to the mainland. As the first man went across there came the familiar whine and crump of a shell. The enemy gunners had the range to a T. In ones and twos 3 Troop dodged across between shells, and pushed on across the railway.

As they approached the cross-roads, the Germans opened up with heavy machine-guns and mortars, putting down a devastating fire. On the cross-roads they could see a big gun pointing straight up the road towards them. 3 Troop fought back as hard as they could, but decided to withdraw when they heard tanks approaching up the road.

Back in town we knew nothing of this. We could hear the firing and knew they had run into trouble, but the forward observation officers with us were unable to contact any British warship to come to our support because the sea water had damaged their radios. We ourselves had only half our normal ammunition with us, and there was no sign of 17 Brigade with whom we were supposed to link up. The enemy, on the other hand, appeared to be sitting on the cross-roads in great strength.

We decided to stay where we were and hold the port until the army did arrive. My section was pushed forward to where the Citadel overlooked the harbour. From there we could command the road forty feet below along which any attack must come. Alec joined me there as it was an ideal spot from which to control his mortars. We settled down to wait, a cold night in front of us and a dawn which we knew we might never see if the enemy attacked in strength.

It was a cold night. All around me the huddled figures of the section stirred restlessly as they tried to grab a little sleep before taking over sentry duty. Even the stars were frozen into the dark blue sky. I shivered. A solitary shell whined over in the direction of the outer bay where we had landed. There was silence. Fifteen minutes later another shell whined over. So it continued throughout the night – one shell every fifteen minutes. We changed sentries by them. I tried my radio again, but it was dead. The batteries had not yet dried out after their wetting coming ashore. I switched off.

In the centre of our position stood a small ornamental fountain, but no jets played from it. That too had died when we landed. The stonework glittered coldly in the starlight. A cold breeze rustled the leaves in the surrounding trees. The Citadel stood out black and forbidding against the night sky. I fell asleep.

Heavy boots tramped through my dreams and I woke with a start. The stars were fading and dawn was near. The man on sentry ran over to where I lay. 'Patrol of six men from 17 Brigade. They've reached the cross-roads.'

'Reached the cross-roads?' I was puzzled. 'I didn't hear any fighting.'

'They say the Germans had pulled out before they got there.'

'OK. Tell the chaps to stand-to while I nip back to Troop HQ and tell them.'

Inside ten minutes I was back. The bleak grey light of dawn had reached out over the harbour and the distant hills. The sun still hung below the far horizon. It was bitterly cold.

Alec had already ordered his men back into the town square. I was about to do the same when there came that familiar '*Wumff – wumff*'. Two puffs of smoke appeared in the air not a hundred yards in front of our position, and shrapnel whined and zinged down through the trees among us. I looked round. We were all flat on our faces. 'Anybody hit?' Nobody was. 'OK. Work your way back to the square.' We started to wriggle back.

'*Wumff-wumff-wumff*.' They were getting nearer but, miraculously, everyone was still unhurt. Obviously there was a battery still to be overrun and, even more obviously, they had an observation post that overlooked our position. We wriggled faster. Back in the square a couple of shells burst inquiringly overhead, then the firing stopped. They had lost us.

We had come ashore without rations. We set about foraging for food. Soon dozens of fires were going on the pavements and the smell of cooking set our nostrils quivering and our mouths watering.

After I had eaten I went down to where we had landed. The sun was shining on an empty sea – not a sign of any ship anywhere. Back in the square someone had dragged a piano out of a café on to the sidewalk and a singsong was in progress. Reaction from the night before had set in. The strain on our nerves released, everyone was now in high good humour.

Two newsreel men appeared from somewhere and, having delightedly recorded the scene, were carried off to do a little celebrating of their own.

Half-way through the afternoon word came that we were to be taken off in two destroyers. In a long column we marched down to the harbour where an old motor boat was waiting to carry us to the destroyers – one Greek and one British.

On board the British destroyer we were given a royal welcome – a hot meal, drinks and cigarettes. Once we were under way I went up on deck. The water was screaming past as we headed for the open sea at speed. I looked back at the harbour we had just quitted. Out of the sun, flying low and fast, came six planes. Huge mushrooms of water fountained into the air as their bombs struck home. We had got away just in time.

In Syracuse harbour the *Ulster Monarch* was waiting for us. All around the bay Bofors guns were getting into position. We felt secure. This time we wasted no time getting down to some good solid sleep. As I lay in my bunk my mind ran over the events of the past three days. For the loss of two killed and eight wounded we had captured the first major enemy naval base to fall into our hands in Europe, together with twenty-seven seaplanes and numerous small ships.

A German military spokesman later described that night in Augusta as 'a night of terror the Germans will never forget'. But perhaps he was exaggerating.

6

Unquiet Interlude

The *Monarch* was sweltering in the hot Mediterranean sun when we awoke next morning. The whole sea shimmered and glistened with dancing points of light. A quivering heat haze hung over the land. The little Bofors guns had discreetly retired beneath their camouflage nets. The events of Augusta seemed no more than a vague dream during our long night's sleep.

After lunch we went ashore in the LCAs for a swim. As I dived from the side of the landing craft and felt the warm-cool water swirl past me I forgot all thoughts of war and fighting. Only later did I have cause to remember that those same waters, angry and turbulent, had battered down and engulfed so many men but five days before, as they swam for their lives from the wrecked gliders.

Towels under our arms, we swarmed over Capo Murro di Porco where we had charged in with rifles and tommy-guns so few days before. Reminiscences were endless. Then, hot and tired, we scrambled back to the shore and headed out to the *Monarch* again . . . As we approached the hospital ship anchored in the middle of the bay, its white paint splashed with green bands and red crosses, a body floated in towards the shore slowly, lapped by the rippling waves. Grey in death and floating face down, it was clad only in a pair of thin cotton pants. A single bullet-hole showed darkly in the middle of the back.

Early next morning we were on the move again, back to Augusta. Speculation was rife. As we entered the harbour we saw lying at anchor the two commando ships,

Emma and *Beatrix*. Perhaps it was coincidence, perhaps not.

From up the coast in the direction of Catania came the dull booming of a monitor's huge guns as she hurled shell after shell into the beleaguered port. Sprawling between the sea and the mountains which crowded the coast, Catania was being stoutly defended by its German garrison. The British troops, forced to make a frontal attack on a narrow sector, were trying desperately to thrust forward. For the first time in the campaign, something approaching trench warfare was developing.

Even so, it came as a shock to hear – as we did, after lunch – that the two commandos and ourselves were to be used to try and break the deadlock. 3 Commando, who had suffered heavy casualties in the campaign, were to land north of Catania and establish a beach-head. We of the Special Raiding Squadron were to pass through them and fight our way the five miles down into Catania and seize the dock area. The Marine Commando were to follow up and throw an outer ring round the docks. A brigade was then to be landed on the harbour mole. The threat of this diversion, it was hoped, would cause the German front line to crack.

To a man we were uneasy about the operation but, whatever forebodings we had, we did our best to keep them to ourselves. There was to be a final conference at five o'clock. Meanwhile we busied ourselves getting ready. Carefully we studied the maps, but there did not seem to be as much information as usual on them. Neither did anyone know the exact dispositions of the German troops. We expected more information about that after the five o'clock conference. Yet it seemed inevitable that long before we had covered that five miles the Germans would see what was coming and we would find the docks heavily defended.

Still, it had to be done and no one doubted that we would succeed – although the general feeling was that the Special Raiding Squadron was about to go out in a blaze of glory.

As five o'clock approached, the feeling of tenseness and anxiety increased. The guns of the British naval forces bombarding Catania rumbled in the distance still. I had a queer bottled-up feeling, and the waiting seemed interminable. I pictured our landing, making our way blindly through woods that stretched from the water's edge to the road to Catania. Half a mile down that road was a defended road-block. There, it seemed likely, we would run into our first bit of trouble. We had blue-printed our attack upon it and we would get past all right, but the sound of the firing would be certain to bring a hornets' nest about our ears. It would be quite a party, no doubt.

I reviewed the odds and accepted the fact that, by the same time on the morrow, I might be lying like so many I had seen – cold, dirty, unlovely and a bit of a mess. Yet something deep inside told me I would live; that same something that tells every man that, up to the moment the bullet hits home or the shell blows him into oblivion.

A tender headed towards us across the harbour. The conference in the *Beatrix* was over. As Paddy came aboard I looked for some sign. Always on these occasions his expression was an accurate barometer of the difficulties ahead. He smiled, and the tenseness fell away. The cry went round the ship, 'Job off.'

In the last five minutes of the conference, word had come from Intelligence that the Germans had moved up fresh troops, and had bivouacked for the night precisely where we were to have landed. We could never have cut our way through to the road, let alone Catania.

Emma and *Beatrix* were still at anchor on the far side

of the harbour. Now, as light began to fail, a 'flak' cruiser moved into position not far from where we lay. It was comforting to know it was there, bristling with anti-aircraft guns. Climbing into my bunk, I fell fast asleep.

I woke to the shrill shrieking of ships' sirens. An urgency in their note sent me hurrying into my clothes and up on deck. Over the loud hailer came the sharp command, 'Make smoke.' Slowly and sinuously a dark blanket of smoke curled its way across the harbour, blotting out ships and shore installations. From overhead came the throbbing roar of bombers. A flash flickered from end to end of the cruiser as its guns roared into action. The curtain of red tracer sailed slowly and majestically into the air. One by one, every ship in the harbour joined in, adding its quota to the red inferno in the skies above the dark fog.

On the *Monarch*, gun crews groped their way through the murk to their posts. The crackle of their cannon guns punctuated the frightful din. Gun flashes flickered back and forth through the pall of smoke like lightning among thunder clouds. The roar of the bombers was louder, more insistent now. Then the bombs. With a shrieking whistle they hurtled towards the smoke-blanketed harbour to burst with a deep concussion that seemed to stop my heart. It was one thing to know that the bombs were meant for us. They could either hit or miss. But to lie hidden beneath that suffocating cloud waiting for a chance bomb to find its billet was far more unnerving.

Already the *Monarch*'s guns were so hot that relays of men were dashing buckets of water over guns and crews alike as they continued to pump their shells into the air. There was nothing I could usefully do, so I went below. As I lay in my bunk, my face little more than a foot from the ceiling, I realized for the first time that my cabin was immediately below one of the Oerlikon cannon. Its frantic hammering seemed to suffocate me. I was slowly drowning in a sea of noise. Every so often a thin whine penetrated through the din and the whole ship shook as another near miss sent the harbour waters cascading into the night. Gradually I sank into a deep stupor, in which only the jangling of my nerves remained to show that I still lived.

Two more nights of these sustained attacks left their mark. We were jumpy and apprehensive. On the third night a bomb falling near one of the commando ships detonated the explosives store on board . . .

That afternoon we went ashore. In an orchard not far from where we had struck the Germans on our first visit to Augusta, we settled down for what we fondly hoped was to be a good night's rest.

Shortly after ten o'clock there came a warning '*Wumpp – wumpp.*' Within a minute the whole of the port defences were in action. A huge umbrella of red tracer spread out over the harbour. Up above, the German bombers droned in. From the leading aircraft dropped a large cluster of blazing flares, picking out our forest white mosquito nets like so many pinpoints of light. Then came the first bombs.

The following morning our kits were lying on the quayside. The *Ulster Monarch* had been ordered to sea. We collected our belongings and moved off to another camp further from the port, on the cliffs.

Now followed a period of waiting; waiting for the fall of Catania. We filled in the time with long marches, and bathing from the foot of the cliffs. We got used to the regular visits of the Luftwaffe. Sharp at ten in the evening and four in the morning they came over, pasted the harbour, and went on their way.

With the fall of Catania we were jolted out of our routine. We were to land and cut the road and railway south of Messina, thus cutting off the fleeing remnants of the German army. It was a rush job. We had no maps, but the CO of a fighter reconnaissance squadron volunteered to fly in at low level to get the necessary aerial obliques. His pictures of a startled Sicilian carter staring up with open mouth showed that he had gone in 'on the deck' to get them. By six o'clock the same evening we were all tee-ed up. We were aboard the LCIs (Landing Craft, Infantry) and ready to sail. Five minutes later news came that the Eighth Army was moving so fast up the coast that it was feared we might cut them off instead of the Germans. It was 'Job off' again.

We set off by train to Canizarro, just north of Catania, and made our camp on the very spot where we were to have landed in the projected attack on Catania. While our troops faced the Germans and Italians on the mainland across the narrow Straits of Messina we explored the town, had our first taste of Marsala and – some of us – our first octopus cake. We climbed to Etna's summit and stared into the huge crater.

We wondered when Italy would be invaded.

7

Better Born Lucky . . .

The little ship shuddered slightly as we left the shelter of
the land. The north Sicilian coast slipped away behind us.
We were alone with the white wash of our propellers, and
that dark smudge ahead of us – the LCI on which the rest
of the squadron had embarked at Messina.

I shivered and snuggled down in the well of the after
gun to get away from the biting wind. Less than twenty-
four hours ago our troops had crossed the Straits of
Messina into Italy. Now we were heading up the Italian
coast towards Bagnara.

The long weeks of waiting in Sicily seemed unreal now.
The dash up the coast from Catania to Messina; our
arrival there but a few short hours ago; the hurried orders
in the dark; the precious time wasted when our LCI
refused to come off the beach: all were vaguely remembered snatches of another existence.

Bagnara lay some thirty miles to the north of where our
main forces had landed. We were to hold the town till
they arrived. With an enemy across their lines of communications, the Germans were less likely to make a stand
in the toe of Italy.

A grenade slipped off my belt and rolled away. In the
darkness I fumbled around for it. I was confused. The
layout of these LCIs was strange to me. It was the first
time we had operated from them. Carrying about two
hundred men, they could run right up to the beach and
drop their two landing-ramps. I prayed they would not
make too much noise. My groping fingers closed on the
grenade. I clipped it back on my webbing.

When I awoke I was cold and cramped. The night was black. On the starboard beam, like a long black cloud low on the horizon, lay the Italian coast. We turned in towards the land. Gradually, very gradually, the Italian hills looked up out of the darkness. A single pinpoint of light ashore moved slowly along and out of sight.

The revving of our engines slowed till we were barely making headway. From the LCI ahead two small dark shapes detached themselves as the beach assault party headed for the shore in assault craft. All we could do was wait. We strained our eyes, watching for the winking light that was to be our signal to close in and land.

The minutes passed like hours. Then it came. Two long flashes and one short. The engines revved up and we moved in. As we took up our positions by the landing-ramps there came a resounding boom from the shore, then silence. 'Demolitions.' The whisper ran round. Had we been spotted?

The Navy men ran out the ramps ready for lowering. Like giant antennae they reached out over the beach as the LCI grounded gently. I held my breath, and scrambled down the ramp with the section crowding at my heels. One of the Navy men was shooing us down. 'Come along, army. Get moving. We want to get out of here. It's nearly dawn. Come along, army . . .'

The beach looked ominously bumpy in the growing light, as if it were mined. We hopped across like scalded cats to the shelter of the promenade that ran along the foot of the cliff. Crouching there, we waited with bated breath while the rest of the squadron scrambled over the beach, waiting for that first orange flash and crash of a mine going up.

One of the signallers from Troop HQ came up at the double. 'Captain Poat wants to see you, sir. I'll take you to him.'

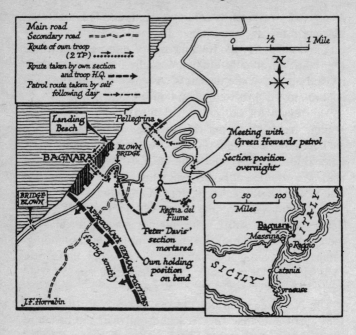

Main road
Secondary road
Route of own troop (2 TP)
Route taken by own section and troop H.Q.
Patrol route taken by self following day

Landing Beach
Pellegrina
BAGNARA
BLOWN BRIDGE
Meeting with Green Howards patrol
Section position overnight
BRIDGE BLOWN
APPROXIMATE GERMAN POSITIONS (facing south)
Regna del Fiume
Peter Davis' section mortared
Own holding position on bend
J.F. Horrabin

0   ½   1 Mile
N

0   50   100
Miles
Bagnara
Messina
Reggio
SICILY
ITALY
Catania
Syracuse

He was huddled down by the low sea wall. I squatted down beside him.

'We've been landed on the north side of the town instead of the south – and we're late. We'll have to work our way into the town from here, and hope for the best. We'll make for the upper part of the town.' He jabbed his finger at the map.

'Tony will lead, with Peter second and yourself in the rear. We'll have to look slippy. It's almost dawn. Any questions? Right then. Get your chaps ready to move straight away.'

We slipped into the town, padding along silently in our rubber soles. Almost immediately the buildings began to take shape through the grey dawn haze. Within a few minutes it was fully light. The streets along which we were advancing led straight inland. At the far end a long flight of broad stone steps led upwards towards the church, like a picture of an Aztec temple.

So far there had been no sign of any enemy. Silently we hurried on. Half-way up the street, on the right, the wooden shutters of a window swung open. For perhaps five seconds the old Italian woman stood there, staring out into the street, stupefied amazement on her face. Then her cracked voice shrilled out excitedly. '*Inglesi, Inglesi!*'

Up and down the street it echoed, more shrill and more excited. Windows and doors flung open as sleepy-eyed Italians rushed to see what the excitement was about. Fingers on triggers we waited for the first German to show himself. Out into the streets poured crowds of Italians: women, children, and old men, shouting and gesticulating wildly. '*Inglesi, Inglesi. Mussolini finito. Inglesi . . .*'

Now they were pushing huge bunches of grapes into our hands. If there was a German within miles we had had it.

'Get them back into the houses,' I shouted, 'and make them shut up.' Roughly and unceremoniously we bundled our would-be well-wishers back into their homes. All along the street other sections were doing the same. Grinning broadly, the chaps herded them all back with their rifles.

'Go on. Get in, you Eyetie bastards . . .'

'Here, just a minute, ma' – this to a fat Italian woman protesting vigorously – 'you can leave those grapes behind before you go. OK. Thanks. Now, in you go.'

Still no sign of the Germans. At the top of the steps we turned through a narrow, dark passage-way into the upper part of the town. Ahead of us huge chunks of masonry blocked the road. A thick white dust had settled everywhere. It was only just possible to make out the shattered arches of the bridge. This must have been the explosion we had heard before we landed.

Tony's section were taking up positions round the bridge. Peter had made his way on to the hairpin bend above us. My own section were strung out behind me as we approached the wrecked bridge. I turned round to make sure the chaps were not bunching too much. Round the corner behind us a file of men marched into view, rifles at the trail.

For a moment the only thought that came into my mind was: Americans. What the devil are Americans doing here? Then something clicked. 'Germans!' I shouted, and pointed. The two Bren gunners swung round, firing from the hip. The Germans were round the corner in a cloud of dust. They had been marching up behind us, blissfully unaware that we were other than Italians, and must have been very shaken when we opened fire. They ran into our fire again as they turned a bend in the cliff road. Those who were not killed were captured when they ran into the arms of another section.

Beyond the bridge a series of hairpin bends carried the road up into the mountains above the town. Round one of these bends we came upon Paddy sitting on a doorstep, pensively studying a handful of aerial photos of the area.

'Come over here, Harry.'

'Sir?'

'Look. We've found that the Germans are holding a hastily-prepared line just south of the town, more or less where we should have landed.'

'Lucky we didn't.'

'Yes. But they know we are here now – and if they are going to counter-attack it will be down this road.' He pointed down at one of the photos. 'See this bend? I want you to take your section up there. If they attack, hold them off as long as you can, then fall back slowly down the road.

'If they attack in strength we cannot hope to do more than that.' He paused. 'Quite clear? Right. Get off with you, now.'

Reaching the bend he had indicated I was surprised to find 1 Troop already in position. I pushed on to the next bend above them. It was a nasty position to hold, overlooked by steep hills. I was showing the last man to his fire position when, from up the road, there came the sharp angry whine of a sniper's bullet.

Over on the left I heard the slow, eerie whistle of mortar bombs. '*Wummp – wummp – wummp – wummp.*' They straddled 1 Troop's positions on the lower bend. Someone shouted and a medical orderly came running up the road.

Up in the hills a gun came into action. A shell whined over to fall in the town. I ducked hurriedly. The sniper was at it again. Someone flopped heavily to the ground beside me. It was Peter.

'Got to push through you to the next bend,' he explained breathlessly. 'What's going on?'

'Sniper potting at us down the road. Can't see where he is, but it might be that shed up there. Watch out for him, anyway.'

'OK. See you later.' He signalled his section forward. Hugging the sides of the road, they trudged towards the turning. There was a sudden deafening concussion. Section and bend disappeared in a cloud of smoke and dust. Two figures came staggering out of the cloud, hands to their eyes. They hesitated for a moment, then turned and went back. When the dust had subsided and the smoke cleared away there was no sign of anyone.

'What's happened?' Harry Poat came running.

'Those Jerry mortars were smack on Peter and his section.'

'All right. Get your section up into the hills and try to locate those mortars. If Peter's pinned down it'll give him a chance to get out. I'll come with you.'

Half-way up the hill someone reported that Corporal McDiarmid had dropped out. Shot through the ankle as we left the road below, he had struggled up the hill with us until pain and loss of blood forced him to stop.

Every so often we rested on the terraced hillside among the grape-laden vines, but the top was reached at last. Under cover of the trees we pushed on towards the sound of the mortars thumping away in the distance. The further we went the thicker the undergrowth, until at about half past two we were forced to call a halt. We were making very slow progress, and the mortars were as far away as ever.

I decided to take up a defensive position among the trees, covering the town below us. We could also overlook the village of Pellegrina, where the enemy were still apparently in occupation. Despite the shade of the trees it was now very hot. We put out two Bren gun posts. Now and then a shell whined over as it plummeted down into the town to burst with a distant crump. Flies and insects droned lazily. We drowsed in the heat . . .

A shout from one of the Bren gunners. A platoon of Germans was moving down the road from Pellegrina, presumably to mop up Peter's section. It was extreme range but a good target. The Brens chattered into life. The Germans broke up in confusion and melted away. They did not try again.

Meanwhile 3 Troop had contacted the enemy on the

southern outskirts of the town. After a sharp, brief engagement, the Germans abandoned their mortars and took refuge in a railway tunnel. Some slipped away into the hills. Their exact strength we never knew, although one of the wounded Germans asked anxiously what had become of the rest of his battalion, and our prisoners numbered among them men from a Grenadier regiment, Jaeger battalion, and sappers.

About two o'clock in the afternoon, the advanced elements of the Yorks and Lancs Regiment, 15 Brigade, reached the southern edge of the town but were held up by a blown bridge. But up in the hills Harry Poat and I knew nothing of this. Shells and mortar bombs were still whistling and whining overhead. One of the shells fell on our position, burying four men. We dug them out uninjured. It must have been a stray but I took my glasses out to see whether I could spot that gun position. I carefully scanned the ridge above us. Trees, trees, nothing but trees, and a grey boulder looking strangely out of place. As I watched, the boulder moved. It was a rather fat German in field grey crawling cautiously along on hands and knees. I counted them. Ten. With the glasses I followed their tortuous journey through the trees. One by one they slipped out of the wood to take cover in a hollow dug into the side of the grassy bank that bordered the wood.

Just before dark we decided to withdraw to a shorter line above the town where we could better defend ourselves during the night. Before leaving our positions I pointed out the hollow to the two Bren guns. Each poured a magazine of tracer into it before pulling out. The shots slammed straight home.

We were awake at first light next morning. No counterattack had developed during the night. I asked Harry if I could take five men and try to find the battery that was giving all the trouble. It seemed to be somewhere over the crest above us.

We arranged to keep in wireless touch. We took a 38 set, with its throat microphone, and planned to get in touch every half-hour with the 11 set that Harry had with him. Keen and full of hope, we set off on the steep climb ahead of us.

It was steep, too. In places we had to pull ourselves up from tree to tree, being careful always to grasp the trees only at ground-level. We did not want our progress marked by a line of waving foliage easily spotted from above.

At the end of the first half-hour we contacted Harry Poat. We had climbed several hundred feet but still seemed no nearer the top, although we had an excellent view out to sea. It was then that we saw the cruiser moving in towards the coast. There was a flash and a rushing sound overhead as her shells searched out the German guns.

For another half-hour we toiled up the slope, getting more breathless, resting every few yards. In a small clearing we ran up the telescopic aerial again. I strapped the throat microphone on.

'Hello, Harry. No sign of anything yet but it looks as if we are getting near the top. We should be over the crest before we contact you again. Anything for me?'

'No, nothing for you. We'll be listening out.'

I took off the microphone and we pushed on. We expected to run into the battery just over that crest. We checked rifles and tommy-guns as we reached it. Lying in the brushwood, I had a good look round. 'Thank the Lord it's wooded,' I murmured to myself, taking in the closely-set trees and the thick undergrowth. In single file we moved cautiously forward.

We must have pushed inland for the best part of a mile,

still through thick woods, when we ran the aerial up again. But try as we could we were unable to make contact. The trees were screening our transmission. We packed up and carried on.

Threading our way carefully through the trees, the growing light ahead showed that we were coming to the end of the wood. On our stomachs now, we wriggled cautiously forward to the edge. The ground sloped away to a deep valley.

On the far side the hills rose even higher. Snaking its way tortuously to the top ran a solitary white road along which, through my glasses, I could see a single truck moving along in a cloud of dust. Then it was gone.

I had been so taken with the view straight ahead that I had completely overlooked the red-roofed houses showing through trees over on the left. Now I had a good look at them. It was a village; quite a big one, too. I decided we would stay where we were and watch it for a while. There was no other way of telling whether or not it was occupied.

We must have lain there for a good half-hour without seeing a sign of a movement. Only the thin wisps of smoke wreathing slowly up from two or three chimneys told that it was inhabited. A closer reconnaissance was needed.

Two or three fields away a line of telegraph poles showed where a road led into the village. Scattered clumps of bushes crowded up to the hedge along the roadside. Crouching low we made for them. Crawling painfully past gaps in the hedge we inched our way slowly towards the village. In the garden of the first house washing flapped idly on the line, but there was still no sign of anyone about.

In this fashion we worked our way right into the village. There was no evidence of German or Italian troops so, emboldened, we stepped out into the road, three on each side, rifles and tommy-guns at the ready. We slipped forward the safety catches. If we bumped anything seconds would count.

'Hiya, Tommy!'

From the ditch where I had flung myself I cautiously raised my head. Twenty yards away, seemingly from a hole in the ground, popped a tousled head with a broad grin all over its face.

'Hiya, Tommy. You are Ingleesh, yes?' The head disappeared. From the depths of the ground came an excited shout.

'They are 'ere. They are 'ere. Ingleesh. *Inglesi.*' The head reappeared. A body wriggled into view. He was an oldish man. Now he stood up, excitedly waving to an invisible horde behind him. One by one, like animals coming out of the Ark, they tumbled into the daylight, staring at us from the road. There were old men, women, and girls, and even two babies. Apprehension and uncertainty showed on the faces of some of them.

By now a sizeable crowd had gathered round, but more and more were coming from their hide-out till there must have been over a hundred of them. It was my turn to get nervous. If we were surprised now, we would have to fire through them or be taken prisoner. The old man I had first seen had appointed himself spokesman.

'Welcome, Tommy, to Regna del Fiume. You are . . .'

Impatiently I cut him short. '*Dove i Tedesci?* Where are the Germans?'

He spread his arms out in a gesture of resignation. 'The Germans? They left, perhaps half an hour ago. But where . . . ? Who knows?' He waved towards the crowd around him. 'Many of us here speak English. We work in America once. But now you have something to eat, yes?'

I groaned inwardly. This could go on all day. 'OK, chaps. We are pushing on.' Unceremoniously we forced

our way through the crowd and disappeared down the
road, leaving them staring after us. We were running into
the woods again now. I was about to tell three of the men
to move a little way into the trees when, round a bend
two or three hundred yards ahead, came a file of men.
Surprise was mutual. My instinct was to drop to the
ground and open fire, but for some reason or other I did
not. Neither did they. Warily we approached each other,
alert for the first false move. If they were Germans our
only hope would be to fire and break for the woods.

As we came closer I could make out the battle-dress
and saucer-like tin hats. They were British. A few
moments later we were exchanging notes with the
advanced elements of the Green Howards. While the rest
of my small party went back to Regna del Fiume to keep
that luncheon date I went on to brigade HQ.

The brigadier and his staff had made their headquarters
in a small house. When I arrived they were lunching on
apples and wine and the brigadier was complaining that
his supporting artillery had not come up. I knew that
some 25-pounders had reached the blown bridge just
south of Bagnara the previous evening but, for some
reason best known to himself, the brigadier refused to
credit my story. He was also out of contact with the Yorks
and Lancs on his left flank.

He did accept my offer to contact them, so filling my
pockets with apples I set off back to Regna del Fiume to
collect the rest of the party. Together we plunged into the
woods. The undergrowth was very thick, and we had to
push and hack our way through it for several miles. In a
clearing we came across a small deserted camp showing
obvious signs of recent occupation by Germans. A little
further on we struck the road.

Along a little track leading from the road we found the
German battery position we had been looking for. The

guns were gone but empty shell-cases littered the place. From here they had been able to shoot into Bagnara over open sights. To the right and far below us we could see the roof-tops of Pellegrina.

So far there had been no sign of the Yorks and Lancs. We scrambled down the hillside towards Pellegrina. Approaching the village we proceeded with more caution, not knowing what to expect. What we did find was certainly unexpected. Sitting patiently on the cross-roads were two Italian soldiers, kits packed, ready and waiting to be taken prisoner.

We searched the place, house by house. From one that had clearly been a German HQ we took several documents of interest, and then moved on towards the cemetery at the other side of the village. A shot whined over our heads. We took cover but no more were fired. A couple of minutes later we ran the culprits to earth, manning a machine-gun in a tiny fox-hole dug into the side of the hill, overlooking Bagnara.

From up the coast came a prolonged burst of rifle fire and the chatter of machine-guns. The Yorks and Lancs had by-passed Pellegrina and were going into the attack. There was no longer any need to deliver my message. With our four prisoners we started back to where we had left the rest of the section that morning. Already the sun had begun to sink towards the horizon and the sea was splashed with orange and gold. We turned once again into the woods.

It was seven o'clock before we got back to the section position. We found them getting ready to pack up, and surprised to see us. Unable to contact us since our last message that we were near the top of the hill early that morning, they had made up their minds that we had either been killed or taken prisoner. The rest of the squadron had re-embarked that morning for Sicily. Only my own section and Tony Marsh's had remained behind to wait for us.

We dropped our prisoners and the documents we had brought with us into divisional headquarters in Bagnara. A meal had been prepared for us and, sitting on the kerb-side, we soon made short work of it before hunting up billets for the night.

We found these in a deserted schoolhouse by the shore and, had it not been for the fleas, we would no doubt have slept well on into the day. As it was, dawn found us outside on the beach. The sea, whipped up by a westerly gale, was pounding the shingle as huge rollers thundered in. It was Tony who first spotted a dark shape tossed high on a wave and wallowing in the trough. It was an amphibious DUKW. Disabled, she was in real trouble. Most of her deck cargo of petrol had broken free and was being swept away. The crew of three RASC men were trying desperately to prevent her foundering as wave after wave pounded her broadside-on.

But her plight had also been seen from the schoolhouse. While some of us plunged into the heavy seas to salvage the precious petrol, the rest busied themselves getting a rope out to the DUKW. Within an hour the petrol was safely stacked on the beach, and the DUKW was again under way.

We marched down the dusty road to the port and embarked for Messina, there to refit and pick up three months' mail.

8

Adriatic Adventure

The three LCIs butted their way doggedly up the Adriatic, riding the heavy swell. Above, low black clouds scudded swiftly by. A fine rain swept the decks.

For the past three weeks, ever since Bagnara, we had been 'resting'. We had celebrated the Italian armistice with a profusion of multi-coloured Very lights, flares, and Italian red wine. Now, exactly a month after the first landing in Italy, we were heading for Termoli, a small Italian port on the Adriatic coast. On the other two ships were 3 Commando and 40 Royal Marine Commando.

The 78th Division were advancing as rapidly as possible up the coast towards the port. On the high ground north of the river that runs into the sea there, the Germans were waiting for them. It was hoped that our landing at Termoli would disorganize German resistance to 78 Division's advance, thus introducing a serious threat to the north of Rome.

At a quarter to three in the morning of 3 October, 3 Commando landed successfully on the beach above Termoli and established a bridge-head. The night was black and the beach particularly narrow and, as 40 Commando and ourselves poured ashore, there was great confusion. Sections and troops were trying to sort themselves out as best they could. A figure challenged out of the darkness.

'Jack Hobbs.'

'Sorry, chum, not this section,' retorted a Cockney voice from the ground. 'Better try the commandos.'

The Marines were going into the town to leave their visiting-cards on the German garrison. 3 Commando, sadly depleted by this time, were strung out along the railway line a few hundred yards inland. Alec and his mortars were to come with my section, and we were to head three or four hundred miles inland to high wooded ground where we could have a smack at the Germans as they retreated from Termoli itself. We were to be in position by dawn. Somewhere on my right were Tony's and Peter's sections. The other two troops were heading for the Termoli–Campomarino road.

We crossed the railway line and started to climb the steep bank on the other side. The rain had stopped by this time but our rubber-soled boots slithered and slipped in slimy mud. It was as much as we could do to scramble to the top, a matter of fifteen feet or so. The mortars gave us most difficulty. Time and again they slipped back to the bottom just when we thought we had made it. We got them up eventually, and headed inland on a compass bearing.

Slowly we threaded our way across thick, heavy plough, sinking in well over the ankles with each step. The thick mud clung to our boots, turning them into leaden weights. About a mile inland we were due to cross a road but, although we seemed to have been going for hours, there was no sign of it. To our right I could make out a clump of trees, but could remember no trees on the map near the road. Through the trees showed a glimmer of light. From the isolated farmhouse came the frenzied barking of dogs. We veered sharply off to the left and the barking died down. Twenty minutes later we hit the road. Now we were passing through an orchard. Beyond lay open fields with a few scattered trees. With a shock I realized that dawn was not far off.

We were out in the open when, from the town on our left, there came the crackle of rifle fire. For a moment I thought we had been seen, but the Germans were far too busy with 40 Commando to be looking our way. Ahead of us I could see our objective, a tree-crested hill rising into the misty dawn. Within a matter of minutes we were pressing into the shelter of a little valley running straight into the heart of the hill.

'That looks a likely place for your mortars, Alec.' I pointed to a spot below a farmhouse ahead of us. Even as I pointed bullets whipped past our heads, the green tracer sailing slowly down towards us. A figure dashed through the trees and into the farmhouse. We leaped for cover in a sunken track some twenty yards in front of us.

Over to the left a thick hedgerow interspersed with tall trees ran straight up towards the farmhouse. Crouching low we made for it now. While I had a good look through my glasses Alec got his mortars into position. The first bomb fell straight into the farmyard. Three more followed in quick succession.

The firing stopped. I raised myself up on my elbows to get a better view, but could see no movement. I lowered my glasses.

'Look.' It was Alec. 'About a third of the way down the hill. Whole column of them. Can you make them out?'

'No, I can't. There's twenty or so of them making their way towards us but I can't make them out.'

'OK. I'll give them a smoke bomb for luck.' Then, to the mortars: 'One round smoke – fire!'

It burst in a thick cloud of white twenty or thirty yards short of them, spraying fragments of burning phosphorus all round. They started to run for cover.

'Good Lord! They're women and children.'

They huddled for safety under an overhanging bank beneath the trees. Risking drawing the German fire we blew our whistles and waved to them to come down. For a while they crouched there, clearly terrified that we would fire on them again. Then one or two of the bolder ones began to pick their way down the hill in our direction. Seeing that nothing happened the rest of them followed at a respectful distance.

I still suspected a trick, but decided to wait until they were within about a hundred yards. Ahead of the women and girls came a grey-haired farmhand. He waved his hand. From the farmhouse came a solitary shot. The bullet buzzed angrily overhead.

'Alec, get your mortars back on that farm. I'm going to take the section up the far side of the hedge and go in from the left flank.'

'OK. Do you want me to give them a pasting as you go up?'

'No. Only if they spot us and start slinging stuff at us.'

We reached the top of the hill without any more shots being fired. In extended line, rifles and tommy-guns ready, we moved warily into the farm. Feathers and dead hens littered the place, proof of the accuracy of Alec's mortars, but of Germans not a sign.

Cautiously we searched outhouses and buildings. The Germans had turned the main building into quite a nice little fortress with some well-sited sniping positions in the attic. I decided to make it our temporary headquarters. I placed one man in the house as a sniper. The rest took up positions in the farmyard while I got out the map and tried to place our positions. I compared the map with the ground and eventually decided that the map was wrong. Crouched in a hollow, the signaller was trying to raise the rest of the troop. He called across.

'I can hear Squadron HQ. They're saying something about Major Melot being wounded.'

'How badly?'

'Don't know. They are very weak. I can only just hear them.'

'OK. Try and get Troop HQ. Here's our position. Try and find out where they are.'

There was a shout from the farmhouse, and two of the section appeared dragging a German parachutist between them. They had seen him skulking around and had gone after him. He wore a white armband with, in gold letters, the word *Kreta*. It was the first inkling we had that we were up against the fellows who had dropped in Crete. During the next half-hour a further eight prisoners were brought in. They seemed a good type of soldier, smart and intelligent, but some of them looked done in. They had been taken completely by surprise, and did not even then realize that we had landed from the sea. They thought we had come overland from Campomarino.

We were in contact now with troop headquarters but, try as we might, we could not make out their position. Harry Poat wanted us to join him there.

'Tell them to fire a Very light into the air,' I called to the signaller, 'and we'll close on that.'

Over the treetops to the right a red light sailed into the air, hung for a moment, and dived out of sight.

'Right. Pack up. We're going over to HQ.' I turned to Alec. 'You coming with us?'

'No. Think we'll try and make Squadron HQ. There don't seem to be many targets round here now.'

We moved off in single file. We found HQ and Tony's section in a farm beyond the trees, on the far side of a ravine-like valley which ran like a gash across the green fields. Standing in the shadow of a haystack was a captured German officer. He was quite at a loss to understand what was happening. It was not war as he understood it.

In the little farmhouse kitchen an Italian woman was preparing a meal of sausages and eggs. From a distance the prisoner watched with growing disbelief as officers and men piled in together with their mess tins. But it was nothing to the shock he got when one of the men grabbed him by the arm, pulled him through the crowd to the kitchen range, and pushed a mess tin into his hand.

'Come on, Fritz. Better grab something before it's all gone.'

But if his feelings were hurt, he was even hungrier. Diffidently he began to eat. Inside five minutes he was one of the family, smiling broadly and uncomprehendingly at the men chattering away all round him.

News was beginning to come in over the radio now in scraps. John Tonkin and his entire section had been captured. There were no details. We had to wait till later for the full story. Bob Melot, our fifty-four-year-old fighting intelligence officer, ex-Belgian flying ace of the 1914–18 war, had been shot through the shoulder. Much to his disgust, Bob was evacuated to the nearest casualty station as soon as the Eighth Army came up around noon. There he caused quite a to-do by refusing to be treated as a 'lying case', and insisting on sitting on the edge of the bed, smoking. He finally registered his disapproval of the whole proceedings by signing his own discharge papers and walking out at six o'clock the following morning to rejoin us.

I had been studying the map again. A few miles inland was marked what appeared to be a small town – Guglionesi. I asked Harry Poat if I could take my section and have a look at it. I had an idea that that would be where John Tonkin's section would have been taken by their German captors. If we could catch up with them . . .

Harry OK'd the idea, but told me to try to keep in radio contact with him. About one o'clock we moved off. As we left the shelter of the farm Tony came running after us.

'We've heard from Peter. He's on the road leading to

San Giaccomo, taking a patrol out parallel to yours. Watch out for him.'

With a last wave we dropped out of sight into the next valley. The descent was very steep but, by hanging on to the occasional straggling bush and tuft of tall reedy grass, we managed to scramble down with nothing more serious than a few scratches and bruises. We pushed inland along the valley for a while, then started to climb the other side towards a lone farmhouse on the top of the far ridge.

An Italian girl of about eighteen was standing at the door. As we approached she started hurriedly to comb her hair and pat it into place. Then, all smiles, she waited for us. From her we learned the approximate whereabouts of the Germans in the immediate area then, while she filled our water-bottles, we rested.

Half a mile on we halted again, to observe the farther ridge. Sergeant Ridler spotted them first – about a dozen men moving around just below the sky-line. As we watched we saw they were digging-in. The Germans were hastily preparing a new defence line.

There was more movement around a small cluster of houses at the foot of the far slope. At first I thought these were more Germans, but as they slipped from the cover of the houses into a nearby quarry, I realized from the way in which they were moving that it was Peter and his patrol. They were working along right in front of the new German front line.

I was metaphorically taking off my hat to Peter when it dawned on me that, from where he was, he could not see the Germans above him. As the signaller tried to raise him on the radio, we watched his patrol working its way nearer to the Germans. In response to my unasked question the signaller shook his head.

'No luck yet. Shall I keep on trying?'

'Yes – no, get Captain Poat instead. I'll speak to him.'

Perhaps, with his more powerful set, he would be able to get the warning to Peter in time. It was now only a matter of minutes before he bumped into the German working party. We waited tensely as the gap slowly closed. The radio crackled. The signaller grinned, and gave the thumbs-up sign.

We advanced now in staggered formation just below the crest of the ridge. A sky-line seemed to be a particularly unhealthy place under the circumstances. We halted from time to time and, while the signaller tried to contact Peter's patrol, Sergeant Ridler and I crawled to the top of the ridge to have a look round.

I peered across the rich green valley towards the enemy-held ridge. The gentle breeze stealing in from the Adriatic tempered the dry heat of the sun. I felt drowsy. I had felt this way before, watching a cricket match back home, with the bees droning round and the birds singing. There were no birds singing here. Come to think of it, I had not heard a bird sing since we first landed in Sicily. For the first time I became aware of the silence; a tangible silence as when a clock stops that has been monotonously ticking away the minutes unnoticed.

A burst of machine-gun fire ripped through the stillness. The sharp echo rolled back along the valley. A German MG 15. No mistaking that sound. They were not firing at us, so I wriggled quickly down the slope to where the signaller lay by his set.

'Anything from the other patrol?'

'Lieutenant Davis is on the other end now.'

I grabbed the mike. 'That you, Peter? Did you hear the firing? Somewhere ahead of us, but I can't see anything.'

'Yes, we heard it. We thought you had run into trouble. We're going back now. What about you?'

'Hello, Peter. Look, I'm pushing on a bit further to see

what it's all about. When you get back, tell Harry what
we're doing. We are out of touch here. See you later.'

A mile further on we came across the marks of a
tracked vehicle. We were examining them when three
Italian peasants, two women and an old man, came up.
They pointed in the direction of Guglionesi. Yes. Yes,
the Germans had gone there. English? Yes, there had
been some *Inglesi* with them.

That was that, then. It was a racing certainty that it was
John's section they had with them. And if they had been
in tracked vehicles there was no chance of catching
them up.

Half an hour later we slipped quietly into a small wood
at the end of the ridge. On the far side the ground sloped
steeply away, rising again gently towards the roofs of
Guglionesi just visible on the horizon where they gleamed
in the slanting rays of the afternoon sun. It was four
o'clock now. We would never make Guglionesi before
dark, so we had better call it a day. It was disappointing
but there was no earthly use in just walking 'into the bag'.

I turned to Sergeant Ridler. 'I'm going to stay here and
do a bit of observation for about half an hour. Remember
that hut we passed a little way back? 2 subsection had
better get back to it and get a brew going. The rest of us
will join you at four thirty.' I crawled into the ditch on
the edge of the wood and got out my glasses.

Below us on the left was the bridge over the river that
had been one of 1 Troop's objectives. Unfortunately they
had been unable to reach it in time. Now its massive white
arches lay shattered, the river tumbling in confusion over
the crumbling masonry. Along the road from the bridge,
running across our front, came a solitary motor-cyclist.
He stopped at a pill-box by the roadside, then disappeared
up the road again.

In a field beyond, near a deserted-looking farmhouse, I

picked out the lines of a German fighter aircraft. An attempt had been made to camouflage it, and I assumed that it had probably crashed. Beyond that there was nothing. Now that the motor-cyclist had gone the country-side was peaceful and quiet. In spite of this, or perhaps because of it, I had a queer uneasy feeling that everything was not quite as it seemed.

Withdrawing carefully, we started back to the hut. I could use a brew of tea. As we came out of the cover of the trees we walked straight into a battalion of the Lancashire Fusiliers advancing towards us in open order. The Eighth Army had arrived. To their CO I explained as briefly as possible what we had seen, then dashed off to get that tea. I was putting the mess tin to my lips when there was a whine and a crash, then another and another. Mortars! There had been something screwy about that peaceful countryside, after all.

From up ahead came the chatter of Bren guns going into action. A mortar detachment of the Lancashire Fusiliers appeared in the middle of our tea-party and began slapping bombs down the barrels as fast as they would go. With the whole of 11 Brigade going into action we felt superfluous. Waiting only to down our tea, we set off back towards Termoli.

9
Counter-Attack

We had spent the previous night on our return to Termoli in the cold discomfort of a monastery overlooking the harbour. Our new billet had been abandoned by its Italian owner. The deep pile carpets and luxurious furnishings contrasted very favourably with the cold stone-flagged corridors and cells. Tonight we would be sleeping in real beds, with real bed-clothes. Through the house came the strains of *Lilli Marlene*. Paddy had found an ancient gramophone and a scratchy recording in Italian.

Throughout the day vague rumours had been floating about of a big German counter-attack that was building up. In a detached sort of way I thought of the Eighth Army lads out in front. If it were true, they would get precious little sleep that night.

Along the corridor came Harry Poat. 'There's a big counter-attack building up.'

'Yes, I know. Leastways, I've heard the rumour.'

'It's more than a rumour. They want volunteers to fill a gap in the line tonight. The main body of the army haven't caught up with the leading elements yet, so they're a bit thin on the ground.

'I'm taking three sections out. We have to cover the gap between the coast road and the beach. Tony's coming, and Sandy Wilson of 1 Troop.'

'OK. I'll come with my section.'

'How are they feeling?'

'A bit tired, but no more than anybody else. When do we move off?'

'At half past five; in about twenty minutes' time. Form up in the square outside the monastery.'

The two three-tonners rumbled out of the town along the dusty track towards the east ridge of Torrente Sinarca where we were to take up our positions for the night. We were to be relieved in the morning. Just short of the ridge the lorries stopped and we tumbled out on to the side of the road. Along the ridge the trees stood out clearly against a rapidly darkening sky. We would have to hurry if we were to be in position before dark.

Tony led the way with his section. A troop of 40 Commando were digging in among the trees when we reached the top. One or two of them waved a hand in greeting but no one spoke. There was silence as we tramped on, except for the crackling of dry twigs beneath our feet. The muffled sound of careful digging faded away.

Ahead, one of the ubiquitous farmhouses loomed up. We halted. Tony explained in an undertone: 'This will be my section position. I'll leave the chaps here and take you and Sandy on to yours. Think you'll remember the place?' Then, in a stage whisper, 'Sergeant Downes.' Hurriedly he gave his orders.

We marched on for perhaps half a mile until we came to another farmhouse. 'OK, Harry, this is your area. Leave your section here with Sergeant Ridler. You had better come with me and we'll see where Sandy is going. Then we will each know where the other sections are.'

Sandy's position was just inland from the railway which ran along by the beach. You could see the gleam of the sand under the culvert ridge. A large farm building on the ridge behind merged awkwardly with the night sky. With a whispered 'Cheerio. See you later', Tony and I set off back to where we had left our sections. We little knew then that we were never to see Sandy alive again.

About fifty yards to the right of the farmhouse in my area a straggly hedge ran up to the crest of the ridge. Now, with Sergeant Ridler, I crawled and wriggled my way along it. Five yards from the top the hedge stopped. The rest was open plough land. Carefully we inched our way forward until we could see the valley beyond.

It was a good commanding position but – I pressed myself flatter against the ground – very exposed. Our only chance of avoiding being sky-lined was to get forward of the slope and dig in. I felt the ground. It was rock-hard. There was only one thing to do: get back behind the crest.

A little way back I had noticed a narrow path running parallel with the crest and cut into the slope some four or five feet. I scrambled back to have a look at it. It might have been made for us. From the cover of the bank, fringed with low, stunted bushes, we had a clear field of fire of thirty yards or so. It was impossible for anyone to approach without making themselves conspicuous targets against the sky – at point-blank range. We started to improve the position.

It was bitterly cold now that the sun had gone. The men would do an hour's sentry duty apiece. We had to keep a round-the-clock listening watch on the radio so Rogerson, my signaller, and I decided to take it turn and turn about, an hour each, throughout the night.

Before leaving, Tony had told me that the LCIs that had brought us ashore were going a few miles up the coast to create a diversion. It was timed for twenty past ten. Coming close inshore, they were to lay a smoke-screen and pour in a barrage of fire on Di Montero for ten minutes, to give the impression that a landing force was in progress. If the ruse worked it was unlikely that the Germans would attack our position that night in face of a new threat.

I decided to stay awake until I heard the ships opening

up. To the minute came the distant crackling of the Oerlikons. I roused Rogerson and handed over the radio to him. We had all brought one blanket with us. I rolled up in mine, curled up on the path and settled down to snatch a little sleep. But sleep would not come. I lay there shivering with the cold eating into me . . .

Rogerson was shaking me. It seemed that my eyes had only just closed. I was stiff and numb with cold. I took the radio from him.

'Anything doing?'

He shook his head. 'Not a thing.'

Every hour we made a 'nothing to report' call to Tony, and got the same back from him. Every hour until, at last, the first flush of dawn lightening the eastern sky brought to an end one of the longest and most miserable nights I had ever endured. I roused the section for stand-to.

From the chimney of the farmhouse wreathed a blue wisp of smoke. We had warned the people there to get out the previous night, but they refused to leave their home. They seemed incapable of understanding they were in the middle of the front line, that there was in fact any danger. Now they were preparing breakfast. It was a good idea. As soon as it was fully light and the danger of a dawn attack was gone, I sent two of the men over to the house with the rations we had brought with us in our haversacks.

To the trees on the far side of the house I took one of the Bren gun teams. It was essential that we should now have some forewarning of impending attack. We found a position for them just forward of the slope. Sergeant Ridler and I would take turns with them while the rest of the section, two at a time, went to the house for breakfast.

We ate in a large dimly-lit kitchen watched by eight or nine dirty, ragged-looking children. Grand-dad, smoking an English cigarette with obvious relish, sat quietly by the huge fire. Mother and the eldest girl busied themselves cooking our meagre rations and washing up the few dishes after us. Again I tried to impress upon them the folly of staying, but they shook their heads and smiled. This was their home. There they were safe. I gave up and went back to the Bren position.

Anxiously I looked at my watch. Nearly ten o'clock. Our relief was late. I picked up my glasses again and swept the valley in front, slowly. There was a certain amount of movement on the far ridge but, although I could see small parties of Germans moving about, they were out of range. Up to the left I could see where the coast road dipped down and crossed the valley. To the right, and nearer, was another small railway bridge. Close against it stood a square whitewashed house, probably a railwayman's home. On the far side of the line was a wooden signal-box.

Suddenly, from behind the white house, strolled a group of four men. I might never have noticed them had not one, probably an officer, been carrying a map board covered with talc. Now, as he moved around, the sun flashed from its polished surface like a heliograph. I could see him through the glasses pointing in our direction, apparently giving orders to his NCOs or junior officers. I made a quick estimation of range.

'Range sixteen hundred – right of arc – white house – just in front – group of four men.' I waited until the Bren gunner signalled that he was on target.

'Fire!'

The Bren chattered. The little group made a quick dash. At the corner of the house one of them fell forward on to his face and lay still. The other three dived out of sight into some bushes. Quickly changing the magazine, the Bren gunner poured a long burst into the clump of bushes. There was no more movement.

Now that the Bren was again still, the silence came down over the valley like a curtain. The minutes dragged on. Across the valley small groups of Germans were still moving around. I watched them, but it was impossible to do more than guess what they were up to. Sergeant Ridler came up.

'Still no sign of our relief, sir. Wonder what's happened to them?'

'Expect they were late getting through. Should be on their way up to us by now, though.'

We walked over together towards the section position. If we were not relieved soon, rations were going to be a bit difficult.

'Duck!' Like a flash we dived for the cover of the haystack we were passing as the German fighter roared overhead, not more than thirty feet up. Had he seen us? It did not seem possible. At that height he must have been on us and past like a streak of lightning. Anyway, we would soon know . . .

From the direction of the port came the crackle of Oerlikons and the scream of diving planes. Jerry was going for the harbour. I broke into a run. As I did so a shell moaned overhead, and another and another in eerie succession. They burst with a quick concussion some way behind our positions. I grabbed the radio.

'Hello, Tony. They're shelling behind our positions. What do you make of it?'

'Hello, Harry. They are bursting some way back. I think they must be going for our relief. Those planes probably spotted them moving up.'

'Hello, Tony. Relief nothing. They are falling just behind us now. The last one was not more than thirty or forty yards behind Sandy's position.'

'OK, Harry. Get dug-in, fast.'

We had only one shovel, borrowed from the house. It

was not then a normal part of our equipment as assault troops. The ground was hard and digging-in slow work. Shells were dropping nearer now and showering our positions with shrapnel.

From the advanced Bren post came news that the Germans had just put in an attack on the other side of the coast road. It had been broken up by accurate fire from our 25-pounders further inland. I went forward to have a look. There came a slow tearing sound through the air. In the valley immediately in front of us spouts of earth appeared as if by magic. 'Thank Heavens,' I breathed. 'Our guns are ranging.'

We did not know, then, that tanks of the 16th Panzer Division had broken through our left flank and that it was they who were responsible for the mysterious spouts of earth. Nor did we know that the panzer division had been rushed from Rome, on the other side of Italy, with orders to recapture Termoli 'at all costs'.

'Message from Captain Poat, sir.' It was Rogerson with the 38 set. I clapped on the phones.

'Harry? Look, the situation is deteriorating over on the left flank. Get your section over there as fast as you can and see what you can do. At the worst the chaps over there will think reinforcements are coming up. Better hurry, though. All the best.'

I snatched off the phones. 'Sergeant Ridler, I'm going over to Captain Marsh's position. Get together the section and join me there as fast as you can.'

I found Harry Poat with Tony. He was looking very serious. Quickly he explained. 'There's a squadron of Recce Regiment over there. Their carriers can't stand up to the Jerry tanks and they're being forced to give ground . . .' He broke off. 'Here's Ridler with your section. Get moving. There'll be infantry following those tanks.'

The trees were thicker on this part of the ridge. In open

formation we advanced towards the danger spot. Grouped round a farm cottage we found the commando troop we had seen the evening before. Along one wall the wounded were lying or sitting propped up against it. Every now and then a shell from a German tank thudded into the other side of the building. Solid shot tore through the air with the sickening sound of tearing paper. Beyond the farm the trees thinned out. Frail-looking carriers were strewn among them. Some had their tracks broken. One had received a direct hit. We had arrived too late. Only their CO remained, and a machine-gun section of the Kensingtons. The leader of the commando troops thought there were a couple of anti-tank guns somewhere whose troops had been knocked out.

If we could man them we could make a fight for it. Bellies to the ground we crawled forward under the fire of the tanks. At the edge of the trees we came upon the guns, but even a cursory examination showed that they would never go into action again. We crawled back to the commando positions. There we prepared with them to meet the German attack, my section spread out on either side of me at five-yard intervals. Rogerson, with his radio, was next to me.

Someone shouted, 'Captain Marsh wants you to get back at once.' Rogerson plucked my sleeve. 'Did you hear that, sir? Captain Marsh wants us back.'

'Who was it shouted?'

'Don't know, sir. Perhaps it was Terry Moore.'

Terry Moore was Tony's signaller and was acting as liaison with the commando troop. I crawled across to where he lay in a hollow with his radio. 'What did Captain Marsh say?'

'Captain Marsh? Nothing.' He looked at me a bit queerly.

'Didn't you call out that message just then?'

'Not me. This set's diss. Haven't been able to raise him for the last hour. Perhaps it came over the commando's set.'

I continued my crawl over to the farmhouse. The commando signaller was quite definite. No message. Yet two of us had heard it, quite distinctly. I made up my mind. We were going back.

'Thank goodness you've come.' It was Tony. 'These damned mortars . . .' We fell flat as the next salvo whistled through the trees. The bombs patterned the earth all around where we lay close in against a small haystack. 'I've been trying to raise you on the radio, but couldn't get through.'

The rest of Tony's section were dispersed among the farm outhouses. My own were lying flat among the trees taking what cover they could against the flying mortar fragments. A bomb burst among the branches overhead. A large fragment ripped through the air, tearing a large hole in the blanket slung like an awning above us.

'We can't stay here much longer like this, Tony.'

'I know, but we can't withdraw either. It could leave the commandos unprotected on this flank.'

'Then there is only one thing for it. We must go forward. At least it has the advantage that it is the last thing Jerry will expect. I'll see if I can find a place down in the valley from which we can cover the front of 40 Commando.'

With my two subsection commanders following about fifty or sixty yards behind, I started to crawl cautiously forward through the trees down into the valley. With uncanny accuracy the mortar fire followed us down the side of the ridge. I was nearly at the bottom when a bomb fell not five yards from where I was lying in a fold in the ground. To my great surprise I was untouched. I signalled up the subsection commanders.

'There's a deep sunken track here. Bring your chaps down it. We'll take up a position along the top of the banking there. It's good cover and we'll be safe from mortars unless one should drop right on to the track, and the odds are against that: it's so narrow.'

While they were gone I busied myself organizing the arc of fire to cover the front of the 40 Commando positions. It was only when I heard the snapping of a twig behind me that I looked up from where I lay. One of the subsection commanders had returned – alone.

'Where the devil are the chaps? I thought I . . .'

'You'd better come and have a look. A bomb's fallen in the middle of them.'

They were lying beneath the trees – four from my own section and one from Tony's. I had a quick look at their wounds. Tony's man and one of mine looked pretty bad. There was little we could do for them except give them a jab of morphine to help relieve the pain. I got the kit out of my haversack, then we wrapped the five of them in blankets and laid them on improvised stretchers – barn doors, bits of fencing. My already weakened section was now further depleted. It seemed I could best use the rest of them to get the wounded back to the nearest dressing-station. Tony agreed.

Slowly they made their way down the valley behind us towards the beach. That way they stood a good chance of getting back unobserved.

I was now without a section so I joined Tony. The mortaring was getting heavier. They seemed to be concentrating on our little position. With bombs bursting all round we lay waiting for the inevitable. They were plastering the area and it was only a matter of time.

The mortaring died down. From forward of the farm buildings came the excited chattering of the Brens. A man came running back.

'German infantry coming across the valley towards us. We've broken them up for a bit, but they are getting ready again.'

Tony swore. 'I thought this would be happening. Well, there's only twenty of us. We can't keep them back for ever. We'll have to fall back on Sandy's section down by the railway. We can hold out there with our backs to the sea.'

He turned to the man. 'Get over to 40 Commando and tell them what we are going to do. We won't move till you get back.'

We collected together all the equipment. It was impossible to take it all, so some of the rifles were left behind in favour of the Brens and tommy-guns. By the time we moved off we were a pretty well-armed band.

Half-way to the railway we came across the two more seriously wounded men. The going had been too difficult with the improvised stretchers, so it had been decided to wait until stretcher-bearers could be sent forward for them. We could see them now, the red crosses on their arms picking them out against the green grass, as they made their way carefully towards us.

We helped transfer the men to the stretchers. Tony's man looked in a pretty bad way. His face was a deathly grey-green. Close by, a small stream trickled down to the sea beneath steep banks. We waded into it. It was a good thing to be out of sight. The Germans must have overrun our position by now.

Slithering down a small waterfall, I saw that the stream entered a culvert under the railway. So far there had been no sign of Sandy and his section. They had either been captured or forced to withdraw. The culvert was, however, full of very frightened Italians sheltering from the fighting who, as soon as they saw us, began babbling excitedly at the tops of their voices. At the point of our guns we made them keep quiet. We had no wish to draw unnecessary attention to ourselves.

A runner from the commandos whom we had picked up on the way was the first to leave the culvert. As he stepped out on to the beach there was a sharp burst of machine-gun fire and a long, dangerous crease appeared in the sand-dune near his head. He ducked down. A few minutes later the two of us crept out together. While he pushed his beret cautiously up above the sand-dune on a stick I raised my head slowly into view some thirty yards away. It was a corny trick but it worked. On the railway line, not fifty yards away, was a German machine-gun post covering the beach. We were cut off.

Tony asked me to go back on our tracks to see if there was any way of escape further inland. After going some way I scrambled up the steep bank of the stream. It was hopeless. The ground was bare and open. I came back and reported. We decided to wait for darkness and take a chance of slipping unobserved down the beach to Termoli – if the port still held out.

The big problem now was what to do with the two wounded men. They needed medical attention as quickly as possible. The stretcher-bearers wanted to risk it and carry them openly down the beach, trusting to their Red Cross armbands. I was against it. The Germans, under their existing circumstances, could not afford to let anyone get back to report their positions. It was the choice of two lives or six. We had a long and anxious debate about it, eventually deciding that darkness was our only hope.

We posted sentries at either end of the culvert and settled down to wait. The corporal in charge of the stretcher-bearers produced a carton of cigarettes. We smoked endlessly. For a while we did not know whether the Germans realized we were in the culvert or whether they had fired to discourage the Italian refugees. But we were not long left in doubt. Creeping down the line came a German, grenade in hand, presumably intending to drop it outside the entrance to the culvert. His heavy boots sent a stone clattering down the embankment. A shot rang out. We had no further trouble.

Along the beach the shadows began to lengthen as the sun dipped lower. The commando volunteered to cover the withdrawal. I went with him. Together we crept out among the dunes. The machine-gun post had been withdrawn, but about a hundred yards away, we could see the outline of a German sentry. We slipped our tommy-guns forward in readiness, and waited.

I peered back towards the culvert. In the growing darkness I could only just make it out. I watched for the little column making its way out on to the beach, but there was no sign of movement. I waited two or three minutes longer, then, with a whispered word to my companion, made my way back.

Twenty yards away from the entrance I saw them coming out. In a whisper Tony told me the man from his section had just died. I hastened back to my post as the group of men disappeared into the darkness. So far no alarm had been raised. When the section were out of sight and some distance down the beach we withdrew a little way and took up another covering position. In this way we progressed down the beach towards the town.

The withdrawal had gone so smoothly we must have dropped our guard. From the high ground outside the town automatic fire opened up on us. We scattered for cover. One of the men, darting under the shelter of the low cliff, started to climb. Firing was sporadic now. The sand was cool against my body as I lay listening to the waves breaking gently on the Adriatic shore. I was a long way off. There came a shout, a realization of present reality. We had bumped our own defences and, miracu- lously, no one had been hurt.

The line was held at this point by a scratch force of about a hundred men under Harry Poat – commandos, our own men, and a number of brigade HQ cooks. Half a mile to the rear, in a large building near the railway station, an advanced surgical team was at work. Our other wounded had already been taken there. The last man, whom we had brought with us, was taken down now.

Inside ten minutes he was on the improvised operating table. The place was heavy with the smell of blood and ether. Across the grimy windows danced the flames of a burning railway shed. Shells moaned overhead on their way into the town. The surgeon, tired, with drawn face, prepared to operate. Tony and I made our way along the dark corridor to a 'ward' where the other wounded men were. The surgeon who assured us they were all right looked us up and down. We were dirty, unshaven, tired out and wet through to the knees.

'You'd better go down to the kitchen and tell them to give you some hot soup,' he added brusquely.

Back outside we stumbled along the railway track to where Harry Poat's little force held the line. The rest of the section were already curled up on the ground. We had no blankets – they had all been used for the wounded – so we lay down where we were and tried to sleep. It was miserably cold and our wet clothes froze to our bodies. After a while we got up and went in search of shelter. In the middle of the goods yard was a small wooden hut. It was bare of furniture but there were two sinks. We sat in these and again tried to sleep, propped up against the wall. Our legs were the first to go to sleep. Hopping around with pins and needles we wrenched two doors from their hinges. These we laid across the sinks and a trestle we had found. Thus suited, we fell into a deep, dream-filled sleep.

We woke with the first light of dawn and made our way back to the line. We could see now that the cliff we had climbed the night before, some fifty yards high, swung inland to skirt the railway yard. The defenders were strung out along the lip of this cliff. Sandy's section, we learned, were holding a position of their own some hundreds of yards further inland. We climbed the slope and took our place with the others.

For two hundred yards in front of the position the ground sloped gently upwards, then dipped away out of sight. To the left, and this side of the ridge, was a walled cemetery. Above the walls towered a number of minaret-like tombs. Further to the left, in front of Sandy's position, stood a large, lone farmhouse. Immediately to our right the railway line and the beach stretched away into the distance.

The hundred of us numbered between us thirty Bren guns and a handful of tommy-guns, so we were able to put up a devastating volume of fire. During the morning the Germans put in a number of abortive attacks down the line of the railway. Every time they showed their heads above the ridge we blasted away at them, forcing them back. But one party got themselves firmly established in the cemetery and sniping started from the tombs.

On our left flank a single Sherman tank moved up to give us a hand, methodically shelling the cemetery. Tombs disappeared in clouds of dust. The new dead mingled their bodies with the dead of past years. Another attack was held. Not till later did we learn that our hundred men and a tank had held up the attacks of a panzer grenadier regiment.

As attack after attack was broken up the Germans fell back on the use of their mortars. A curtain of mortar bombs now crept down the slope towards us. We crouched low in our shallow trench. It was inexorable. Fifteen yards, ten yards . . . The barrage lifted. Over the ridge came the German infantry, to meet a withering fire. It was their last counter-attack.

Now came the news that Sandy Wilson had been killed fighting off an attack on his position. Of the rest of his section every man but one had been wounded. This man had dragged all the wounded to safety and returned to hold the position himself.

I had moved now into the rough broken ground at the top of the railway embankment. From here I could see right down the railway and beach to the culvert from which, only the night before, we had made our escape. Among the dunes where we had lain to cover the withdrawal I could see German heads moving about incautiously. I started sniping with a Bren gun.

About half past two I noticed a good deal of activity in the goods yard behind me. Jeeps and men of the London Irish Rifles were moving up. Word came round. They were to attack through our positions. We were to give all the covering fire we could put down.

Five minutes before three o'clock one of their company commanders, a major, flopped down beside me.

'Can you show me their positions? My company is attacking through here, between the cemetery and the railway.'

I pointed out the positions among the dunes and warned him that there were probably a number of them still in the cemetery. But it was not an ideal start-line. He would be attacking blind.

Three minutes to the hour we started to pour a withering fire into the known German positions, two or three men refuelling the magazines for each Bren gun. The barrels became red-hot. There was no time to change them. Exactly at three o'clock the London Irish Rifles went into the attack. Five minutes later the company commander was carried back on a stretcher, shot in the back by a sniper in the cemetery. He waved weakly as he went past.

A section of machine-guns came up, looking for a target. I got them on to the men among the dunes, where there was now a considerable amount of activity. They fired off half a belt, then moved away to the cemetery. Ten minutes later I would have given my right arm to have had them back again. The Germans were streaming back up the beach in hundreds. We had one of Alec's mortars rushed up to engage them but, though he bent the base-plate in his efforts, he was unable to do more than reach the near fringe of them. At twenty-two hundred yards they were a perfect machine-gun target.

Now a small party of commandos, with more zeal than discretion, chased up the beach in pursuit – a daring move doomed to failure. Two of them pitched forward on to their faces, to lie still on the sand, before they had gone more than a hundred yards.

At half past five we were ordered to return to the town. Our job was over.

10
Prisoner of War

There was a deserted air about the billet now. The rooms were the same. The strains of *Lilli Marlene* came once more from the old gramophone. But there was a difference. It was like returning to an old haunt many years after to find everything thick with the dust of time. Here lay the fine dust of crowded, already half-forgotten memories – the fleeting memories of forty-eight hours. Many lifetimes had come to an end in those short hours since we had marched into the square, to take our place in the line.

In the monastery gardens a burial-party was busy. A shell had scored a direct hit on a truck crowded with men on their way to reinforce us at the height of the battle. The position had been signalled to the German guns by a spy from the tower of the coastguard station. He had been shot after summary court martial.

For a week we hung on in Termoli, licking our wounds. We had landed originally with two hundred and seven all ranks. In that operation and the subsequent fighting we had lost twenty-one killed, twenty-four wounded and twenty-three missing. The missing were John Tonkin's section, now prisoners.

Early on in the landing John's section surprised a small German convoy which they attacked. The Germans, intent on escaping from the town, fought back fiercely. Other Germans escaping on foot surrounded the small British party, firing down on them from the high ground around their position. John did the only thing open to him. He ordered, 'Every man for himself.'

Crawling on hands and knees from bush to bush up the small valley in which they were trapped, John suddenly paused. He was staring at something that looked uncommonly like a German jack-boot. He looked slowly upwards, to see a huge German grinning down at him. With the rest of his section, he was taken by his captors, men of the German 1st Parachute Division, to Guglionesi. There the treatment was excellent, due to the fact that they, too, were wearing parachute wings. After food in the German mess, John was taken to Campobasso for questioning. The interrogating officer came forward, hand outstretched, and smilingly bade John 'Goodbye'. As John said later, 'I defy anyone to carry on after that.'

He was awakened next morning by a German corporal who brought him his washing water and told him in precise English that General Heidrich wished to see him, as it was his custom to entertain all captured British paratroop officers. This raised a new problem. John was totally ignorant of the correct etiquette as between a junior British officer and a German general under the existing circumstances.

Heidrich was of medium build, with light hair and pale eyes. He was a little chubby and, although pleasant enough, gave an impression of ruthlessness. He started off by inviting John to lunch, asking him if he would prefer chicken or pork. He added that it was immaterial which he chose as both were 'borrowed' from the Italians. He smiled. 'You, I have no doubt, would call it looting.'

John hastened to assure him that he called it 'living off the land' – and plumped for chicken.

Conversation during lunch was tricky, so he kept to two subjects remote enough, he considered, to be safe – Russia and Crete. Heidrich immediately launched into hair-raising accounts of fighting on the Russian front. On his second tour there, he told John, the Russians had been able to bring a concentration of thirty mortars to bear on any one point of the line at any time of the day or night. The wounded, unless treated within ten minutes, died.

One story Heidrich recounted with relish concerned an officer and two of his men taken prisoner by the Russians. As was usual, the men were separated from the officer before interrogation. The men were terrified, but, to their surprise, they were treated courteously as prisoners of war, no 'persuasion' of any kind being offered them. Instead, the Russians stressed the need for all men like themselves to understand and accept their common brotherhood, and so on and so forth. They wound up by telling the German prisoners that they were to be released and sent back to their own lines in order that they might spread the good news.

The Russians insisted that they mark their new-found brotherhood with a little celebration dinner before their return. And what a dinner! It was a dinner to be dreamed of. Certainly they had seen nothing like the food put before them since the war began, with more meat than they had had during the whole campaign. Perhaps not the best meat, but there was after all a war on.

Replete and satisfied, the Germans leaned back in their chairs. It had been a wonderful evening. Their Russian captors had put their seal on the brotherhood pact in a way that left nothing further to be done. So the Germans were quite unprepared for what came next. With a flourish, the doors of a cupboard were flung open. There, propped up, were the butchered remains of their officer.

From atrocity stories Heidrich turned to the present. The Termoli landing, he said, had been perfectly timed and perfectly executed, and had upset the German plans considerably.

That afternoon John was sent back to German corps headquarters. All night through the pouring rain the trucks rumbled north carrying their loads of prisoners. He gave up all thoughts of trying to escape that night and went to sleep. He had been told by one of the German parachutist officers that, while he was in army hands, he had nothing to fear, but that once he fell into the hands of the 'civilian' authorities he would be for it. He decided to make his escape the following night.

There was little chance of escaping during the halts when the prisoners were allowed out of the trucks. The Germans were on the alert for any false move. There were a number of halts, however, for the benefit of the drivers.

During these halts, drivers and guards came to the tail of the trucks where they could smoke while keeping an eye on the prisoners. They halted on the second night on a road leading through thick woods. The rain of the previous night had cleared up during the day but thick clouds obscured the moon. At the rear of the truck the Germans were smoking and talking. As arranged with John, the rest of the prisoners crowded to the tail of the truck to afford him a certain amount of cover. He crawled forward and, fumbling a bit in the dark, managed to undo some of the fastenings of the tarpaulin cover behind the driving cab.

Cautiously he put his head through the opening. No one about. A quick wriggle and he was through, standing behind the cab. Another quick check. The only danger now was from the guards at the rear of the truck in front. Now! He dropped quickly into the ditch at the side of the road and rolled away.

So far his escape had not been noticed. The next five minutes were like five years as he lay there in the grass, hugging the shadows, fists tightly clenched. A sharp, guttural order and guards and drivers climbed back into the trucks. This was the final hurdle. Would the guard notice he was not there? He waited tensely for the first sign that he had been missed, heart thumping wildly despite himself. The engines broke into life and the convoy rumbled on into the night.

John had not planned beyond this. Now he took to the hills, away from the roads and villages, to find himself one of a large wandering army of escaped prisoners seeking shelter and food from isolated farms and cottages. The majority of the men were content to keep alive and wait for the Allied armies to overrun their hiding-places. The Italians, for their part, were only too willing to give what assistance they could in return for a note saying that they had helped the Allied cause.

For the best part of a week John lived like this, moving from one farm to another, too wary to stay long in one place. There were nights when rumours of an impending swoop by German security forces would send him out on to the bleak hillside, there to lie low till all was quiet again. Then the inevitable happened. The Germans did swoop on a village in the area. Where he had formerly found assistance he was now met with, if not hostility, indifference. Joining up with another escaper, he decided to make for the British lines. They made a pact that, whatever should happen, they would keep moving south, and only south. In this way they were bound, sooner or later, to reach safety.

Moving by night and lying up by day, they travelled south for several days, skirting villages and farmhouses as they realized they were getting near the front. Then they came to the village that was different. Even before they reached it they sensed a difference. It was silent, deserted. There were no old men at the doors, no noisy children playing in the sun and the dust. Driven on by the thought of food, or even wine, left in the deserted houses, they decided to investigate instead of by-passing the village.

John went first. Hugging the walls of the houses, he moved warily from street to street. Ahead was a small cross-roads. He eased his head slowly, cautiously, round the corner – to stare into the startled eyes of a tin-hatted British sergeant.

They had made it. A minute or two later a jeep came tearing up the road in a flurry of dust. The officer who was driving leaned out as he brought the jeep to a halt.

'Jump in. I'll take you up the road to HQ.'

John was about to climb in when a thought struck him. 'Which way is headquarters?'

The officer pointed. John jumped back into the road. 'Thanks all the same. I think I'll walk. I'm only travelling south.'

The officer shrugged, and drove off. A minute later came an explosion that rocked the street. John swung round. The jeep had hit a mine.

Had it not been for this, perhaps ridiculous, insistence on the letter of the pact he would never have rejoined us; would not have been there when General Montgomery came to Termoli to inspect the Special Service Brigade to which we then belonged.

We were drawn up on the quayside. After the inspection 'Monty' made a short speech.

'I hope – I hope soon to be going back to England.' He paused. 'I make no promises but, wherever I go, I like to take with me the men who have fought with me.'

It was only a straw, but what a straw to clutch at. Blighty! Home!

Lieutenant-General Dempsey, commander of 13 Corps, under whose command we had operated since our landing in Sicily, came to say goodbye. We packed into one of the rooms in the monastery to hear him. He spoke in a quiet voice.

'It is just three months since we landed in Sicily, and during that time you have carried out four successful operations.

'You were originally lent to me for the first operation – that of Capo Murro di Porco. That was a brilliant operation, brilliantly planned and brilliantly carried out. Your orders were to capture and destroy a coastal battery, but you did more.

'I left it entirely to you what you did after that, and you went on to capture two more batteries and a very large number of prisoners. An excellent piece of work.

'No one then could have foretold that things would have turned out as they have. You were to have returned to the Middle East after that operation, but you then went on to take Augusta. You had no time for careful planning; still, you were highly successful.

'Then came Bagnara and finally Termoli. The landing at Termoli completely upset the Germans' schedule and the balance of their forces by introducing a threat to the north of Rome. They were obliged to bring to the east coast the 16th Panzer Division which was in reserve in the Naples area. They had orders, which have since come into our hands, to recapture Termoli at all costs and drive the British into the sea. These orders, thanks to you, they were unable to carry out. It had another effect, though. It eased the pressure on the American Fifth Army and, as you have probably heard, they are now advancing.

'When I first saw you at Az-zib and told you that you were going to work with 13 Corps, I was very impressed by you and by everything I saw. When I told you that you had a coastal battery to destroy, I was convinced that it was the right sort of job for you.

'In all my military career, and in my time I have

commanded many units, I have never yet met a unit in which I had such confidence as I have in yours. And I mean that!

'Let me give you six reasons why I think you are as successful as you are – six reasons which I think you will perhaps bear in mind when training newcomers to your ranks to your own high standards.

'First of all, you take your training seriously. That is one thing that has always impressed me about you.

'Secondly, you are well-disciplined. Unlike some who undertake this specialized and highly dangerous job, you maintain a standard of discipline and cleanliness which is good to see.

'Thirdly, you are physically fit, and I think I know you well enough to know you will always keep that up.

'Fourthly, you are completely confident in your abilities – yet not to the point of over-confidence.

'Fifthly, despite that confidence, you plan carefully.

'Last of all, you have the right spirit, which I hope you will pass on to those who may join you in the future.'

General Dempsey paused before explaining that he had a further six points, which he always tried to bear in mind when handling the unit.

'These principles,' he continued, 'if I may call them such, are:

'First, never to use you unless the job is worthwhile. That is to say, unless the effect to be gained more than compensates for the risk taken in putting you in; and there is always considerable risk in using troops like yourselves.

'Secondly, never to put you in too far ahead of the army. Always I must be able to reach you in twelve to twenty-four hours: if you are a small party, in twelve hours; if a large party, at the most in twenty-four hours.

'Thirdly, I must be prepared to use the whole of my

force, including artillery and tanks if need be, to reach you within that time. One reason is that you always seem to stir up trouble wherever you go.

'Fourthly, I always try to give you as much time as possible for careful planning.

On the other hand, I bear in mind that I must not hesitate to use you quickly if the opportunity suddenly arises. Such a case was Augusta, and you succeeded as only a well-trained unit could succeed.

'Finally, once you have carried out your job, I must get you out as quickly as possible to enable you to refit and to reorganize.'

General Dempsey expressed regret that the association of the Special Raiding Squadron and 13 Corps was to end.

'I hope', he concluded, 'that the association may be renewed at some later date.'

A day or two later we left Termoli for Molfetta, on the first stage of our journey home. But it was Christmas morning before we finally sailed from Algiers on the last lap.

11

Action Stations

It was raining when we reached Manchester. After a month's home leave, twenty of us had been packed off to Ringway aerodrome to do our long-delayed parachute course. One or two in the party were new recruits but the majority of us were still 'wingless' because we had had neither the time nor the opportunity to do our jumps since joining the unit in the Middle East.

Now the great moment had come, I was looking forward to it with very mixed feelings. Somehow I did not see myself jumping out of an aeroplane. There was something unnatural, I felt, in throwing oneself out in mid-air. It was against all instincts of self-preservation. I wondered if the others felt the same.

If they did, they did not talk about it. No more did I. We hid our feelings under a forced air of bravado. Openly we discussed with professional detachment the chances of the 'chute not opening, how long it would take to reach the ground from seven hundred feet if it did not, and what sort of a mess we would look when we hit.

'There was blood upon the harness, there was blood upon the 'chute.'

'The paratrooper's intestines were hanging from his boots . . .' – this we chanted to the strains of *John Brown's Body*.

'Glory, glory, what a helluva way to die . . .' We roared the chorus with astounding fervour, privately wondering if we would go out that way, and hoping we would not. Only one accident in every thirty thousand jumps, said the instructor. We believed him then, and inquired anxiously if there had been any accidents in recent courses. We did not want to be the thirty-thousandth.

It was a three-week course with the first fortnight given over to synthetic, or ground, training. In a large hangar fitted up like a super gymnasium, with a multiplicity of gadgets ranging from 'Kelly's Circus' to the 'fan' and the awe-inspiring 'cable-railway', we learned to control our 'chutes and land without hurting ourselves. On the coconut matting we sneaked up on one another, to give a sly, forceful push. If you felt yourself falling you were supposed to collapse gracefully, do a neat forward or backward roll, and come up smiling for more.

'Kelly's Circus' was a refinement of this parlour game. You sat in a loop of rope, one end of which was held in the hand, while willing, malicious hands propelled you round and round as on a roundabout. Suddenly the instructor shouted your number. You let go your end of the rope. The loop collapsed. You hurtled to the mat, did a neat roll and got out of the way of the next man down.

On the second day we were introduced to the mock aperture. This was a replica of the jumping hole in the aeroplane, built into a wooden platform some eight or ten feet high. 'Action stations!' roared the instructor. I swung my feet into the hole, gripping the edge nervously with my hands. 'Go!' The last word was fairly bellowed. Staring straight ahead I pushed off with my hands and hurtled through the hole to land on the mat below.

Trussed in dummy parachute harness, we swung backwards and forwards from the hangar roof, learning to turn this way and that, covering up with hands and legs when the instructor shouted 'Trees!' and struggling out of the harness in mid-air when he shouted 'Water!'

Climbing a tower at one end of the hangar, we hurtled down the overhead cable clinging to a pulley. Running at maximum speed we released our hold and rocketed down to the mats, rolling over and over.

Then the fan. In a platform about forty feet up were cut six holes. Above each one of these was suspended a drum-wound cable. On the end of the drum were the fan blades. I strapped myself into the harness at the end of the cable and waited.

'Action stations.' I tensed.

'Go!'

Down and down I shot. The drum spun madly as the cable unwound. Then, air resistance against the fan blades checked the speed of my fall. I touched down comparatively lightly, did the roll that was required of me, and tried hard not to look as if I had achieved something.

Before the end of the first fortnight, 'action stations' and 'go' were the only two operative phrases in our vocabulary. On the buses it was 'action stations' – not 'this is where we get off'. We leapt for the pavement from still-moving buses with wild yells of 'Go!' Only with difficulty did we restrain the temptation to do a forward roll as we touched down.

We were just beginning to enjoy ourselves when the blow fell. The instructor looked at us keenly. 'Just a word of advice before you dismiss. Lay off the beer tonight. Weather permitting, you'll be doing your first balloon jump in the morning.' He paused to let it sink in. 'Take it from me, beer and jumping don't mix. If you don't believe me, just try it. OK, that's all.'

Trussed up in our parachutes we waddled over towards the motor winch to which 'Bessie' was tethered. 'Bessie' was a silver-grey barrage balloon with a difference. Slung below her glistening belly was the cage, a metal platform with a hole in the centre and with four canvas sides. In ground training the hole of the mock aperture had seemed all too small. Always with us was the dread of hitting our nose on the edge as we went out. Now, as I climbed into the cage, it seemed just one big hole and little else.

Outwardly calm we sat round the gaping hole, holding on grimly to a bar as the instructor hooked us up.

'Up seven hundred, five to drop,' he sang out and, with a gentle whirr, the winch started up. Hypnotized, I stared through the hole at the rapidly receding ground.

'Look up at the balloon, it's safer,' counselled the instructor. 'When she stops, hang on tight. She'll rock a bit.'

Up and up we went until we were at the right height.

'Action stations, number one!'

'Number one,' I, thought. 'Lord, that's me.' Long tedious hours of training came to the rescue. I swung my legs into the hole and braced myself for what was to come. There was a bellow from the instructor.

'Go!'

Before the word was properly out I was rushing earthwards, the wind tearing at my face and clothes. Down, down I went. A moment of panic swelled into sheer terror.

'It isn't going to open,' I thought. 'It isn't going to open.'

One small portion of my brain, however, remained cool and clear. Calmly and quietly it seemed to be saying 'Stand stiffly to attention. Grip the seams of your trousers with your hands.' Then the nightmare was gone. My downward rush was halted and I swung gently to and fro. I looked up. There was the 'chute. What a beautiful sight it was. I looked down. Trees, houses, people: all were dwarfed into insignificance. There was no sensation of falling, no dizziness. 'Glorious,' I murmured to myself.

But the ground was getting nearer. Forty, thirty, twenty feet – whack! I was down and no bones broken. Wriggling out of my harness I looked up. Just above me the second man came hurtling through the hole. Almost immediately, it seemed, the canopy blossomed above his head like a gigantic flower. 'Gosh. What a thrill it's been,' I thought. 'What a hell of a fellow I am.'

As I started to roll up my heavy parachute, I suddenly realized that I was hot. All morning I had been frozen. Up in the balloon, less than a couple of minutes before, my fingers had been blue with cold. Now I was actually sweating. The tension of waiting to drop was over. All the surplus energy I had called upon to help me to jump was burning itself up.

Carrying the heavy 'chute I hiked over to the Nissen hut under the trees in the far corner of the dropping zone, where the YMCA women were waiting with mugs of piping hot tea. Everyone was talking at once.

'. . . made a beautiful landing.'

'Did you see me come down? I was still kicking out the twists . . .'

'Did anyone ring the bell?'

'Ringing the bell' was the term used when anyone hit his nose on the far side of the hole while jumping. It was caused either by looking down as you pushed off, or by not pushing off smartly enough. It was drinks all round if you walked in with the unmistakable signs on your face of ringing the bell.

Proudly and perhaps a little self-consciously I fastened one of the silken parachute ties to the zip of my jumping jacket. It was the 'done thing' – one tie for each jump. I was now a one-jump man. Not till I had seven to my credit would I qualify for my parachute wings.

A few days later we did our first jump from a plane. The planes were old Whitleys. The jumping hole was half-way down the fuselage. I was number four to jump. As the plane became airborne a cage of butterflies was let loose in my stomach. Approaching the dropping zone I stared steadfastly at the signal lights above the hole – red for 'action stations', green for 'go'. Seven hundred feet below, the countryside slid slowly by.

There it was. The red light. My heart leapt to my throat. Green! Number one on the far side of the hole disappeared from view. The man sitting next to me was preparing to follow him. I felt him tense. Then he, too, was gone. The lights went out. The plane banked as we circled round for the next drop.

'Running in.' The instructor shouted the warning above the roar of the engines. Red light! . . . green light! I caught a glimpse of number three as he shot through the hole. Automatically I swung my legs into the hole after him – and pushed off.

Immediately the full blast of the slipstream caught me. Instinctively I shut my eyes. There was a roaring in my ears that threatened to suffocate me. The wind plucked and tore at my clothes. Then silence, peace. I opened my eyes. I was alone between heaven and earth. I did not bother to look up at my 'chute. It was enough for me that I was no longer hurtling towards earth. Down below, on the edge of the dropping zone, I could make out the red cross of the 'blood wagon'. Then with a thud that knocked all the breath from my body, I was down. I staggered to my feet, rolled up my 'chute and, with fumbling fingers, tied on to my zip the second silk string.

Our third jump was a night jump, from the balloon. I was in the third stick. As I waited for the first man to drop I could just make out the balloon against the dark sky. Faintly through the night came the sound of the instructor's voice. Below the cage the white 'chute blossomed out, faintly perceived but getting clearer as it drifted down until, of a sudden, it disappeared. He was down. We waited for his voice. 'Number one OK.' We breathed. No damage done.

I was jumping number one in our cage again tonight. I hung on tight to the floor handles as we rose through the night air. We rocked to a standstill. The instructor checked my parachute, made sure I was properly hooked up.

'Action stations.'

I swung into the hole and waited.

'Go!'

I was away. Down and down. Faster and faster. Tightly I clung to the seams of my trousers. Still I was dropping – a dead drop. No slipstream this time. Just a dead drop. Don't panic, don't panic, I muttered to myself. With a crack like a whip the 'chute opened. I was floating down.

I stared anxiously towards the ground. Where was it? All I could see was blackness. Was I drifting backwards or forwards? There was no way of checking. I looked for lights that might help me. There were none to be seen. I tried to remember what I had been told. Adopt a correct position in the air. Don't anticipate the landing. If your position is correct you won't come to any harm. Hell! If I did not know which way I was drifting how could I adopt a correct position? Which way to turn my feet? Why hadn't I thought of asking that while I was still on the ground?

I pulled down on the forward lift webs to stop myself swinging. The ground. Was that the ground? Gingerly I pushed my feet out to feel. It was the ground. With a crash I landed on my back. My head whipped back. There was a blinding flash before my eyes. Dazed, and with a splitting headache, I got to my feet. Where the devil was my 'chute? A figure loomed out of the darkness.

'You all right? Didn't hear you call out. What's your number?'

'Number? Oh, 145763,' I answered, reeling off my regimental number.

'No, no. Your jumping number.' Then: 'Say, did you bang your head when you came down?'

I nodded.

'OK, I'll get your 'chute. You'd better come over and get yourself a cup of tea. You sound as though you might be a bit concussed.'

For three days we hung about waiting for our last jump. Good old Manchester. Fog and mist. We spent hours in the stand-by room at the end of the hangar staring out through the window into the white mist. Sometimes it would begin to clear and everyone brightened up. Then it would close in again as thick as ever. We began to wonder if we ever would make that seventh jump.

'Fog's clearing.' Someone managed to raise enough excitement in his voice to bring us once again to the windows. It *was* lifting. One of the instructors put his head inside the door.

'Come on, chaps. Get your 'chutes on. The weather boys say we'll just have time.'

Grabbing our parachutes we dashed out on to the tarmac. The big Whitley bombers lumbered up into position. The first plane roared down the runway and disappeared into the distant haze.

I was in the second plane. A few minutes later we were droning towards the dropping zone. Mentally I urged the plane on . . .

'Action stations!' Red light . . . green light. I was out. I was a parachutist.

12

Dress Rehearsal

Heavy boots clattered sharply on the hard metalled road. Our breath frosted the air as we raced down the hill. The slopes of the Scottish hills glared white with the thick hoar frost. Below nestled the little village of Darvel, snugly sheltered by the steep slopes of the Irvine Valley.

Darvel had been our army home ever since our return from disembarkation. Not many miles away, the 2nd SAS, recently withdrawn from North Africa, were settling down to training too. Our two British units had been joined by a Belgian SAS Squadron and two French battalions of SAS – the 3rd and 4th.

This rapid expansion into a brigade group had been carried out to enable us to meet our heavy commitments in the forthcoming Second Front. At 'Hush-hush House', attached to brigade headquarters, plans were already being laid for our part in the invasion but we, as yet, knew nothing of these. For us it was training, training, and yet more training.

Now reconstituted as the 1st SAS, still under the command of Lieutenant-Colonel Paddy Mayne, we had seen considerable changes ourselves. Each troop of the old Special Raiding Squadron had become a squadron, each section a troop. Harry Poat, now a major, was second-in-command of 1st SAS. Tony, also a major, commanded C Squadron, with Peter and myself as his two troop commanders.

Apart from my own small headquarters, I had now three sections to look after, commanded by officers who were all new to me, having joined us while I was on leave.

First there was Roy Close, slim, dark-haired and debonair. His careful consideration of everything he did, his keen sense of responsibility, contrasted strangely with his bantering couldn't-care-less attitude. The other two, 'Titus' Oates with his deep, villainous laugh and husky voice, and Stewart Richardson, had been friends before they came to SAS, and were remarkably alike in character if not in looks. They were keen as mustard, conscientious in their work and as irresponsible as schoolboys off duty. Once we got to know each other we got on very well.

There were many little difficulties to overcome, of course. There were no textbooks on SAS work. Everything had been developed in the light of experience and from our mistakes. The whole fund of knowledge of this type of work lay in the minds of the 'old operatives'.

Although there was a certain amount of good-humoured sarcasm in the way the more experienced members of the unit were referred to as 'old operatives', we knew that unless we could get over to the newcomers the full force of what our *esprit de corps* meant to us, we were in danger of splitting into two camps, the old and the new.

In passing on the lessons of our experience we had to avoid giving the impression of superiority. It was not easy. All the time it was 'Now when we landed in Sicily . . .' or 'I remember on one occasion . . .' Reasons for going against the book had always to be backed up with personal anecdotes. The appeal was all the time to experience. But these teething difficulties were gradually overcome, although much of what we taught had to be taken on trust until it could be proved in action. The successful building up of the new SAS was as much a victory for the new boys as for the 'old operatives'.

For three months we slogged over the hills and moors of Scotland, learning to find our way across some of the most difficult country in Britain, through mist and rain, and carrying heavily-laden rucksacks.

After dark, working by compass, we headed out into the desolate Scottish countryside, our rucksacks weighted with filled sandbags to get us used to travelling long and arduous miles with heavy loads. With small token charges of explosives in our pockets, we made for distant roads, railways and bridges, sinking up to our knees in bogs, wading through the icy waters of fast-running burns. In the dark hours before the dawn we crept up on our objectives and laid the charges. Sleepy Scottish hamlets awoke to the sound of the explosions. We melted away again into the mists and headed back for home. Like this we learned to make our way with unerring accuracy to places that were little more than pinpoints on the map.

We made several more parachute drops to keep us in jumping trim and train us in the use of leg-bags. These leg-bags were roughly the same shape and size as an ordinary army kit-bag and were used to carry the equipment we dropped with. Secured to the right leg with two straps, a pull on the quick-release cord freed it immediately, allowing it to swing from the belt at the end of a twenty-foot length of rope. Although heavy and cumbersome in the extreme, it avoided the danger of having to run the gauntlet of the enemy fire while dashing to and fro undoing supply containers dropped separately. Hanging there twenty feet below, the leg-bag had the added advantage of 'feeling out the ground' on a night drop. As the bag touched down the 'chute, released from the extra weight, billowed and 'breathed', giving a lighter landing and warning of its imminence.

Despite these advantages we were at first irked by the need to drag the dead weight of some ninety-six pounds along the plane's length to the jumping hole. The ideal would have been to land with the bag on our backs but, as the parachute was already there, that was out of the question. We began to look round for an alternative. Eventually we struck upon the idea of strapping the leg-bag, with quick-release, to our chests and upside down. Our legs free, we felt less encumbered.

About this time the commander of the aerodrome at Prestwick, from which we took off to do our jumping in Scotland, asked if some of us would do a jump actually over the aerodrome. He felt it would give the staff a greater interest in the work. So far they had only seen us arrive and take off. The scheme was debated and eventually it was decided that sticks of six – that is, parties of six men in a plane – from each of the SAS units would compete against each other for a bottle of whisky, the quickest stick out of the plane to be the winner.

Stewart, Titus and I managed to get into the 1st SAS stick, so we decided to try out this new idea with the leg-bags. The planes we were jumping from were Albemarles. We were very cramped for space while in the air, mainly due to the larger jumping hole, which was coffin-shaped. But, unlike the Whitleys in which we had trained, we could stand up to jump. The idea was mooted that the first three should stand legs astride over the hole and, on receiving the signal, snap to attention one after the other, plummeting straight down. I was against the idea because I felt there was a danger of the 'chutes fouling and, though it was only a slight risk, a bottle of whisky was not worth a life. We decided to do a normal jump, relying on the leg-bags to give us the extra speed.

A number of distinguished visitors, civil and military, with their womenfolk had been invited to watch the demonstration. It was a perfect day – warm and clear, with a ten-mile-an-hour breeze. Standing as far out over the hole as I could, I looked down as we started the run-in. The far end of the concrete runway swung into view beneath the plane. Red light! Green light! I was out. I looked round. Not far away, the other five 'chutes were sailing down, perfectly spaced.

As soon as we landed an RAF truck drove up. One of the instructors jumped out. 'Never mind folding your 'chutes, just sling them in the back and jump in. You're going to be inspected by the big-wigs. They've never seen a real live parachutist before. By the way, the Belgians won.'

The truck pulled up and we piled out. The visitors, about a dozen of them, were standing self-consciously around. We lined up and, from the pockets of our jumping jackets, we produced for inspection some of the gadgets we intended to take on operations – commando knives, special wire cutters, fuse wire for short-circuiting telephone wires and so on. Our Colt automatics escaped inspection when we explained that they were loaded.

We carried out innumerable training schemes against local Home Guard units and troops stationed in the area. Even the police were dragged in to act as opposition and entered into the spirit of the thing admirably, from Chief Constables down. We enjoyed ourselves immensely on those schemes, and the stories told of what happened on them were legion if sometimes apocryphal.

Often quoted against another squadron was the story of one of their parties, intrigued with the idea of cutting telephone communications with fuse wire. They decided to try it against a village they were 'attacking'. Unfortunately, it was so successful that when one of the villagers tried to call the fire-brigade he was unable to get through and his house burned down.

On another occasion a party bent on sabotage entered a dockyard and, eluding all the sentries, slept the night on board a submarine, much to the consternation of the authorities. These and other stories were ably illustrated for us by Ian Fenwick, the well-known cartoonist, who commanded D Squadron, 1st SAS.

The most ambitious of these schemes, however, was Operation Castle Douglas. We were dropped – from trucks as the weather was unsuitable for jumping – a few miles from Castle Douglas with orders to blow up the railway, railway station and certain bridges there. The Home Guard were defending the area. My own party, delayed by heavy going, arrived on the objective some five minutes after midnight. Unaware that the time limit had expired, we crept along the edge of the road leading to the station. Footsteps approached. It was a lonely road, and very dark. The Home Guardsman, no doubt thinking longingly of his bed, plodded heavily along the centre of the road. We melted into the shadows and waited. As he passed we slipped up behind him. One man pinioned his arms, another pushed the muzzle of his Colt in his back. With a fearful cry he flung his hands to his throat. For one awful moment I thought someone had over-zealously slipped a knife between his ribs. With explanations and profuse apologies we went on our way.

We were now faced with a journey back to base of some seventy miles, on foot, with the whole of the police and Home Guard mobilized against us. We were to hide up by day and carry out attacks on specified objectives each night. For food we carried seven small cardboard packets, each with sufficient potted rations for twenty-four hours. Each box contained sweets, biscuits, tea, soup cubes, oatmeal blocks and meat blocks. Also included was a small tin of cheese and another of dripping. The crushed oatmeal blocks mixed with boiling water made a passable porridge. The meat blocks similarly treated gave us mince, and a queasy stomach. That, with the monotony of the diet, started us looking round. With every man's hand against us, at least for the next seven days, we turned to poaching – and very successfully, too.

On the fourth evening six of us lay hidden in the woods outside a small town. Somewhere nearby five other parties waited. We were to combine and sabotage all the key points in the town. The attack was to go in at six o'clock while it was still light. Each party was to work out its own scheme for getting into the town past the defences.

Outside the town we laid a double row of bricks across the road. Hidden in the hedgerows we waited. An Army truck came belting down the road. With a screaming of tyres it pulled up as it saw the obstruction. In a trice we were out, menacing the occupants with our Colts. They were on their way to join a course of instruction at a nearby Army school and were already late. I regretted I would have to delay them still further. We climbed into the back of the truck.

'Right. Now drive into the town slowly and quite openly so that everyone can see you. If anyone stops you, tell them you're going to this course and show them your papers.

'When you get into the town look round for the nearest hotel and drive into the courtyard. We'll do the rest.'

Peeping under the hood as we drove into the town I saw heads pop up from slit trenches by the roadside to scrutinize the truck as it went by. Apparently satisfied, they disappeared again. The truck took a sudden swing to the left and pulled up. Peering out of the back I saw we were in an old-fashioned coaching yard. I called out to the driver:

'Back up against the open stable door. This is where we get out.'

He backed up and we scrambled over the tailboard into the stable. The truck drove off. Opposite the courtyard was the back door of a house. We slipped across and pushed open the door. Going through to the front we found ourselves in a small general stores. An elderly woman was standing behind the counter. She cottoned on pretty quickly and when, less than a minute later, one of the Home Guard came in for cigarettes she served him and saw him out of the shop while we crouched out of sight behind the counter.

On our instructions, she shut up the shop and drew the blinds. This done we made a careful reconnaissance of the street. Our luck was in. Outside the door, unattended, was a small baker's van. We crept out of the shop and into the back of the van. All we had to do now was wait for the unsuspecting driver. It was a local van, and in it we could drive round the town without attracting attention.

Meanwhile another party had made its way to the house of the local Home Guard commander. Three of them entered the front door. They found him in the kitchen just finishing his tea before going on duty. He snatched up his pistol as they walked in, and a heated argument ensued as to who was covering whom. The question was settled by the arrival of the rest of the party via the back door. Protesting that the scheme had not really started, the 'enemy' commander was dragged off to the local jail.

But our life in Scotland was not all schemes. We visited the Kilmarnock power station, where we made a study of the entire undertaking. We were shown how we could cause the most damage with the least trouble to ourselves, from large-scale demolitions to nuisance-value sabotage.

At Kilmarnock railway station we studied the working of the railway system. Railway officials went to great pains to show us the easiest way to derail trains so that the greatest possible damage would be done to the track and other installations. In the sidings we realized our schoolboy ambitions by learning to drive an engine.

Outside lecturers came to explain the difference between SS, SA, SD and other German military and para-military organizations. Officers who had escaped from Germany or had spent considerable time in enemy-occupied territory came to give us the benefit of their experience.

'If you know no one in the area,' they stressed, 'never go up to two or more people together. They may be suspicious of each other and give you away, fearing to be given away themselves.

'The best way to ensure that they are alone is to tackle them on their way to the outside lavatory – preferably after dark so that you cannot be seen from the house.

'The women are more trustworthy than the men, the young more than the old.'

Illustrating this, one lecturer told how he was travelling across France by train without papers when the German security police swooped. Posting guards round the train they started working their way through, compartment by compartment. There was no escape so he decided to take a chance. In hurried undertones he explained his predicament to a young woman alone in a compartment. Without a moment's hesitation she took him along the corridor to the toilet. There she hid him behind the door while she stripped to the waist. A few moments later the Germans hammered at the locked door. Coyly clutching a rather inadequate towel to her, she opened it a little way and, wide-eyed, asked what they wanted. The German officer, considerably embarrassed, went on his way.

We learned how to locate underground telephone and telegraph cables, how to put them out of action for a considerable time by destroying the junction boxes, replacements for which were in short supply in France. Though we did not know it at this time, this was the role we had then been assigned in the coming invasion of Europe.

We were to drop prior to the landings and cut the main communications between the beach-heads and German rear headquarters. It would be a 'blind drop' with no one on the ground to receive us and guide us in. Dropping only a few hours immediately prior to the invasion we would have our work cut out to place our exact position, locate these hidden cables, dig for them and blow them. The only alternative would have been to drop twenty-four hours before the main landing, but that idea was scrubbed because capture, or even discovery of our presence, would have endangered the security of the whole invasion. That particular operation was, therefore, scrapped as being impracticable.

We had now been issued with miniature radio receiving sets 'For the reception of instructions and reports from England – not for listening to Vera Lynn'. Everyone was taught – with indifferent success – simple phrases in French and German. No doubt this was the basis for a German report, later captured, that stated that all members of the SAS were linguists.

It says much for our security-mindedness that when, towards the end of May, a small party of officers and men disappeared from our midst, it was several days before we realized that they had gone, nor did we know where they had gone.

13
D-Minus-One

We guessed they had 'gone on a job', but it came as a shock nevertheless when we heard over the radio that Allied troops had landed in Normandy.

On D-minus-One, Lieutenants Poole and Fowles with four men had dropped into France just south of Carentan. Dummy parachutists were also dropped into the area. The job of these six men was to create a diversion by giving the impression that a large-scale airborne landing was in progress, and thus draw the enemy forces away from the real point of attack.

They jumped forty minutes after midnight on 6 June in conditions of very good visibility, but landed some two kilometres from where it had been intended they should drop. On landing, the men found that neither of their officers was with them. A hurried search failed to reveal their whereabouts. Neither could they find any of the containers that had been dropped with them, although they covered a very wide area looking for them.

Without the equipment they contained it was going to be very difficult to create a diversion on the scale envisaged. However, the four men had between them twenty Lewes bombs. These they laid out in an area about five hundred yards square and ignited. It was now after three o'clock in the morning and beginning to get light, so they quickly made their way to the north, firing their carbines in the air. Half a mile away they hid up in a hedge and waited for the explosions.

There was still no sign of the missing officers, so they decided to lie up where they were during the following

Above: In training for the assault on Europe: SAS men practise cliff-scaling on the coast of northern Palestine

Below: Dress rehearsal for Sicily in the Gulf of Akaba: assault craft leave the *Ulster Monarch*

Above: Capo Murro di Porco: John Tonkin and his men regroup after the fall of the first battery

Left: One of the lucky ones. Many gliders were lost at sea in the airborne invasion of Sicily

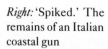

Right: 'Spiked.' The remains of an Italian coastal gun

Right: A lull in the street-fighting for Augusta, the first major European port to fall into Allied hands

Left: After the battle: the battered street outside the Fascist head-quarters in Augusta

Right: Musical interlude: SAS men amuse themselves in the captured port while waiting to be taken off by destroyers

Left: Bob Melot, intelligence officer of the 1st SAS and First World War Belgian flying ace

Right: Peter Davis and Friend

Left: 'Titus' Oates

Bagnara from the air. SAS troops, landing on a beach at bottom left, captured and held this town behind enemy lines in southern Italy

Right: 'Paddy' Mayne, four times a DSO, who commanded the SAS after David Stirling's capture

Below: Tea and dice en route for the Termoli landing. Left to right: Bill Fraser, the author, Alec Muirhead

Below: In the 'cage' at Fairford, waiting to go to France. Left to right, seated: Peter Davis, Tim Iredale and Colin Rosborough. Standing: Tony Marsh, Roy Close, Stewart Richardson, 'Titus' Oates, Tom Bryce, the author, John Reynolds, 'Mike' Mycock

Above: SAS raiders eighty miles behind the German lines in France. An hour after this photograph was taken, 'Curly' Hall, second from left, was dead and the author (left) was fighting for his life at Les Ormes

Below: The scene of the pitched battle with SS troops at Les Ormes. Sixty were killed and wounded by the two heavily-armed SAS jeeps

Above: The author in camp

Left: SAS troops and their maquis guides meet the Americans at Courtenay

Right: In this firing range in Antwerp, patriots were tied to the planks and shot by the Germans. Between the planks is a coffin

Below: Near the end. Sergeant McDiarmid and the author in Holland, 1945

day. Apart from a German patrol which cycled slowly up the main Carentan road, they saw no signs of enemy activity throughout the whole of the day. However, about eight o'clock that evening they were contacted by a Monsieur le Duc, a member of the French Resistance who had been out looking for them. He told them he would get them away that night.

He returned about eleven and escorted them to a ruined abbey some two miles to the west. Here, safely hidden, he left them while he went in search of food. About one o'clock in the morning he returned with food and cider.

During the morning of the 7th they saw Monsieur le Duc approaching again, but this time there was another man with him. It was Lieutenant Poole. Poole had 'rung the bell' on leaving the aircraft and lain unconscious for three quarters of an hour while the rest of the party searched for him. He had jumped with a carrier pigeon strapped to his chest and, as soon as he recovered, had sent it off with a message saying what had happened and that he was out of contact with the rest of the party.

For the next three days the little party carried out numerous patrols within a four-mile radius of their hide-out but saw no activity to report. On the afternoon of the 10th Monsieur le Duc turned up again, this time with Lieutenant Fowles. Chick Fowles had landed some little way from the rest of the stick and, search as he might, had been unable to contact them. Left on his own he began sniping German troops in the area but without any marked success. He also cut the telephone lines leading into a nearby German HQ.

Now that they were all together they held a council of war and decided they could do worse than work from their present hiding-place. But, although they carried out many patrols in the next three weeks, they could not make contact with any of the German forces. Then, on

28 June a German parachute regiment moved into the neighbouring village of Remilly-sur-Lozon. From Monsieur le Duc they learned that the Germans knew of their presence in the area. With the Frenchman as guide they made their way back to their original dropping zone where they stopped for the night, moving on the following night about two kilometres to the south. There, in an old brushwood cabin, they stayed for three days and nights.

A few days earlier they had been joined by three American parachutists who had escaped from the Germans when a POW convoy had been strafed by American planes. Food was becoming a difficult problem. They decided they would have to try to make their way back to their own lines some six kilometres to the north.

Moving by night, they covered the distance in six days. Extreme caution was needed because of the large number of enemy patrols now in the area. On the night of 9 July they lay up about four hundred yards from a German position that was being mortared by Allied troops. They decided to make a break for the Allied lines the following night.

They rested during the day, saving their strength for the coming ordeal. Then, about noon, they were horrified to see two Germans walking straight for their hiding-place. They were so close their parachute badges were clearly visible. That it was a chance encounter was obvious. The Germans were as startled as they were and, before anyone in the little party could do anything, the Germans flung a couple of hand grenades and made off as fast as they could.

Chick Fowles, Troopers Hurst and Merryweather and two of the Americans were wounded by the exploding grenades. The other four carried them to a farm about a hundred and fifty yards away, but the farmer, fearing for his own life, refused them shelter and went off to fetch the Germans.

While he was gone they held a quick council of war. Carrying the wounded men, they would have no chance of getting clear. It was equally unthinkable that they should leave them. They could defend the farmhouse for a few brief minutes before they were overwhelmed. They decided to stay and await developments. No one noticed that Chick Fowles had disappeared.

It was now half an hour since they had arrived at the farm. The farmer had not returned. They began to think that he had thought better of his decision when there was a movement among the nearby trees. A quick check round the house was enough to confirm their fears. Forty German parachutists, all young and looking very jumpy, had surrounded the farmhouse. They were armed with light machine-guns and machine-pistols. The sergeant in charge called on them to surrender. They had no option. Carrying the wounded they came out and were marched off down a sunken road, through an orchard and up to an old hut that had been turned into a headquarters by the Germans. Here they were interrogated by a captain before being sent back to a dressing-station.

Having had their wounds dressed they were given a handful of cigarettes and some sweets and moved on again to an old monastery now being used as a hospital. In a filthy room, full of straw, they were operated upon. Just as Hurst was about to be dealt with, Chick Fowles was carried in with a bad wound in the back. Although already wounded, he had left the farm where the others were captured in a one-man attempt to find the two Germans who had surprised them. Without their story as corroboration the Germans might well be too busy to listen to the ramblings of a French farmer.

Four days later they were removed in trucks to the

hospital at Rennes where they stayed until released by the Allies early in August.

Monsieur le Duc was shot by the Germans for the help he had given the SAS party.

14
The Cage

Meanwhile those of us who had been left in Scotland nursed our wounded professional pride. As each day passed we chafed at the agonizing delay. Without a word of warning A Squadron packed up and left in the early hours of one morning. It was not until 17 June that we of C Squadron got our orders. We entrained in the evening, not knowing where we were going, glad only to be on our way at last.

All through the night our train sped on, along cleared lines. All through the night the pale yellow beams of the lamps and lights that rushed past the windows fled across the carriages, flickering over our faces. We slept fitfully. At dawn we were on the outskirts of Birmingham. It was afternoon before we reached a wayside halt, where we transferred to the big army trucks. In silence we rolled along the quiet country lanes towards 'the cage'.

Before us, out of tune with Nature's easy arrangement of clouds, trees, fields and hedgerows, the neat rows of dirty white tents stood to attention across the slope of a long gentle hill. The barrier swung up, the trucks turned in and rumbled to a halt. The barbed wire closed in around us. Here we were to be briefed for the operations ahead of us. Once briefed, the barrier would be closed against us until we left for the aerodrome and – what?

But action was not yet for us. There was equipment to draw, light carbines with folding butts, lightweight sleeping-bags, new Colt automatics, operational radio sets and other special items. We went for marches and runs. We spent hours practising with the Colts and carbines. In the evening we strolled down to the little village of Fairford for a drink, or took the bus into Oxford. We made the most of what freedom remained to us.

A number of parties from A Squadron had been briefed. For them life was more restricted. Twice a week we had a cinema show in one of the marquees in the camp, and there was no shortage of beer. This considerably eased the burden of waiting, but there was, nevertheless, a keyed-up feeling throughout the camp.

A number of our old parachute instructors from Ringway had come down to join us as dispatchers. The chance of coming on operations with us was something they had looked forward to as they had seen hundreds of men passing through their hands as trained parachutists. Now they flew with us, one to each plane, seeing that our leg-bags were properly fastened, that we were correctly hooked up, and that we left the plane OK.

Each day they were eagerly sought out by the parties waiting to leave. 'Are we flying tonight, Frank?' 'What's the weather going to be, Leo?'

Then it would come. Weather reports OK. Intelligence reports OK. Immediately there was intense activity in the tents of the lucky ones. Personal kit was packed and taken down to the store tent. Operational equipment was stowed away into the rucksacks and these, with much heaving and straining, were forced down into the leg-bags. Quick releases were tested and checked. Automatics were belted on beneath jumping overalls. Parachutes were drawn and adjusted. With envy in our hearts the rest of us watched them climb into the trucks that were to take them to the aerodrome and freedom. Then they were gone.

Afterwards we strolled round the tents they had left. Here and there would be the fragments of a torn-up letter, some small piece of equipment which at the last

minute they had decided not to take, a bowl of still-warm
shaving water.

We were next door to the aerodrome. At take-off time
we stood around in small groups listening to the roar of
the planes warming up and taxi-ing across the field.
Beyond the trees on the edge of the 'drome the red and
green navigation lights lifted slowly into the air as the
planes took off and circled round before fading away into
the night. That evening as we lay on our camp beds
looking out through the tent flaps at the star-filled sky, we
thought of them winging their way over France, wondering what lay before them.

The following morning we heard from the dispatcher
what kind of drop they had had, whether there had been
any trouble from flak. Sometimes the empty tents filled
with life again. The men who, the evening before, had set
off so light-heartedly and eagerly were back again. Some
parties made as many as five trips before they jumped.
Either the weather closed in over the dropping zone, or
the plane was unable to pick up the signal fires or the
code letter from the dropping zone.

Most of the drops were made to reception committees
on the ground. These were arranged either by SAS
advance parties, SOE,* or Special Forces. Informed by
radio of the estimated time of arrival over the dropping
zone, these men arranged to light three fires in line at
intervals of eighty or a hundred yards. Some twenty or
thirty yards to the flank of the third fire a pre-arranged
code letter was flashed by torch to the approaching plane.
The men jumped as the plane ran-in over the fires. The
same procedure was adopted for the dropping of supply
containers.

---

* SOE – Special Operations Executive.

Unless everything went off as planned, the men were not dropped. It might be that the wrong code letter had been signalled, that it was impossible to light the fires due to the proximity of German troops, or that the reception committee had been captured or compromised. Whenever any of these things happened we found the party back in the camp again next day.

Sometimes the plane did not return at all and we would wait anxiously for days for some news, not knowing whether the plane had been shot down, had crashed into a hillside, or had force-landed. And it was also possible that the men had been able to parachute to safety before the crash.

Some of us spent very pleasant evenings up at the aerodrome getting to know the pilots who would be taking us over. There were also a number of glider pilots on the 'drome, for whom we had a healthy respect. Few parachutists would willingly trust themselves to a flimsy glider without a parachute. The glider man, as a rule, recoiled similarly from the idea of jumping. However, the glider pilots needed some live loads to train with. They asked if we would like to go along. For want of something to occupy us during the waiting period, we agreed.

The whole squadron was going up. Dividing into glider loads we trooped aboard. The towing plane taxied along the runway. The glider swayed and lifted. We were airborne. The door in the side of the glider had been left open. Through it I saw the ground dip and slide away. I went for'ard and peered between the heads of pilot and co-pilot. The tow-rope stretching out to the plane ahead sagged gently. We were higher than the towing plane. The pilot turned his head.

'Like to take over for a while?'

'Who – me?'

'There's nothing to it. Just hold the stick as it is.'

He moved over and I slid into his seat. The stick twitched a little in my grasp. I gripped it tightly.

'Whoa! Relax there.' The glider bucked and swerved like a bronco. I relaxed and she steadied down.

'Now take her down to the low position, beneath the plane. Just forward with the stick, gently.'

Gingerly I eased the stick forward. Like a swallow the glider swooped down, shuddering from stem to stern as she dived through the slipstream of the towing plane. Then all was still again. Someone else was at my shoulder ready to take his turn at the controls. I slipped from the seat and handed over.

Making a wide sweep over Oxford we turned and headed back for the aerodrome. The pilot was back at the controls now. 'We're casting off in a minute or two,' he called over his shoulder. 'Fasten your seat belts.' We pulled them very tight. The roar of the plane stopped. We were in free flight. It was uncanny gliding silently and effortlessly through the air. The lack of noise brought back again all my fears and doubts about gliding. It was only now that we were alone with the silence that I knew we were gliding, without engines, without parachutes. It was only now that I realized that we were in the hands of the pilot, that our safety depended solely on his skill. If he misjudged first time there was no question of making a second circuit.

The aerodrome was ahead of us. We went into a gentle dive. Despite the reassuring feel of the safety belt I clung on to the seat as we gradually lost height. Then, with a suddenness that brought my heart into my mouth, we plunged steeply to earth. Just as it seemed we must crash, the nose of the glider came up and we were bumping and bouncing heavily across the landing field, to come to a standstill among the gliders that had already landed.

We made several other trips in the gliders after that, and went on firing practice with the big Stirling bombers from which we were to drop. It all helped to while away the time until our turn should come.

We were getting a certain amount of briefing now on conditions inside France, how to read French and German maps, and odd scraps of information that might be useful to us. But as yet there was no indication of where or when we were to be dropped.

As days drifted into weeks, scraps of news began to filter back to us from France. For the first time we got an idea of the work the parties already over there were doing.

15

First Blood

Ian Fenwick, the commander of D Squadron, parachuted into France on the night of 16–17 June with six men, landing south of Pithiviers. An advance party consisting of Lieutenant Riding and five men had dropped into the area two nights previously.

He started operations immediately on landing. Working on foot, he attacked and blew up during the first twelve days the three main railway lines running through the area, successfully derailing a goods train on the Malesherbes–Puisseau line. Moving his camp to the Forêt d'Orléans he again attacked the railways in his new area, derailing yet another train, this time on the Bellegarde–Beaune line.

The railway lines were guarded by *milice*, French renegades in the pay of the Germans – men with an unenviable reputation for brutality and treachery. But bravery was not one of their qualities. They took to their heels immediately they learned that an SAS party was going to blow the line. On no occasion did they engage the sabotage parties. So scared were they that when, later, jeeps were parachuted to the SAS parties, it was possible to drive right up to the railway line, walk down the track to a suitable spot, lay the charges and drive away.

German vehicles in the area, heavily camouflaged with foliage, drove around with headlights blazing. Ian Fenwick took a leaf from their notebook and removed all masks from the jeep lights, driving around in a blaze of light on the principle that the Germans would hardly expect British 'terrorists' to drive around so openly.

The jeeps enabled Fenwick's parties to extend the area of their operations. They blew the railway lines as fast as the Germans could repair them, attacking first in one direction and then in another.

It was, of course, impossible to carry out work like this without a certain amount of contact with the civilian population, although on the whole SAS parties tried to remain independent of their aid. It was inevitable, therefore, that here and there they should run into the occasional black sheep. This happened to one of the parties operating in the Fontainebleau area.

Reconnaissance had indicated a profitable venture at a nearby railway yard. Their first objective was the locomotive shed. Without much difficulty they eluded the sentries and, working fast, placed their bombs and broke the time pencil detonators. It all seemed too easy. They were about to move on to their next objective when there was a shot. That they had been given away by one of their contacts did not seem to be in doubt, and was later confirmed. Now their immediate problem was to extricate themselves. The first shot had apparently been loosed off at random, or else it had been a signal. A force of some two hundred Germans was closing in on them, but they did not dare break off the engagement in case the Germans should discover the bombs. Keeping just out of trouble the little party put up a fierce fight until they judged the bombs were due to go off. As the roar of explosives rocked the locomotive shed, destroying one engine, they slipped away before the horrified Germans could gather their wits.

Warned by radio about the end of July to expect an important drop, and to make the base safe, they carried out a series of wider sorties in the jeeps. These jeeps were armed with twin Vickers K guns, front and rear, firing tracer, incendiary and armour-piercing rounds at a rate of about twelve hundred a minute.

These sorties were marked with considerable success. At Ascouy a large German transporter was destroyed. On the Orléans–Pithiviers road two German trucks were set ablaze with machine-gun fire. On the following night on the same road they ambushed a petrol lorry, the first burst from the jeeps catching it fair and square. It blew up with a loud explosion and the sheet of flame lit up the surrounding countryside for miles.

Ian Fenwick now decided to disperse his parties until he received word that the 'important drop' was imminent. Three stayed at the original camp. Ian, with his own party, and Watson with his, moved off into the blue. Bateman and Parsons took their parties to a French Resistance base at Thimory. Jock Riding, who was based on the original camp, went with them.

On the way Riding passed four or five Tiger tanks on their transporters, travelling without lights. With his own lights off he passed them without incident. However, the road seemed a bit too busy to be healthy, so he decided to turn off on to a smaller road, but in doing so upset the jeep. Unable to use any lights but the occasional flash of a torch, they sweated and struggled to right the vehicle. Three Frenchmen who happened along stopped to help. Between them they had done little more than unload the guns and stores when, along the road, came a German convoy of trucks and cars packed full of troops. It happened so quickly the decision was taken out of their hands. There was no chance of making a break for it. With a silent prayer they carried on, sweating and cursing to themselves as the jeep remained immovable and as truckload after truckload of Germans passed by. In all, eighty vehicles went by, and by great good fortune not one stopped to lend a hand. Eventually, after two hours' work they got the jeep back on the road and continued their journey.

Meanwhile Watson's party had been having considerable success in their sorties. A railway train was attacked and set on fire, destroying some thirty wagons. An officer of a German patrol searching for them in the woods was ambushed and killed. Another train was attacked at Ascouy and its sixteen wagon-loads of sugar left blazing.

Passing through Fourdan, Watson surprised a German convoy drawn up in the market-place and guarded apparently by only five men. These gave no sign that they had recognized the jeep for what it was, so Watson decided to return and engage the convoy with his machine-guns as he drove past again.

Foot right down, he drove back into Fourdan at speed. Clammy with anticipation, front and rear gunners slipped over the safety catches of the guns. They raced into the market-place. Too late Watson saw they had misjudged the situation. As, guns blazing, they raked the enemy trucks with murderous fire, the Germans opened fire with machine-guns mounted on the trucks, hitting their French guide. Wounded, he toppled from the moving jeep into the road. Despite his wounds and his age, for he was an elderly man, he managed to drag himself into the garden of a nearby house where he lay low while the Germans searched for him. Two days later he reported at Watson's camp for further duty as a guide, having made his way back to them on foot.

On the morning of the first Sunday in August a radio message was received from England. Colonel Mayne was to drop that night if a DZ could be given. Usually a number of dropping zones were used, turn and turn about, depending on enemy movements in the area and according to the nature of the drop. There was also the matter of a code letter to be decided. All this information would be signalled to London on the afternoon schedule. The message was never sent.

At three o'clock that afternoon the Germans attacked the main camp in force. The three small SAS parties found themselves ringed by six hundred German troops. For seven hours they fought a bitter battle to break out of the trap. Every man for himself, and rendezvous with Lieutenant Watson were the orders.

Captain Riding and Sergeant Bunfield, the signals sergeant, managed to cut their way through the cordon. They lay up in cover about four hundred yards away from the battle until midnight when they moved to a new locality.

The following day, 8 August, news of the attack reached Ian Fenwick through Resistance channels. Unfortunately the details he was given were completely distorted and garbled, a not uncommon thing when dealing with the Resistance. Most of the men had been killed and all the jeeps lost, he was told. In point of fact, every man had managed to break out from what had seemed a certain death-trap.

Immediately, Ian Fenwick set out in his jeep for the scene of the attack to verify the details for himself. With him were Sergeant Dunkley, Corporal Duffy, Lance-Corporal Menginou of the 4th French SAS and a sergeant of the FFI.

He had not long been on the road when a German spotter aircraft located his jeep. The pilot passed the information back to the Germans at Chambon where they prepared an ambush for him. Unaware of what lay ahead of him, Ian drove the avenging jeep on towards its appointment with the enemy. Then Fate played her last card. Into the road stepped the slight figure of a woman. As the jeep lurched to a halt she gasped out her breathless warning. The Germans were waiting in ambush further up the road. They must turn back.

But Ian's blood was roused. 'Thank you, madame, but I intend to attack them.' He met the ambush at Chambon with all his guns firing. He was almost through the first body of Germans – there were others further back in the village – when a 20 mm cannon shell hit him in the head, killing him instantly. Out of control, the jeep careered wildly towards the woods and crashed. Menginou and the FFI sergeant were killed.

Corporal Duffy lost consciousness. When he came to he saw Sergeant Dunkley being led away by the Germans, handcuffed and with blood on his face. This much he saw before he swam into unconsciousness again. When he regained his senses once more he was lying in a German truck on his way to Orléans hospital, from where he was later moved to another hospital just north of Fontainebleau.

This second hospital had been either a convent or a school before being pressed into service by the German army medical corps, and Duffy found himself sharing a ward with German wounded. These men mistook Duffy for a Typhoon pilot and were the sole survivors of a German battery that had decided, rather unwisely, to shoot it out with some Typhoon tank-busters. There was a bit of a dust-up that resulted in Duffy being moved to another ward.

His companions in the second ward were eight Germans and a Russian. The wards of the hospital were being kept clean by a number of French girls employed by the Germans. He had been there for some days when one of the girls approached Duffy and suggested he might try to escape. She offered to help, and Duffy jumped at the chance.

It was a fortnight, on 22 August, before an opportunity arose. The girl told him that the advancing American troops were at Chartres and that, as the hospital was going to be evacuated by the Germans, he had better be on his way. She purloined for him a German medical officer's uniform and brought it into the ward in a bucket which she put down at the side of his bed.

A number of the other girls came into the ward and busied themselves round the beds of the Germans, shielding him from their view while he retrieved the uniform and hid it under the bed-clothes. Later that afternoon, while the other patients were having forty winks, he examined the uniform. To his dismay there were no shoes. Climbing out of bed he hobbled to the door. The corridor outside was deserted but after a few minutes one of the French maids passed. In elaborate sign language he motioned to her that there were no shoes, then hobbled back to bed again.

In due course the shoes arrived in another bucket. As the Germans were now awake again, the same precautions had to be taken to prevent them seeing what was going on.

Now followed a nerve-wearing time as he waited for the eight Germans and one Russian to fall asleep again. Tensely he lay there in the hushed ward listening to their measured breathing. At last he judged they were all asleep. Like a shot he was out of bed. In no time at all Corporal Duffy, wounded British POW, became a fully-fledged German medical officer. Walking with great difficulty because the shoes were too small, he tiptoed out of the ward.

The rest was easy, or so he insisted when he later told his story.

'I walked across the courtyard which was crowded with wounded and vehicles ready for the evacuation. As I got to the gate I saw there was a sentry standing there but, as I passed him, he drew himself up and saluted me. Naturally, out of courtesy, I returned it.'

Once clear of the hospital he walked quickly in the direction of Milly, down the main Milly–Fontainebleau road. Then, taking to the woods, he stopped and got rid of the shoes which were crippling him. In his stockinged feet he pushed on through the woods, stumbling and crashing through the undergrowth. He was nearly all-in when he chanced on a log cabin in a clearing in the woods.

He lay watching it for a while but could see no sign of life. Cautiously he made his way to the door, and pushed it open. It was deserted. He lay down and slept.

The sound of firing startled him from his sleep. The dawn light was creeping through the trees. He set off in bare feet – the socks had long since ceased to serve any useful purpose – towards the sound of the fighting. The going was hard and painful until he struck the road again just south of Milly. Shortly after, he met an elderly man leading a horse and cart. He managed to make him understand that he was an escaping British prisoner, whereupon the man helped him on to the back of the horse.

They had gone only a few hundred yards down the road when they saw two Germans approaching on motorcycles. They pulled up alongside the cart. With sinking heart Duffy realized that even had he had the strength to make a dash for it he had no chance of getting clear. The Germans were pointing down the road. It suddenly came to him that they were asking the way to a nearby town. Duffy had no idea where it was but he, too, pointed vaguely down the road. The Germans thanked him and drove off. Soon after, he was picked up by a party of Resistance men who took him to a neighbouring house. There he was seen by a doctor and his feet swathed in bandages – there were twenty-one blisters on his left foot and twenty-eight on the right. Later he was passed on to the Americans at Milly and, while in hospital there, was awarded the American Order of the Purple Heart.

Back in Thimory the two parties under Lieutenants Bateman and Parsons were still awaiting news of the 'important drop' when they heard of the death of Major Fenwick. They now contacted 'Agrippa', a local maquis leader, and moved into his camp of five or six hundred maquisards. Two days later they heard that Colonel Mayne had arrived in the area. From him came orders that Parsons was to return with his party to the main camp. Bateman was to remain with 'Agrippa' in a liaison capacity, as the Germans were believed to be planning a large attack from Orléans.

On 10 August the Germans did attack the maquis base in great strength, using infantry and patrol cars. From the first it was a hopeless struggle. The patrol cars were engaged with bazooka rocket guns but, after the first salvo, they wisely stayed out of range. Finally the French officer commanding decided to abandon camp.

Thanks to the German flame-throwers, the woods were burning well by this time. Piled into a civilian car, the SAS party followed the three maquis trucks through the flames, striking the road about a kilometre from Ouzouer-sur-Loire. With the British party was an American airman who had crashed two days previously.

Almost immediately they were attacked by eighteen German patrol cars. The first of these overtook the escaping SAS car, opening fire as it passed. Those who could, piled out of the doomed car and broke for the safety of the woods.

One of the men, Wilson, in the back of the car was hit over the eye and in the jaw by the first burst and lost consciousness. When he recovered he found himself alone in the car. The American, who had also been wounded, lay outside on the road. As Wilson watched, he tried to crawl under the car out of sight of the Germans. He was seen. Two sharp bursts of fire and he lay dead.

Four of the Germans now began to approach the car with an explosive charge in order to blow it up. So far they had not noticed Wilson in the back. He waited until they were within fifteen yards, then raised his Colt and fired. Three of the Germans dropped where they stood. The fourth took to his heels and fled.

All this time heavy machine-gun fire had been directed against the others of the party who had taken to the woods. This fire was now turned on the car. The windscreen was blown in and Wilson once more hit. Again he passed out. He came to, to find himself tied to a tree, his hands behind his back. All his personal effects had been taken away.

As he wondered what was to happen next, a staff car drove up and six Gestapo men got out. One of them questioned Wilson closely as to the number of SAS men there had been with this particular maquis. Receiving no answer he struck him viciously across the jaw. With one of the maquis men, Wilson was then driven to Orléans where he appeared before a German company commander for further interrogation. The questioning followed the same lines as the Gestapo men's.

As Wilson still refused to talk, the interrogator was at pains to point out that in the eyes of the Germans, SAS were classed with men of the maquis as terrorists – and there was only one way of dealing with terrorists. He made a sign with his hand and the Frenchman was led out. There came the sound of a single shot, then silence.

Wilson was then taken by two of the Gestapo men to

another large building in the town for still further interrogation. From then on he remembered nothing until he
awoke in Orléans hospital. Two days later the Americans
marched in. He was free.

16
Special Mission

My turn had come at last. On the large wall map in the intelligence room Tony pointed out the area in which I would be operating. It was not far from Auxerre, about the geographical centre of France. He also handed me several large-scale maps of the area for detailed study.

What I was most interested in was the possibility of finding good cover in my area, somewhere where I could establish a firm base for operations. Small copses and woods may have been all right for schemes in Scotland but something larger was needed when operating two or three hundred miles behind the German lines.

In this I was lucky because the area was quite heavily wooded. I decided that the forest of Merryvaux would do very well, at least for the first few days while I had a look around. My next move was to choose a suitable dropping zone within reasonable reach of the forest.

There was a flat, open stretch of country on the outskirts of Aillant, a large village seven or eight miles from my prospective base. Although it was quite possible that the village was occupied by the Germans there was, immediately to the west of the dropping zone, a large stretch of heavily wooded country into which we could quickly disappear. I banked on being able to get clear before any alarm could be raised.

As soon as I had made up my mind a special reconnaissance sortie was flown, and in forty-eight hours I was handed a complete set of aerial photographs covering the area. Through stereoscopic glasses I studied the photos with painstaking care. First of all, the dropping zone.

There was a small road running right across it from the woods to Aillant. Along the road was a single line of telegraph poles. It would be tricky if we got caught up in the wires but it was a chance that had to be taken. The dropping area was quite big.

Next I had to decide where we would rendezvous after the drop. Just on the edge of the woods a clearly-defined track bent itself into a perfect 'U' shape. It would be quite simple for each man to follow the track to this U-shaped bend. From there we would strike through the woods towards the area I had decided would be our base.

I traced the route we would have to take. A compass bearing would keep us roughly on our course, but I knew only too well the obstacles we would meet up with in the dark. It would be slow work checking and re-checking with the compass. Yet we had to make good speed if we were to reach our proposed base and get under cover before dawn.

The route began to take shape in my mind. A rough bearing of 200 degrees from our rendezvous should bring us to a large rectangular clearing in the wood. It was sufficiently big that there was little chance of missing it even if we wandered slightly from our bearing. From there all we had to do was head due south. Given a clear night we could do this stage of the trek by the stars. Four miles on was a valley that would cut across our route at right angles. This looked like being our first hazard. The woods ended half-way down the slope. The only cover was afforded by a strip of hedge that ran down into a sprawling village. What to do? Run the gauntlet down the moonlit slope, or follow the hedgerow and risk blundering into the village? I decided to wait until we faced the situation on the ground.

Tony told me I was to drop with my own headquarters as an advance party for the rest of the squadron. That meant there would be six of us dropping: myself, Sergeant McDiarmid, Corporal Payne, Lance-Corporals Hall and Myler and Trooper Weymouth. I was first of all to reconnoitre the area to judge the possibility of employing the whole squadron there. Failing this I was to decide how many men it could support operationally and make arrangements to receive them by glider. This came as a surprise. It meant I would have to find quite a large landing ground for them, and one where the gliders could quickly be dragged out of sight. We did not want a pitched battle on our hands as soon as we landed. The jeeps would be loaded into the gliders ready for driving away.

I was also to set about building up a petrol dump for the jeeps – in fact, two or three spread over the operational area. I began to work out a tentative network of subsidiary bases so that, should one base be compromised, we could continue to operate from the others. I also tried to arrange them so that the furthest dumps could be used as jumping-off points if and when we wanted to extend the area of our operations.

With Tony I went up to London to see what Combined Operations HQ could tell us about the area, then round to Special Operations Executive and Special Forces for yet more information. What I heard did not make me feel any the happier. The area was in the centre of five radio direction-finding stations. If they got a fix on our plane we would be lucky to reach the dropping zone.

Next, a factor we had not yet taken into account – enemy troops in the area. They seemed to be pretty evenly distributed in all the surrounding small towns. As I placed the trace over my map and noted where the circles fell I saw we were going to be more or less bottled up once we landed. I noticed, too, with a little uneasiness, that there was quite a percentage of SS troops in the area while in the nearest sizeable town, Troyes, were two thousand White Russian troops.

These White Russians were used by the Germans mainly to carry out repressive measures against the French civilian population and against the maquis, and the stories told of them were not pleasant. The men of the maquis used young boys and even girls as couriers. It was work of the utmost danger and, if captured, these youngsters faced 'persuasive interrogation' designed to wring from them the last ounce of information. Marcel was a courier and he was fifteen. He had been carrying messages between two maquis camps for about a month when he blundered into a White Russian patrol. This much we know. They hung him, alive, by his heels over a fire and left him to die in torment. Tools of the Germans, unwanted by their own country, they were regarded with horror by the French – and not without cause.

We spent days memorizing the route we would take on landing, the largest concentrations of troops in the area, and the road network. We could take no risk of losing our way and stumbling into trouble. I was given the code designation 'Sabu 66' and a code pad. I was told at what times and on what frequencies to listen for instructions and information from London broadcast through one of the BBC transmitters. In the marquee next to the intelligence hut, our little party practised for hours encoding and decoding until we were word perfect.

Up to this time I had been expecting to do a blind drop, without a reception committee to meet me on the ground. Now came news that Bob Melot, our intelligence officer, with Duncan Ridler his sergeant, was making his way across France to my area. He had dropped a little earlier and had been down with A Squadron at 'Houndsworth', the area in which they were operating in the Department of Nièvre. My own area was to be known as 'Kipling', and Bob would investigate our dropping zone and arrange for our reception.

Bob had with him a radio operator, and all we could do now was wait for word from him. It came at 2 P.M. on 13 August.

'Tony wants to see you,' someone called out as I walked to my tent. I found him on what we euphemistically called the cricket pitch, a bumpy patch of open ground between the NAAFI tent and the quartermaster's marquee.

'You're dropping tonight, Harry.'

'Tonight? But I thought there was no flying from Fairford tonight.'

'You're going from another 'drome. Better get ready. You're leaving at six o'clock.'

Sergeant McDiarmid was in his tent. 'It's tonight, Mac. Leaving six o'clock. Tell the chaps to get ready, and take a jeep round to the 'drome and draw six 'chutes. We're taking off from another field.'

On the way to my own tent I bumped into Stewart and Titus. I told them the news and they came along to help me pack. I needed their help, too. There were last-minute things to draw from stores – rations, escape kit, escape wallets, maps and ammunition. From the intelligence room I drew French and American currency. It was five o'clock before, sweating, swearing and straining, the three of us forced my bulging rucksack down into the leg-bag. Last of all in went my carbine, fifteen rounds in the magazine. Last in, first out, ready for action.

As we finished, up came McDiarmid with the 'chutes. I grabbed one and started to adjust it. By the time it was to my satisfaction I was sweating like a pig. A parachute is no light weight and I had on, besides my battledress, my thick, camouflaged parachute smock with my Colt belted over it and, over the lot, my jumping overalls. These overalls, zipping right the way up the front, were an added precaution against any of the equipment fouling the rigging line as the 'chute opened, and were jettisoned on landing.

Shortly before six o'clock the three-tonner which was to take us to the aerodrome drew up on the cricket pitch. We threw in the parachutes and leg-bags and clambered in after them. A number of chaps had come to see us off. Over their heads I could see Tony and Harry Poat walking over towards us. Harry beckoned.

'There's been a change in your briefing. I want you to listen carefully. Your DZ has been changed. You will be dropping at a place called Les Placeaux.' He pointed to his map. 'This is it, here. Just on the edge of the Forêt de Merryvaux. Bob Melot will be waiting on the ground.

'When you get down you're to lie low until you hear from us. You can send for some more men if you need them. Whatever you do, though, do not draw attention to yourself even if it means passing up big targets.

'There's a big airborne landing being planned. I can't tell you where. The rest of the squadron will be going down with them in gliders. As soon as you hear from us you are to set off to get through to wherever the landing has taken place.

'Never mind anything else. Your job is to get through as quickly as possible, gathering as much information on the way as you can about German defences and troop dispositions. You are to report with that information to "Boy" Browning.

'Now have you got that all clear?'

'Yes, I think so. Don't draw attention to myself. Get through with all the information I can as soon as I hear where the landing has been. Report with it to General Browning.'

'That's right. Well, best of luck.'

I climbed into the truck. Slowly we rumbled off. The

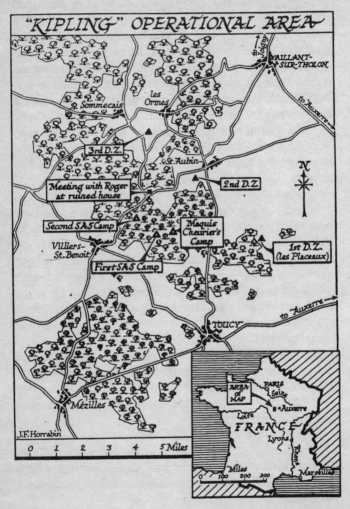

The Forêt de Merryvaux, centre of SAS operations near
Auxerre

barrier of the cage swung up for the last time. The adventure had begun.

I had a queer churned-up feeling inside as we rolled down the country roads. Odd inconsequential thoughts came to me. Little things seemed to take on an added significance. It was a perfect summer evening. The whole countryside was bathed in soft golden light from the setting sun. The grass seemed greener than I had ever seen it before. The cool shade cast by the roadside trees seemed more inviting than I had ever known. For perhaps the first time in my life I realized what this England was.

I wondered what the others were thinking. Swinging past a country pub I had an overwhelming desire for just one last glass of English beer. Already I was feeling cut off from England. After the sun had gone down the moon would ride high into the sky, casting its pale yellow light over trees, fields and cottages, while we would be floating down into enemy-occupied France. Perhaps – and for the first time I faced up to the thought – perhaps I would never see the English countryside again.

A man in RAF blue stepped from the little sentry-box by the side of the road. A few whispered words from the driver and the black-and-white barrier swung up. We pulled up before a low stone building. A squadron leader came out to greet us. 'OK, chaps. Pile out. We've got a bite to eat for you and lashings of hot tea. They're only sandwiches but your people said you wouldn't want a hot meal.'

I wondered bitterly which in particular of 'our people' had said that. A hot meal would have been just the job. However, we tucked into the sandwiches not knowing when we would get our next meal, but somehow the food stuck in our throats.

About nine, as it was getting dusk, we climbed back into the truck to go down to the dispersal point where our plane was waiting. The engines of the giant Stirling bomber were revving up with a thunderous roar. The grass lay back in the slipstream like the ears of a frightened rabbit. Bits of dust and paper swirled into the air. With the captain of the aircraft I checked the DZ to make sure he had the new one. The navigator showed me the route we would be taking.

We were due to take off at 10.14 P.M., and we would arrive over the dropping zone about midnight. I suddenly remembered it was the thirteenth of the month. I crossed my fingers and hoped it would be after midnight when we dropped. It would be my thirteenth jump, and I had qualms about making it on the unlucky day.

We struggled into our 'chutes and waddled over to the plane. Leg-bags were passed up and stowed inside, for'ard. They would not be strapped on until we were nearly there. Next was passed up a stone jar of rum. We would probably feel like a tot after we landed. Last of all, we climbed in ourselves.

On a word from the pilot we bunched for'ard for the take-off. The big black bomber rolled forward on to the runway. The engines roared with new life and we were taxi-ing along, bumping a little and swaying from side to side. The bumping and the swaying stopped. We were airborne.

Next we distributed ourselves along the fuselage in our jumping order. One of the sergeant instructors from Ringway was our dispatcher. I had not met him before. He squatted almost opposite me.

'You can look out of the windows if you want to, now,' he informed us, 'but once we cross the coast I'll have to pull the curtains across.' Nobody wanted to look. I imagine we were all far too busy with our own thoughts. The atmosphere inside the plane was eerie. Dim lights served just to show up the vague outlines of the others. My head nodded forward and I slept.

How long I slept I do not know. When I awoke it was with a start. The plane was bucking and wheeling. Against the window opposite there was a sharp, bright flash. Flak, I thought to myself. Someone murmured, 'We're crossing the French coast.' I dropped off to sleep again.

When next I woke it was to find someone shaking me by the arm. It was the dispatcher. The steady, monotonous drone of the engines brought me to a realization of where I was.

'What's up?'

'Half an hour to go. Better be getting your leg-bag on.'

I struggled to my feet and groped around in the dim light for the bag. Grunting with exertion and swearing under their breath, the rest of the chaps had already got theirs on and were fighting to keep themselves steady as they tried to fasten the straps. I felt terribly drowsy. I lugged the heavy bag up and settled it over my right foot. I was fumbling with the lower strap when the dispatcher returned.

'Here. Let me give you a hand.' He went down on his knees and got to grips with the reluctant buckles. 'How's that? Say if it's too tight.'

I wriggled my leg around. The top of the bag swayed away from my knee. 'Not tight enough.'

He took the strap up a couple of notches. 'That any better?'

I wriggled it around again. 'Yes, perfect.'

He wandered down the fuselage checking the others, then made his way once again to where I was standing. 'OK, number one, let's hook you up.'

I handed him the webbing static line that peeped from the top of my parachute. At the end was a large clip like that on a dog lead. He clipped it on to the strap which hung in the plane, slipped the safety pin through and fastened it. He dangled it in front of my eyes. 'Satisfied?'

I took a squint at it. Yes, it seemed all right. Before the safety pin had been introduced there had been cases where clips with weakened springs had been whipped off as the men jumped – with regrettable consequences. There was no chance of that now if the pin were properly fastened. The dispatcher moved on to number two.

For the first time since waking up I began to come out of my daze. I glanced down at my watch. Just past midnight! The dispatcher and flight engineer moved down towards the tail of the plane. Shooting back the bolts in the floor, they raised the two inner flaps covering the jumping hole. At the bottom of the shallow well now revealed lay a long metal handle and yet more bolts. Carefully these last bolts were shot back, then, heaving up on the handle, they swung the outer flap back into the fuselage.

A gust of cold night air rushed into the plane. Like a douche of cold water it swept away the last traces of sleepiness. I looked down into the night. The jumping hole in the Stirling was about eight feet long and three feet wide. Not much chance of ringing the bell, thank goodness. The woods below stood out like dark shadows against the grey background of fields. Here and there a thin ribbon of lighter grey showed up where tracks and lanes wound their way across the countryside. I was trying hard to make out where we were when I spotted a distinctive U-bend in one of the tracks. It was immediately below and there was no mistaking it after the hours I had pored over those aerial photographs. That was our original rendezvous. We must be nearly there.

Shuffling along – it was impossible to walk with that dead weight on my leg – I made my way to the edge of the hole. Clinging with one hand to a small girder above my head and holding the top of the leg-bag with the other, I edged my feet as far over the hole as I dared. The weight of the bag threatened to snatch me out of the plane. I braced myself and waited. Now that there was nothing else to do but wait, that awful dragging feeling in my stomach returned. My heart began to pound heavily, thumping out its beat even above the roar of the engines. I wanted to speak, to say something, anything, but all I managed was a croaking noise in my throat. I always felt like this just before I jumped.

'Running in!' the dispatcher yelled in my ear. I glued my eyes to the signal apparatus in front of me on the far side of the hole. It fascinated me. I longed to tear my eyes away but dared not in case I missed the warning light. I was afraid even to blink. Just as my eyes seemed to be popping out of my head with the strain, there was a flash.

Red light! 'Action stations!' I tensed.

Green light! I was out before the dispatcher had time to shriek 'Go!' I flashed down through the hole, through the slipstream, and into the peace and quiet of the French night. There was a sharp crack as the 'chute opened above me. Lazily I swung to and fro.

But there was no time to enjoy the sensation. I fumbled for the quick-release cord. I had to get rid of that leg-bag. Where the devil was it? I was all fingers and thumbs. I found it at last. Now the securing rope. Must hold it with the other hand. Must pay it out slowly in case it snaps. Last-minute check. Everything OK? Right! I jerked the quick-release. The weight fell from my leg as the bag swung free. Slowly, slowly, the rope slipped from its sheath as I paid it out through my hands.

'Damn!' I put all the feeling I could into that one word. The rope had jammed in the sheath. The bag was swinging round my feet not four feet below me. Frantically I fought to free the rope as I drifted nearer to earth. With a sudden rush the bag shot away. The coils of rope whipped free from the fingers of my left hand. The rope jerked tight as the bag reached the end of its drop. I gasped with pain and snatched away my hand. The middle finger at least was broken.

So much had happened during my descent that I had had no time to look round for the three fires that should have been burning on the ground. I looked down now and saw with dismay that I was about to land. I heaved down as hard as I could on my lift webs . . . and hit. All the breath was knocked from my body. I had a vague feeling of flattening a sturdy young prickly bush of some kind. I picked myself up.

My broken finger was forgotten. Wriggling out of my harness I pulled out my carbine and laid it in readiness against my leg-bag. Crouching low I ran to the top of my 'chute and started to roll it up. As I did so I noticed that one or two of the panels had ripped on the way down.

I was wrapping the 'chute in its rigging lines when I heard a noise. Quick as lightning I dropped to the ground. My eyes were not yet accustomed to the dark. All I could see were dark blobs of shadows, the prickly bushes and the dark mass of the woods about two hundred yards away. Then I heard the noise again. Voices. Almost at the same time I saw the silhouettes of two soldiers, their steel helmets and rifles outlined against the sky, moving towards me. Quietly I stretched out my hand for my carbine. I had the advantage of surprise. Two quick shots and a break for the woods. My groping hand found nothing. The carbine was just out of reach. My Colt was still under my jumping overalls.

I was debating what to do when they spoke again – in French, as I now recognized. As they hurried forward I called out, '*Anglais. Je suis anglais.*' One of them grabbed my 'chute and the other my rucksack and started to lead me across the field. They asked no questions, but, as they obviously knew what they were doing – which was more than I did – I followed them. As I stumbled along I tried to get my bearings. The woods were behind and on the right. But where was the dropping zone? Certainly this was not it. We were picking our way through a maze of small prickly bushes. We blundered through a hedge. I put up my hands to shield my face from the thorny tendrils that plucked and tore at my clothes.

It was difficult to make out anything much in the dark but, as soon as we got through that hedge, I saw we were on the DZ. I must have drifted into a neighbouring field. I wondered where the rest of the stick had landed. The field we were in now appeared to have been recently ploughed. It was hard going and it was as much as I could do to keep my feet. Another hedge loomed up somewhere in front, and I could hear the murmur of voices. Beneath a solitary tree standing in the corner of the DZ were the other members of my party.

Bob Melot was there directing a group of Frenchmen in the search for the containers that had been dropped with us. They were a mixed bunch, these French helpers. Some were members of the local maquis, but a large number were farmers and labourers from the neighbouring village who had turned out to give a hand to the 'British parachutists'.

Beyond the tree a small track ran along the edge of the dropping zone. On the far side lay the woods. As the containers were brought in they were loaded on to Bob's jeep and taken down the track to a tunnel-like, tree-lined lane where two large trucks were standing.

'That Harry?' Bob peered at me through the dark. His face wrinkled up into a smile. 'You dropped a bit wide.'

He nodded to where the others were lying. 'Better get some rest while we get the containers in.'

I held out my left hand. 'Anybody around who can dress my hand? I think I've broken a finger.' He took a look at it. It was swelling badly round the joints. A girl came forward out of the shadows, twenty-five-ish, dark-haired and rather plump. Bob asked me for my escape file. Flat, about four inches long and wrapped in greased paper, it made an ideal splint. He handed it to the girl who produced some bandaging from somewhere and in no time at all had the finger neatly splinted up.

Feeling happier now, I took Bob's advice and lay down. Someone handed me an apple. It was lying by my side uneaten when I woke up, frozen to the marrow, to find the first flush of dawn lightening the skies.

The jeep was roaring along the track with the last container on board. The Frenchmen were hurriedly carrying 'chutes and loose pieces of container into the woods safe from prying eyes on the ground or from the air. Before daylight there would be no trace left of the night's work.

I looked at my watch. It was six o'clock – just twelve hours since we left Fairford cage. In that short time I had stepped into a new and strange world as completely divorced from England and home as moon from earth.

In a couple of short hours my wife would be starting her daily round unaware that this day was any different from the others. And here I was, bumping along narrow, dusty tracks in the middle of enemy-occupied France in a British jeep, wondering when I would get any breakfast and what I would get – if I got any.

17

Maquis Chevrier

Clinging to the jeep we swept along the forest tracks, swaying dangerously from side to side, ducking low to avoid overhanging branches. The willowy undergrowth, brushed roughly aside by the lumbering jeep, whipped back against our legs where they hung over the side.

'Where are we going, Bob?' I called out as he swung the jeep on to a minor road and put his foot hard down.

'The camp of Maquis Chevrier,' he shouted back without turning his head. I fell silent. We were still driving down the road and it was now quite light. I did not know quite what to expect . . .

With a sudden lurch and hardly any slackening of pace we swung right, off the road and on to a small track leading into the forest again. As we passed, two men with large leafy branches stepped out from among the trees and set-to to erase with them all signs of our tracks leading into the forest.

We drove on for about two hundred yards until the track dwindled away and nothing remained but trees and undergrowth. Under a screen of overhanging leaves Bob pulled up. 'Jump off, lads. We walk from here.'

We climbed down and stretched our limbs. Nearby I could see the containers that had been dropped with us lying among the trees with branches and leaves thrown over them to hide them from the air. With Bob leading we set off through the trees, following the bed of what, even in wet weather, must have been a tiny trickle of water hardly deserving the name of stream. For perhaps half a mile we followed it, then branched off left. What

Bob was following now I had no idea but, after about a quarter of an hour, we struck a muddy path. Up to now the ground had been dry and hard, so that meant there must be water nearby, and water meant a camp like as not. Following the path up a steep banking we marched straight into the camp of Maquis Chevrier.

Immediately in front and to the right were the sleeping quarters. These were shaped like bivouac tents but were made of branches and twigs. A few of them had bits of tarpaulin or groundsheets spread across them. All were built in among the trees, only the minimum of under-growth having been cleared to make way for them.

To the left were the 'dining tables' and seats. These were made from straight, stripped branches lashed together and supported by forked branches driven into the ground. Beyond was a long trench fire, round which the cooks were busy.

Commandant Chevrier came forward to meet us and led us to the tables, where we sat down to breakfast. With his erect bearing and precise speech he was obviously a Regular officer and equally obviously the man to take over this maquis, which had been first raised by the mayor of the nearby village of Villiers-St Benoît. After breakfast we sat and talked until nearly nine o'clock, when he excused himself and made his way to his quarters, there to listen to the nine o'clock broadcast from London.

While he listened, his second-in-command took us on a tour of the camp. It was far more extensive than I had at first thought, with sleeping quarters extending some way into the forest. In an improvised lean-to, well protected with tarpaulins, were the arms. Rifles were neatly stowed in racks. Two Bren guns, well oiled and clean, stood on the ground. Near the entrance lay a box of ready-primed hand grenades. The Frenchman dragged out another box which had been badly damaged. 'You see, it had been damaged in the parachutage. We have not touched it because we do not know what these things are.' He turned to Bob. 'Perhaps, Commandant Melot, you would instruct us?'

'These things' were Hawkins grenades, a small and very compact type of mine particularly effective against wheeled vehicles. There being no time like the present, Bob got down to the job of explaining their mechanism and use. The rest of us wandered on round the camp. A large canvas sheet slung between four trees, its centre just touching the ground, caught my eye. When I peeped over the edge I saw that it held a number of rabbits, very much alive. No shortage of fresh meat there.

A little way beyond the camp we came upon two men with a Bren gun crouching in a well-concealed weapon pit, covering the approaches to the camp along the two tracks which entered the area on that side.

Returning to camp we were in time to find a platoon of maquisards drilling in a small clearing. Like Alice, I felt that things were getting 'curiouser and curiouser'.

Thirsty after our well-seasoned breakfast, we went in search of water. The Frenchmen grinned, motioned to us to hold out our mess tins, and filled them to the brim. I drank mine down almost in one draught. I choked. My throat and stomach were on fire. I gasped for air. The maquisards roared with laughter. They had given us a drink they distilled themselves. They called it 'gut', but it was wood alcohol.

The following morning I went with Duncan Ridler in the jeep to have a look around and get the feel of things. Bulldozing our way through the forest we did a wide circuit of the camp area. If it did nothing else it knocked one idea out of my head for all time. It showed me there was a world outside the maquis camp and outside the protection of their outposts. I think that then, for the first time, I really realized that we were not on just another scheme, that we were on German-held territory, out to kill and very liable to be killed if we made one false move.

After lunch Bob and I talked things over and I decided to send for more men, and for jeeps. We could then set up our own camp. This was a wise precaution as my instructions were to lie low without attracting attention to our presence. There was more chance of succeeding if we kept ourselves to ourselves.

A signal was sent to London arranging to receive Stewart and his section that same night on the DZ at Les Placeaux where I had been dropped. We also asked for one jeep to be dropped to us. Bob approached Commandant Chevrier and he readily agreed to lend his men again to help at the reception.

It was nearly midnight when we arrived at the dropping zone. Two of the men had been left in camp while the rest of us had piled into Bob's jeep. Two maquis trucks loaded with helpers had arrived before us and were now drawn up in the same tunnel-like lane where they had waited on the previous night. The men were standing about on the edge of the DZ waiting for instructions.

Bob wasted no time. I followed him around, watching everything he did. It was the first time I had been at a reception and I was more or less under instruction. One party of helpers was detailed to spread out along the length of the DZ on one side at intervals of about eighty to a hundred yards. Another party was detailed for the far side. A third group was ordered to watch along the track at the end of the dropping zone. A fourth was already standing by to load the containers when they were dropped.

Before placing the men Bob tested the direction of the wind. It was blowing up the DZ from the track end. With Duncan Ridler I walked out on to the dropping zone to help place the three fires for which the plane would be searching. These we decided to put at eighty-yard intervals, with the first fire about a hundred and fifty yards up from the track.

Thirty yards to the flank of this first fire Ridler was to stand with his signalling torch ready to flash the recognition signal into the air as soon as the plane was heard approaching. The plane would then fly down the line of fires towards the flashing light letting go its cargo of men and supplies. By flying towards the light the pilot would know he was flying into the wind and that the 'chutes would be carried back on to the dropping zone.

On the site of each fire a bundle of brushwood was dropped and by each bundle a man was stationed with a tin of petrol. On receiving the signal – a light flashed straight up the DZ, or a shout of 'fire' – they would splash petrol over the brushwood and throw a match in.

Estimated time of arrival of the plane over the DZ was 0200 hours. I looked at my watch. Fifty minutes to wait. We made our way back to the tree which had become the focal point of our operations on the DZ. Bob was there with an officer of the maquis. The four of us sat in the jeep smoking endless cigarettes, waiting for two o'clock. Somewhere around us in the dark were the maquis outposts.

As the minutes dragged on it got colder and colder. I zipped my smock up tight and snuggled down low in my seat. The moon dipped lower in the sky. The shadows in the woods grew deeper and deeper. At ten minutes to two we stirred ourselves and hurried over to the first fire. Ridler took up his position away to the left with his torch.

Five to two! We were quiet now. No more whisperings. All ears were strained for the drone of the approaching plane. The minutes ticked away slowly.

Two o'clock! Still not a sound. One minute past . . .

two minutes past . . . three . . . Faintly in the distance came the sound we had been waiting for. The steady rhythmic throbbing of a plane's engines approaching.

This was it. Or was it? It might be a German plane and, if we lit the fire, we were almost certain to be machine-gunned. All it had to do was run down the line of fires. It had happened before. My heart beat a little faster.

The droning was louder. Bob nudged me. 'Sounds like ours. What do you think?'

I shrugged. 'I wouldn't like to swear to it.'

We fell silent again and waited. Like a huge black bird against the lighter background of the sky the plane swept in above the woods. We stared up at its silhouette. 'Halifax,' we breathed together. Then with one voice, 'Fires!'

Ridler's torch jabbed up through the night sky. Dot dot dash dot. Dot dot dash dot: 'F' – 'F' for Freddy – the recognition signal. The three fires flared up suddenly as the petrol ignited. The plane swept on above our heads. The drone of its engines died away again into the distance. Had it seen us or had we been too late with the fires? We waited, ears alert for the returning sound of its engines. After what seemed hours but could not have been more than seconds we picked up the sound again.

'Ready with more petrol.' The fires flared up anew as the plane droned in again. At five hundred feet the Halifax circled round, then flew off to make its dummy run-in over the fires. On its second run-in it would start to drop.

Here it came. From beneath its belly a large black shape detached itself. Four white 'chutes billowed out, one from each corner, checking its fall. It was the jeep. The plane, released from its weight, leapt upwards as a cork in water.

Round went the plane again. Containers this time. One

– two – three – four – five . . . I started to count as they fluttered and billowed out behind the plane. The jeep had floated out of sight behind me, but now I was waiting for the men to drop. Like black specks they fell away from the plane, gradually becoming larger as they floated nearer to earth, disappearing as they merged with the dark woods behind.

The lines of helpers whose keen eyes had been busy picking out and marking where the men and containers nearest to them had fallen now moved forward. Another gang was already searching for the jeep. Its forward momentum, assisted by its weight, had carried it beyond the dropping zone into the woods on the far side of the track.

A shout from the woods told that the jeep had been found. It had landed about twenty yards from a track running through the trees. Smashing aside young saplings in its fall, it had come to rest in the midst of about the thickest undergrowth in the woods. With hatchets and rifle butts the Frenchmen were hacking and beating a way through to it. But it was one thing to get to it and another altogether to get it on to the track. It took two and a half hours of sweating and struggling before the task was completed and, miracle of miracles, the jeep was driven away to our camp.

I did not stay with the jeep. As soon as I saw work was in progress to get it out I made my way back to the DZ. Stewart Richardson was there with his men, or some of them at least. The rest, he said, were in a second plane which had not shown up. One of the men had lost his leg-bag. The rope had snapped when he pulled the release cord and it had plummeted to earth. It was not found for nearly a fortnight. Meanwhile he had nothing but his Colt and the clothes he stood up in. I made a note to send for fresh equipment for him.

Brearton, Stewart's driver, was looking rueful. Like the jeep he had overshot the DZ and landed in the woods. Unlike the jeep, however, he had not crashed through to earth but had remained strung up in a tall tree by his rigging lines. Dangling in mid-air, he had seen the men searching for the jeep below, but did not know whether they were French or German.

At last he could stand it no longer and he hollered out. Immediately a group of them gathered at the foot of the tree shouting gratuitous advice to him in French, none of which helped him to get down to earth.

'Get Captain Harrison!' he yelled at the top of his voice. 'Get Major Melot, get Mr Richardson.' Then, as nothing happened, 'For Lord's sake get somebody, get somebody who speaks English.'

He was eventually rescued, but his opinion of the French was never the same afterwards.

Similar experiences of being tree'd had already befallen two other members of the unit. Our padre, Fraser McGlusky, finding himself swinging lazily to and fro from a tree in another part of France, whipped out his knife and cut through his rigging lines. He dropped twenty feet to earth and sprained his ankle, but considered that preferable to being found roosting in a tree by passing Germans.

Major Bill Fraser was the other victim. As he dangled there, his 'chute inextricably entangled in the branches of a tree, he thought of what had happened to the padre. He stared down towards the ground but saw nothing but inky blackness below him. He decided to hang there till daylight rather than risk the plunge into nothingness. For more than two hours he swung idly in the night breeze. With the first flush of dawn he gazed down into the depths below – and found his feet no more than three inches from the ground.

But though there was a humorous side to this business of parachuting into occupied France, there was a job to be done. Men, containers and our new jeep were back in camp before dawn. This time we brought with us several parachutes which we intended to use as makeshift tents.

Bob spent the morning looking for a site for our first independent camp. He returned about two o'clock in the afternoon. He had found a good spot about two kilometres outside Chevrier's outposts with a fresh-water spring nearby, and a concealed track for the jeeps. As we loaded our equipment and stores on to the jeeps I looked at the one that had been dropped to us and wondered more than ever that it had been possible to drive it an inch. The force of the landing in the trees had bent the whole framework over at an angle of twenty degrees from the vertical. However, although it would never carry guns it would be valuable for parachutage work. By half past four we were installed in our new camp.

I had already decided to send for the whole of my own troop to join me and, while we had been moving camp, had received a signal from London confirming our request for further parachutage that night. Code letter was 'H' and estimated time of arrival of the first plane was 0240 hours. Apart from men and supplies, two more jeeps were to be dropped.

Having had a parachutage two nights running at Les Placeaux we decided we had better change the DZ in case the Germans had got wind of our operations. Bob had already marked down this new dropping zone against such an emergency. It was three or four miles away, a long rectangular field from which the corn had been recently cut. The stooks still littered the field, but damage to the crops had to be risked. The biggest danger, of course, was fire. In addition, a second-class road ran along the end of the DZ, while, just over the hill about a mile and a half away, ran one of the main roads used by the Germans. Altogether it was not a perfect spot, but it was the only other DZ of sufficient size to take the jeep drops.

We arrived just after midnight. Up one side of the field ran a narrow, overgrown track overhung with trees. Up here we drove the jeeps and, as on the previous night, set about laying the fires and detailing the helpers. The big maquis truck could not get up the track so we had to leave it standing at the side of the road. It was asking for trouble if the Germans should chance along, but it was a risk we had to take.

Bob had stayed back in camp so I found myself in the position of instructor to Stewart. I had also taken over the job of flashing the recognition letters to the plane. Shortly before half past two we heard the sound of an approaching plane. I alerted the men at the fires. Here it came.

'Fires!'

I sent a jab of light up the DZ. The fires blazed into life. The plane roared over the field and disappeared into the night. I waited for the sound of it returning. A minute passed and still no sound.

'Dowse the fires!' I yelled to number one fire. Number one passed it up the line. The fires went out. Either the plane had been German, in which case . . . Or it had been carrying a British agent to some other rendezvous. I prayed it might be the latter.

At 0241 the first Halifax arrived. There was no mistake this time. I snapped out the code letter on my torch. As the plane ran-in I saw that it was not over the fires but away to the right, nearly where our jeeps were parked. The jeep, slung in its open bomb bays, dropped away and floated to earth to land with a splintering crash among the young trees on the other side of the track. What a record! Two jeeps, two tree landings.

On his second run-in he let go the containers. He was

over the fires this time but too late in dropping them. They floated way past the dropping zone towards the top of the hill. His third run was better, the men dropping all round us. Men, leg-bags and 'chutes were hurried off the DZ. The second plane was due over.

Steady and low it flew in. Away went the jeep. Down, down, a perfect drop, to land right on the third fire. Fortunately its crating smothered the flames, and we were spared the sight of it going up in one big blaze.

We were knocking away the chocks to drive it off the DZ when from the road came a frantic shouting. A man came running up. '*La jeep. Où est la jeep avec les mitrailleuses?* Quick! The jeep with the machine-guns.'

It was one of Chevrier's men. I grabbed him. 'What's the matter? What's wrong?'

'Quick, *mon capitaine*, the jeep. The White Russians are coming.'

I went cold in the pit of my stomach. We were in no position to put up much of a fight. White Russians! We knew all about them. The jeep drove up, Stewart at the wheel. I jumped on. Down the dropping zone we roared. The Frenchmen with their Sten guns and one or two of our men with their carbines sprinted down behind us. Those who could jumped on to the jeep and hung on precariously.

Now that action was imminent the cold feeling had left me and my mind was already planning what to do. We pulled the jeep in about thirty yards from the road under a couple of low trees, its guns pointing up the road. The rest of us flung ourselves down into the ditch alongside the road. Two of the Frenchmen, carrying one of our Brens, scuttled up the ditch towards the approaching lights, ready to take them in the rear when we opened fire.

Round the bend it came. It was a battered old coach.

As it sped towards us I prayed none of them would spot the two Frenchmen lurking in the ditch. As it passed them I held my breath. Suddenly the two men leapt to their feet.

'Don't shoot! Don't shoot!' they yelled at the tops of their voices.

With a screaming of brakes the coach skidded to a halt. The Frenchmen came running up, out of breath. 'They're French. It is the FFI. Don't shoot.'

Dazed by this sudden turn of events we stood up, carbines and Stens at the ready, still not sure that it was not a trick. I saw that the coach was packed tight with some forty or fifty steel-helmeted troops of the FFI – French Forces of the Interior. They were crammed in their seats, unable to move, their rifles between their knees, looking very scared. They thought they had run into an ambush by the Germans.

The situation was soon explained. They were part of a force that had been moved into the area to protect our parachutages, with their headquarters in the neighbouring village of Sommecais. But no one had told us. It had been a big scare on both sides and it was with no little feeling of relief that we saw the coach carry on down the road.

We returned to the immediate job of collecting the containers. Dawn was fast approaching and we had to work against time. As fast as the containers were brought in they were loaded on to the big maquis truck. The two new jeeps were sent off under escort to our camp, together with the men who had dropped that night. Last of all, the truck lumbered off down the road in the approaching light.

Three containers were still unaccounted for. A small party of us stayed behind to find them. They must have landed far up on the hill overlooking the main road. At all costs we had to have them. If the tell-tale parachutes were seen by a passing German convoy the jig would be up. There would be a sweep of the area to rout us out.

German man-hunts were very thorough. They would ring the suspected area for a distance of some four kilometres out, then close slowly in. Escape along the roads would be impossible. In the woods the Germans would bring up their flame throwers to burn us out. We had to find those missing containers.

We found them, shortly after daylight, on the hill where we thought they would be. They were loaded on to Ridler's jeep and as many of the men as possible were packed on. Sergeant McDiarmid, one of Chevrier's lieutenants and myself stayed behind. Ridler would return for us. We took up positions on the edge of the wood overlooking the road. From now on we had to be doubly alert. Smoke wreathed up from the chimneys of a nearby farmhouse. A woman came to the door and looked over towards the DZ. I looked myself. We had done a good job. There was no sign of the night's work. The charred remains of the three fires had been covered over with stooks which lay carelessly tumbled all over the field. There was nothing to attract the attention of passing Germans.

Mac gave a stage shout. 'Here comes Ridler.' Down the road at top speed came the jeep, a flurry of dust spinning into the air behind it. Hardly slackening pace it swept off the road and pulled up under the trees.

'Come on, quick. Jump in.'

'What's wrong?'

'We've left a jeep 'chute strung up on the trees. You can see it for miles.'

We roared up the track as fast as we could go, coming to a halt about half-way up the DZ. Ridler was first off the jeep and plunged into the trees. 'Here it is.' We plunged in after him. I could see the webbing dangling from the lower branches. Looking up I could see the huge expanse of the white silken canopy sprawled out across the top of the trees. Together we started to pull like madmen on the rigging lines.

'It's no use, we can't shift it.' Ridler eyed it thoughtfully. 'There's only one thing. We'll have to burn it.'

It was a risk, but the lesser danger. As it was it was a permanent beacon for all to see. If we burned it, the flames might be seen beyond the hill if anyone happened to be looking this way. Quickly we splashed petrol on it and lit a match. It blazed up almost in one flash. As we stood back to admire our handiwork there came the sound of an approaching tracked vehicle from over the hill.

We leaped into the jeep and beat it back to camp as fast as we could. My instructions were still to lie low – and wait.

18

Rendezvous with Roger

It had been a hot, backbreaking job but the containers were at last out of sight. We had ferried them from Chevrier's main dump in the jeeps. Now they were hidden in the deep ditches running alongside our own camp. Over the top we had pulled branches and leaves. Later on we would have to break them up into their cells. These cells were smaller cylinders carried inside the containers. In some there was ammunition, in others food. Clothing and weapons came packed in containers with no cells. Petrol came in jerricans. All these would have to be sorted out in time, but there were other things to do just now.

With Bob's little party, we were now nineteen strong. I made my way up the narrow track into the camp to see if the ten men who had dropped during the night were yet awake. The new jeeps had to be fitted up. The first thing to do was to allocate crews to the jeeps – driver, commander (who was front gunner), and rear gunner. As soon as this was done the crews set to work on the vehicles. Auxiliary petrol tanks had been fitted, one under the commander's seat and two over the lockers in the back, giving each jeep a capacity of forty-eight gallons and a road range of some nine hundred miles at one filling. But the feed pipes had to be connected.

The guns, too, had been parachuted separately. Mountings had to be assembled and guns aligned. These mountings, made from tubular steel, were a heavier type than those used in the desert and, we were to find out later, much less satisfactory. The guns, mounted in pairs, were the Vickers K gas-operated aircraft guns, with a rate of fire of around twelve hundred a minute. The hundred-round magazines were loaded up with tracer, armour-piercing and incendiary bullets. One or two magazines were loaded up exclusively with ball, or ordinary bullets. These were for use when it was particularly important not to give away our position to the enemy when firing.

Apart from the twin Vickers front and rear, there was a single Vickers mounted by the driver which could be fired while he drove one-handed. Carried loose in the back for dismounted action was a Bren gun. Hand grenades were tucked away in various odd spots all over the jeep. They were ideal for breaking off an engagement with a pursuing enemy who was in too strong a position. Pins withdrawn, and dropped over the back of the withdrawing jeep, they worked wonders. Finally, close by each member of the crew, easily accessible, were his carbine and escape haversack.

We had made these escape haversacks up ourselves. Besides the normal escape equipment issued to us, there was medical kit, extra ammunition for the carbines, maps, water-bottle, chocolate and cigarettes. In the event of having to bale out of the jeeps in action, all we had to do was grab carbine and haversack and carry on with the job on foot.

I looked up from working on my jeep to see Bob deep in conversation with a man in dark blue uniform leaning over a bicycle. As I did so I caught the sound of engines in the distance. Everyone else heard it too. All work stopped. We picked up our carbines. Roaring and spluttering up the track to the camp a motor-cycle came into view between the trees. Its rider was dressed in dark blue uniform. Within half an hour we were crowded out with blue uniforms. They came on bicycles and on foot. As they gathered wide-eyed round the jeeps, Bob pulled me aside.

'I don't like the way things have turned out, Harry. These are local gendarmes. It seems the Germans gave them twenty-four hours to join the Waffen SS – or else. This morning their chief told them each man would have to make his own decision, but that he was going to take to the maquis.' Bob waved his hand in their direction. 'They all followed him.

'But this isn't the worst. There's another big batch of them at Chevrier's place, about three hundred altogether. And the damned fools coming up in daylight will probably bring half the German army on their tails. There's only one thing for it. We'll have to move camp again. There won't be an attack tonight, but we'll have to get moving tomorrow.'

'Any idea where?'

'No, not yet. You and I had better recce for a site first thing.' Bob gave a deep, long-suffering sigh. 'Oh, and there's another thing. I met Commandant Roger this morning. He's in command of the FFI you tangled with last night. They're about battalion strength and Roger says he has instructions to start offensive operations in the area.'

'Offensive operations?' I was staggered. 'He can't do that. What hope have I of getting through if he starts messing around before the landing? The place will be like a hornets' nest.'

'I know. I told him you had contrary instructions and I've arranged for us to meet him again tomorrow evening. He's got two Special Forces men with him – Americans – and they're coming along too. He won't do anything till after the meeting.'

We had a supply drop that night. No men, just petrol, food and ammunition – but mostly petrol. When it was all over I realized for the first time that, since dropping four nights before, I had had no sleep at all. There had been more than enough to keep the days filled and there had been a parachutage every night. I was hoping for a drop of more jeeps and men the following night.

Next morning Bob and I set off early, on foot, to find a new base. It had to be somewhere with well-concealed exits for the jeeps, and with a nearby water supply. Ideally we would have liked to keep its location secret but, still needing Chevrier's help for our parachutages, we would have to take him into our confidence with at least one of his lieutenants.

We had already sent a signal to London for onward transmission to the organization concerned, explaining the gendarme situation and asking for arms and ammunition to be dropped for them. With that we felt our responsibility was ended. The majority of the gendarmes were no doubt admirable men, but we could not lose sight of the fact that they had taken to the maquis only to avoid pressed service with the German forces. They were now friendly towards us mainly because of the protection we could afford them, but there needed to be only one spy among them for our number to be up, or on its way up.

To have left camp by jeep would have attracted too much attention, which is why we slipped away on foot. As things turned out we were to be thankful for that decision, but for an entirely different reason.

The new camp had to be reasonably close to at least one suitable DZ. The one at Les Placeaux, being so close to Chevrier's camp, we had to consider as compromised now that there were so many 'strangers' in camp. We decided to work the area round our alternative dropping zone in our search for a new base.

By eleven o'clock we had covered a lot of ground. Grimed with sweat and dust, we were lying on our stomachs on the edge of a small copse overlooking the nearby Route Nationale. Five German trucks passed along and out of sight. I was thirsty. So, it seemed, was Bob. He jerked his head. 'We'll get some wine at the farmhouse back there.'

It was cool in the house. The wine was cool. Round the bend in the road came the five German trucks we had seen, in a smother of dust. We downed our drinks in one go, scuttled out of the back door, tell-tale glasses in hand, and went to ground behind the compost heap. The trucks pulled up. Colts in hand, we were prepared to make a fight of it if necessary. As far as we could tell from the voices, not more than two or three Germans had entered the house. But we were not anxious to fight, for two good reasons. My orders, and the fact that any brush with these men would bring reprisals on the farmhouse. We blessed the fact that our jeep was not standing outside.

The hand that clasped my Colt was clammy with sweat. The compost smelled to high heaven. We dared not raise our heads to see what was happening, nor to get a breath of fresher air. But at last we heard the trucks start up, turn round and head back towards the main road.

When we set out on our renewed quest for a base five minutes later, I had learned a lesson that was to stay with me throughout my work in France.

We found a suitable site at last. It was about a mile or so from our first camp, and the approach from that direction was along an almost impassable track, deep-cut with old ruts and strewn with outcropping boulders. We thought we would be able to get the jeeps through, but only just. On the other side was a tree-sheltered track leading on to a third-class road. Branching from this track at right angles and in opposite directions were two more tracks leading back into the woods.

The only drawback was water. There was a farmhouse near where the track met the road. Bob contacted the farmer and decided he was safe. There was little doubt we could get water from them, but it would have meant short shrift for the whole family if ever the Germans connected them with us. We decided to rely on the spring near our old base, sending a jeep every morning to fill up the water-cans.

By three o'clock we had moved to the new camp, lock, stock and barrel. Stores of ammunition and petrol were in new camouflaged hide-outs. The duty cook was busy with a hot meal. We cooked all our meals over open fires but there was no danger of the smoke giving away our position, the heavy foliage of the tall trees effectively dispersing it.

Leaving Stewart to make the necessary preparations for the coming night's parachutage, Bob and I now set out in his jeep to keep our appointment with Commandant Roger of the FFI. The meeting was to take place, rather melodramatically, at a ruined house at a cross-roads not far from our camp. We were first there. To guard against any possible trap, we first drove straight past and over the junction. Stopping at the top of the hill we had a good look round through our glasses. Seeing nothing to arouse our suspicions, we drove slowly back again and swung off the road through the ruined gateway to draw up in front of the house.

Placing the jeep where it was in the shadows and where it could fire along three branches of the cross-roads, we left Ridler on the guns to make sure we were not taken by surprise. Bob and I had a good look over the deserted house, then made our way to the back garden. Here the grass and nettles had grown several feet high, making a complete wilderness. We settled down to wait.

Perhaps five minutes passed before we heard a rustling

in the hedgerow leading down from Sommecais. There was a low whistle and a head appeared at a gap in the hedge. It was one of Roger's men. Apparently satisfied with what he saw he signalled back to an unseen companion. We heard the noise of a car starting up and a moment later a black Citroën drew up. Out of it stepped Commandant Roger followed by two uniformed Americans with the Special Forces flash on their arms. The car turned round and disappeared as the three men approached. Squatting in a circle among the grass and weeds we got down to work.

Bob and Roger immediately tangled in a fast, wordy exchange of which I understood hardly a word. From time to time one of the Americans broke in with his slow, drawling French to ask a question. He was a rather thin, pale-faced individual, with rimless spectacles perched on the bridge of his nose. It would be rather difficult to imagine a greater contrast to Roger, tall, thickset and ruddy-complexioned. Like myself, the other Special Forces man had kept silent during these preliminaries. Now the first American turned to me.

'Well, it seems to me we've both gotten different instructions. Our orders came from General Koenig and said we were to start making nuisances of ourselves right away down here. Your instructions came from London, you say?'

'Yes, I was given them before I dropped. I was to lie low, do nothing to attract attention until I had a further message by radio from London. I have not yet received that other signal.'

'D'you know why you have to lie low? I mean, is the reason sufficiently strong for us to set aside our instructions?'

'Yes, the reason is very important . . .' I hesitated.

'Wouldn't care to tell us what your mission is?'

'Sorry, I can't do that.'

'OK. Fair enough.' He turned to speak to Roger, who nodded thoughtfully as he explained. He turned back to me.

'That's OK, then. We won't do anything to upset your plans. Roger, though, would like to know just how long this is going on.'

'That I don't know, but I can promise him this. He can raise merry hell within twenty-four hours of my receiving my orders. That'll suit me down to the ground. The bigger the stink the more I'll like it.'

'That's settled, then.' He got to his feet and held out his hand. 'Be seeing you around.' At a signal the black car drove up. The three men climbed in and, with a last wave, disappeared up the road.

Back at camp we found all set for the night's parachutage. Captain David Barnaby and ten men were dropping, with three jeeps. We were using the Les Placeaux DZ again because we had not had time to radio London with the change. Estimated time of arrival of the first plane was 0220 hours, code letter 'L'. There was also a little Frenchman waiting to see Bob. Vivier, one of Chevrier's lieutenants, was with him.

After he had gone, Bob called me over. 'That fellow I was talking to was in the French Intelligence. Chevrier vouches for him. He has offered to supply us with detailed information of enemy movements in the area just north of here. Seems a useful sort of chap.' He unrolled a map. 'He's got a house in this village, here, next to the blacksmith's. If we are in the area and need any help, guides, information, or if we need hiding, we're to tap three times on the front window and give the password "la jeep". You never know, it might come in useful.'

With three jeeps dropping that night we needed more men than usual on the DZ, so Chevrier agreed to send along a number of the gendarmes to help in addition to his own men and the usual local people. The first plane arrived overhead dead on time, dropped its jeep and containers squarely across the DZ and disappeared again into the night. No sooner had the sound of its engines died away than the second plane arrived. Another jeep, more containers and the first of the men floated down to earth.

It was ten minutes or more before the third and last plane came in and, when it did, we realized with dismay that it was running up the lights in the wrong direction. Away went the jeep, to land in the hedgerow at the top of the DZ. I crossed my fingers and hoped that the pilot would realize his mistake, but no such luck. In he came again, against the lights. The container 'chutes blossomed out behind him and drifted slowly away up the dropping zone and out of sight among the distant trees. A third and last run-in, and the men went drifting away after the containers.

Search-parties were immediately detailed to go and bring them in. Chevrier's men set off at once, knowing only too well the danger of leaving tell-tale 'chutes around, but the gendarmes would not budge. They seemed scared of moving from the comparative safety of the DZ and unwilling to unbend themselves sufficiently to get down to the hard work of bringing in the containers.

While one party struggled to free the third jeep from the hedgerow where it had fallen, the men who had dropped wide wandered in in ones and twos. One had concussed himself either when leaving the plane or on landing. He did not know which. When Bob offered him his favourite brandy flask he drank greedily from it and, without realizing what he was doing, flung it away into the darkness. Bob was inconsolable until it was found again.

When dawn came there were still five 'chutes missing – three containers and two hampers. The hampers were particularly important because they contained much-needed wireless equipment. As soon as the jeeps and other containers were cleared from the DZ, we set off to search for them. All morning we beat through the thick woods to the west of the DZ while two jeeps stood guard, their guns trained on the road. It was half past twelve before the last one was run to earth.

Back in camp I once again took stock of our position. Excluding Bob's little party we were now twenty-seven strong, and I considered I had enough men to carry out any task ahead of us. Without Bob's jeep, which had anyway been more or less run to death by this time, and not counting the 'leaning' jeep which was hardly in operational condition, we had five jeeps available. I decided that when I got word from London to link up with the airborne landing, the five jeeps should set off along different routes, in the hope that one of them at least would get through. The remainder of the men would stay behind to co-operate with Roger and Chevrier in creating a diversion. Meanwhile I kept the details of the job to myself. The fewer who knew anything about it the better. What I had heard from the men who had just joined us left me in no doubt at all as to what our fate would be if captured.

One of the bases in the Poitiers area had been attacked at dawn on 3 July by a force of about five hundred SS with mortars and artillery in support. The Germans had ringed the area during the night, and the first warning that anything was amiss came when artillery and mortars crashed out as they searched the woods. Then the lorried infantry closed in.

Realizing the impossibility of fighting a pitched battle against such odds, John Tonkin gave the order for the men to disperse as and when they could disengage. All who dispersed made good their escape, eighteen in number, and carried on their work from a new base.

Thirty-three of the men, some of them wounded, were taken prisoner. One of the wounded officers was taken by the Germans to a neighbouring village. There the assembled villagers were forced to watch as he was clubbed to death with rifle butts. His crime: being a 'terrorist'. Of the rest of the men there was no news but a SHAEF court of inquiry later established that sixteen were definitely murdered a few days afterwards, and the rest were almost certainly murdered too.

Small wonder, then, that I decided to keep the details to myself.

Later that afternoon the signaller came to my 'tent'. 'Message for Sabu 66, Captain Harrison. Have you your code pad?'

Bob came over and stood looking over my shoulder as the signaller spelled out the message and I started to decode.

'There's a wrong letter here. Look, ABAC in this group.'

'Let me have a look.' I leaned over to check for myself. 'That's OK. It must be either ABAB or ACAC. The context will tell us which.'

We carried on in silence for a while. 'Hell!'

'What's wrong?'

'That misspelled group, Bob. A chance in a million. Either one of them makes sense. One of them means "Put operation into effect . . ." and the other means "Operation cancelled . . ." Now which in blazes is it? We'll have to ask for a re-coding on the next transmission.'

'I've already tried on the emergency schedule and we can't get through. Static is terrible.'

'Oh, Lord. We're properly up the pole now. Of all

the . . . We'll just have to sit tight till we can get through. Let's hope they're not sitting out there waiting for us.'

The following morning we got the re-coding. 'Operation cancelled owing to pressure of troops in the area.' The proposed airborne landing in the Paris–Orléans gap was off. We immediately radioed back for permission to start offensive operations in the area and received the OK the same afternoon.

The first patrols we sent out were mainly reconnaissance though McDiarmid, driving down the Mezilles–Toucy road, ran slap into a German cycle patrol. The surprise was mutual. The first burst from the jeep's guns went wide. In less time than it takes to tell the Germans were off their bikes into the woods that bordered the road. Mac and his crew grabbed their carbines and went in after them. The undergrowth was thick and tangled, hindering the Germans' escape. There was a sharp exchange of fire and McDiarmid and his men emerged a few minutes later with eight very frightened prisoners.

He now had a problem. What to do with them? Had they made a fight of it they could have been killed in battle. We were obviously in no position to set up a POW cage in camp. It would take more than half our number to guard it. He decided to take them into the nearest town not occupied by Germans.

The Germans had recently vacated Auxerre, and on arrival the patrol found that the Resistance had taken over. Mac explained his predicament and asked them if they would take care of the prisoners.

'*Mais oui, mon ami*. But certainly we will take care of them,' the leader of the Resistance assured him. 'Have no fear, we will take very good care of them.' They had drinks all round, then, with a last word of farewell, the patrol set off. They were driving out of the town when there came the crackle of Sten gun fire. As McDiarmid explained when he got back to base, 'They must have misunderstood what I meant by "take care of them". Been seeing too many American films, that's their trouble.'

Information now began rolling in from neighbouring villages and maquis outposts. The Germans were in such and such a place. There were several hundred moving along such and such a road. We investigated all these reports. Most, we found, were very much exaggerated. Only small bands were encountered. On principle we began to divide by ten. For tanks we read 'broken-down trucks' and for cavalry 'cart horses and bicycles'. In this we were never far wrong.

One prisoner was, in fact, brought back to camp by a patrol. This patrol had been sitting in ambush on a nearby road waiting for a German convoy reported heading our way. Instead of a convoy, a solitary German, footsore and so weary that he did not even see the jeep, stumbled into the wood where they were lying up and went to sleep within a hundred yards of them.

Karl, as we called him, was a short thickset man of about fifty. At first he was terrified, thinking he had fallen into the hands of the dreaded maquis. His relief when he found we were British knew no bounds. He much, much preferred the British terrorists to the French. In civilian life he had been a blacksmith, so we set him to work modifying the rear gun mountings on our jeeps. This was much more to his taste than soldiering and he set to with a will. He was a glutton for work and made a first-class job of them. He was a good cook, too. The question of a guard for him was soon solved. We told him that while he was with us he would be safe, but the moment he stepped outside our camp the maquis would get him. That was enough for him.

On the 20th Bob came back from Chevrier's camp with

the news that they had two prisoners. A German plane had crash-landed in the area and the maquis had snatched two of the crew before a large force of Germans arrived to guard the plane. Bob had asked for permission to interrogate them, but Chevrier's intelligence officer had taken this as a slight on his own abilities. The most he would allow was that Bob should be there during the interrogation. The maquisards had bound the two men to a tree and proceeded to hurl questions at them instead of interrogating them separately. The senior of the two prisoners, a warrant officer, refused to answer questions and ordered the other to do the same. The sequel came next day.

I had run my jeep to the spring to fill up the cans with water before breakfast. As I was about to drive away, a solemn procession came down the track from Chevrier's camp. At the head was the village priest; behind came the two prisoners. Behind them came a squad of six maquisards with Sten guns, and one of Chevrier's officers.

They came to a halt among the trees less than a hundred yards from where I was standing. Spades were handed to the two prisoners. Without further ado they began to dig their own graves. The voice of the priest droned through the woods as they dug.

Their task accomplished, they straightened up and flung away the spades. The priest moved to one side and stood with bowed head as they took up their positions at the foot of the graves. The scent of strong, newly-turned earth came to my nostrils as I watched.

The six men of the firing squad took up their positions, Stens at the ready. The officer's arm dropped. Through the morning air came the familiar crackle of the Stens. The Germans slumped back into the earth. The French officer stepped forward. Two pistol shots rang out.

The little party formed up and marched away. All but

two. These picked up the spades from where they lay and slowly began to fill in the graves. Justice had been done. It was a quicker, cleaner death than that meted out to men of the maquis or men of the SAS falling into German hands.

After breakfast I went out on a routine patrol of the area with two jeeps. Everywhere was quiet. It seemed incredible that, so far behind the German lines, we should be able to drive around in broad daylight in jeeps without let or hindrance. We soon found out that the Germans were not as thick on the ground as we had imagined. Our biggest danger on these patrols, especially when operating at any considerable distance from our base, was from the maquis. They were apt to look upon all transport as German and there was the ever-present danger of running into a maquis ambush. To protect ourselves we took to flying silken Union Jacks from the jeeps. Approaching sharp bends and other places that lent themselves to ambush, we sounded 'dot-dash-dot' on the horn – the letter 'R' for Resistance – a fairly general recognition signal among the maquis.

Whenever we fell in with maquis or Resistance groups in other areas there was always the difficulty of convincing them that the jeeps had been parachuted from planes. It was too much for them to swallow. They much preferred to believe that we were the advanced guard of the main Allied army – preferably the Americans – and that the war was all over bar the shouting.

Another very real danger, ironically enough, was from our own aircraft. In the beginning we were inclined to look up at the Spitfires overhead and make the classic remark about being 'one of ours'. Uncomfortable encounters soon taught us to look on Allied planes as rather more than potential enemies. Anything moving on the roads behind the German lines was fair game to them. Fair enough. But it was hard on us.

We investigated the Route Nationale before returning to base, but it was deserted. Not even a pedal cyclist passed our way and our guns remained silent.

Bob and I had been invited by Roger to have lunch with him at his headquarters at Sommecais. In the interests of closer liaison we decided to take time off to fulfil this social engagement. About two miles from Sommecais we passed through the FFI outposts. Roger evidently meant to hold his area against all comers and make the Germans fight for it.

The village straggled along the edge of the hill road. Outside the butcher's shop we were signalled to a halt by a young French lieutenant. He took us across the road to a rather larger house. Pushing open the front door we found ourselves in a large, badly-lighted room, with a low raftered ceiling. Roger introduced us to his officers and we sat down to a first-class luncheon. The meal over, Roger pushed over a packet of French cigarettes. Bob produced a tin of English ones. Everyone brightened up immediately. 'Ah! English cigarettes! Thank you, Commandant Melot.' Bob threw away the empty tin.

'That reminds me, Commandant Melot.' Roger puffed appreciatively at his cigarette. 'I had hoped to introduce you and Capitaine Harrison to my personal courier, "Claudine". She is an English girl who carries messages for me between here and Paris.

'Unfortunately,' he shrugged his shoulders, 'she had to leave for Paris just before you arrived. She has not had an English cigarette for a long time, and I am afraid she does not care for our French cigarettes. She had hoped, perhaps, that you might have some.'

Bob slipped out to the jeep and returned with another

tin. 'Perhaps you will give her these when she gets back, Commandant Roger.'

'But certainly I will. I thank you for her.' He paused. 'It is possible you saw her as you came up the road. She was riding a bicycle.'

We left Roger about three o'clock and returned to camp. We were passing the old ruined house where I had first met Roger when we heard the sound of firing. It was not so far away either. Bob put his foot hard down and we broke all records back to camp. Arriving there we found David and Stewart putting the camp in a state of readiness. A runner from Chevrier had brought the news that a German force was behind, held by his outposts at Villiers-St Benoît. He feared an attack on the camp.

'Not much use sending the jeeps to help, is there, Bob? If it's an attack on the camp the place will be surrounded and they'll have road blocks up.'

Bob shook his head. 'No, the best we can do is sit tight and defend our own camp. We can't afford to lose jeeps like that and, from the direction of the attack, it looks as if it is Chevrier they're after. They may not know we are here.'

'That's what I feel. If they do come this way we may be able to beat them off. If the worst comes to the worst, we'll have to dump the jeeps and break out on foot, but I hope it won't come to that.'

There were three jeeps in the camp, the others fortunately being out on patrol. Within minutes we had dispersed them as best we could for the defence of the camp. Two we drove deep into the forest so that they were between us and Chevrier's camp, pushing them for the last couple of hundred yards in order not to draw attention to them.

From the sound of the firing the Germans were skirmishing round in a flanking movement. I hared back to camp. Bob had sent the third jeep up a narrow track towards Villiers where it had a clear though restricted view of the road from the village. Bob, Ridler and I now took up positions on the edge of the woods covering the road between Villiers and St Brisson. On the outskirts of Villiers two patrols from Chevrier's camp were heavily engaged with about a hundred Germans. We could hear the sounds of the fighting but it did not seem to be getting any nearer.

I glanced at the others, at their set faces, at the slight look of strain. A figure flitted among the trees on the far side of the road. I slipped my carbine forward to the ready and reached for my binoculars. They were Germans all right, but it was by no means certain that they had seen us or even knew of our existence. I signalled the men to hold their fire. Minutes passed. Then from our right came the excited chatter of a Bren gun. I dashed down to see what was happening.

'What is it, man?'

He pointed to a gap in the line of trees about three hundred yards away leading up to the woods from the road. Through the glasses I scanned the trees. A number of men slipped quickly across it. There was another gap, nearer our positions. I pointed it out to the Bren gunner.

'Get your Bren on that gap but hold your fire till I say.'

I switched my gaze to the nearer gap, and waited. Almost immediately the first man came into view. I dropped my glasses.

'Hold your fire. They're French.'

It was one of Chevrier's patrols withdrawing through our positions. We covered them into the woods but that one burst from the Bren gun had apparently discouraged pursuit. The distant firing became sporadic. Within half an hour it had stopped altogether. A runner came from Chevrier to say the attack had been beaten off.

19
Dangerous Encounter

The morning after the attack, the sun was shining brilliantly. The nervous tension of the previous afternoon had gone. Immediately after breakfast the remaining jeeps went out on reconnaissance patrols but found the area again free from Germans. As we sat on the hillside overlooking the deserted Route Nationale, I talked it over with Bob.

'I've got a feeling this area is played out.'

'I don't know, Harry.' Bob pulled out a cigarette and lit it. He stared reflectively at the smoke. 'We don't see the overall picture here. Maybe we're doing a lot of good in just denying the use of the area to the Germans. Remember, we're not the only party over here. If Jerry goes round us he'll walk into someone else's arms in another area. Still, I'm inclined to agree with you on one thing – it's not very exciting.'

'That's what I feel. It's no use blowing up the railway even. The Germans aren't using it. The rails are red with rust. I feel like asking London if we can try another area.'

'No harm in trying.' Bob warmed to the idea. 'I know a very good spot between Paris and the Belgian frontier. Up there we would get any reinforcements going to the beach-head, and later we would be on the main axis of their withdrawal.'

We sent off the signal as soon as we reached camp.

That afternoon the son of the mayor of Villiers-St Benoît came with a message from the intelligence officer Bob had been talking to a day or two earlier.

Heavy German traffic was using the road from Courtenay to Sens. Could we send the jeeps?

We looked it up on the map. 'It will mean an early start, Harry, and will take you the best part of the day. I suppose you are going yourself?'

'Yes. I'll take Stewart's jeep too.'

The rest of the daylight we spent checking over the jeeps. With a long journey ahead we did not want breakdowns. Last of all, we loaded up and cleaned the guns.

We were away by eight o'clock next morning, heading for Aillant. It was outside Aillant that I had originally intended to drop into France. Remembering the flat, open country I decided to give it a wide berth. The map showed a track through the woods to the east. We took that, only to find that it petered out in the middle. There was no way round. Aillant it would have to be, Germans or no Germans.

We approached it cautiously, safety catches off, fingers on the triggers of the guns. The town lay spread-eagled across the plain, one arm stretching out towards us. Partly to avoid kicking up a cloud of dust we travelled slowly down the road to where the first few cottages clustered, and it was with a feeling of relief that we reached them without incident. But we had still to get safely through the town. I walked over to Stewart's jeep.

'I think we'd better risk a few inquiries here rather than find out when we're in the middle of the place and it's too late.'

Stewart swung out of his jeep and together we approached the nearest cottage. No sign of life. We made our way round the back of the second cottage – right into the arms of a young girl. With admirable presence of mind, she summed up the inadequacy of our French and dragged us quickly over to the schoolhouse. The door was opened, in response to her impatient banging, by an elderly woman: the teacher, we learned. She told us the Germans were concentrating in force at Joigny on the far side of the river Yonne, on the high ground overlooking the river. As far as she knew, there were none in Aillant.

On the other side of the town we struck a good road and were soon bowling along at a steady pace. The country on both sides of the road was quite open but there was nothing in sight. Then I began to get a bit uneasy. The road was too good. I checked with my map but could not see where I had gone wrong, if indeed we had. As we breasted a rise in the road I caught sight of a signpost – 'Joigny 4 Km'. To the left was a small track doubling back the way we had come. Without wasting another minute I had the jeeps turned round and hurtling down that track hell for leather. Thick clouds of white dust billowed into the air behind us. There was not a stitch of cover and we were overlooked by two hills which the Germans would undoubtedly be using as observation posts. I crossed my fingers.

We were now hopelessly lost. All we could do was head in the approximate direction until we struck some place we could identify. We wandered all morning from one track to another, each worse than the last. All I knew was that we were heading in the right general direction.

Shortly after noon we saw a cluster of houses ahead. We stopped the jeeps and, creeping as close as we dared, scrutinized the place carefully through our binoculars. It seemed quite normal. There were a couple of kiddies playing in the road. Further down, a woman was hanging out some washing. We returned to the jeeps and drove slowly in.

Our arrival electrified the place. Crowds appeared from nowhere, all talking at once. We were the advanced guard of the Allied armies. The war was nearly over. In vain we tried to explain that we had been dropped by parachute. They pointed to the jeeps, shook their heads and smiled knowingly.

I did not fancy being caught in the middle of that crowd if a German patrol should come our way, so we drove the jeeps through the nearest gates into a kind of forecourt. Immediately one of the men dashed into the house, to return a minute later. We must have something to eat – some wine. He insisted. Lending action to his words he seized me by the arm and dragged me from my seat. I signalled the jeeps to drive over against the wall into the shadow where they would not be so conspicuous. Then we filed into the farmhouse.

The room to which they took us was barely furnished. The woman of the house was there looking as happy as if the gods had come to earth. It was, apparently, a great honour that we had agreed to accept her hospitality. For my own part, as I looked round at the signs of poverty that were only too obvious, I felt uncomfortable at the thought of taking her food. However, the neighbours all rallied round, bringing eggs, bacon, bread, milk and other titbits until there was enough to feed a regiment.

We sat at the table, but before we could eat, the room was invaded by scores of women who crowded round to watch. Those with children pushed their way to the front and held them out to be kissed. We coped as best we could. Finally, a heavily bearded man shouldered his way through to the table. He was, he told us, the local schoolmaster. In faultless English he made a long speech of welcome liberally interspersed with quotations from Shakespeare. I thanked him and he withdrew.

A moment later, from the crowded passage leading to the room, came terrifying shrieks. Grabbing our carbines we leapt to our feet. The only window in the room was a small one high up in the wall. No way out there. We dashed into the passage determined to shoot our way out to the jeeps, for we did not doubt for one moment that a German patrol had arrived in the village.

Instead, we found a young woman in black fighting like a wildcat with a man near the door. I had not the faintest idea what it was about, only that it had to be stopped. Holding my carbine upright in front of me I pushed between the two of them. The girl took one look at me and slipped to the floor in a dead faint. Whether she was a *collaboratrice* being brought to 'trial' or whether we had offended local susceptibilities by eating at the 'wrong' house I did not know. We pulled out at once.

We had been travelling perhaps half an hour when we heard the crackle of cannon fire. Over on our right, towards Joigny, Allied fighters were ground strafing. They circled round like buzzards, peeling off into their dives and swooping into the air again. As we watched, two of them broke away and came streaking in our direction. We did not wait to argue. Straight into the ditch with the jeeps. In double-quick time we baled out and ran for the shelter of a nearby orchard. I had just time to grab a yellow smoke recognition signal. I struck it as we ran and pitched it back on to the road. The planes saw it in time, circled once and flew off again.

We were met in the next village by a group of cheering Resistance men who said they had been expecting us. Someone had telephoned from the village where we had stayed to eat. I was furious. If the Germans had the lines tapped we were for it. There was no help for it. To be on the safe side we would have to strike across open country again.

We took along two of the men who said they knew the district well. Inside an hour they had us well and truly lost. The maps were no use, none of the tracks we were using being marked, so we had to fall back again on compass bearings.

At three o'clock we halted for a rest. While we had a cigarette we studied the maps again. There were no obvious landmarks. We might, in fact, have been in any one of six or seven places. But, by studying our mileage and allowing for detours, I calculated that we should not be far off our objective. The road from Sens to Courtenay ran more or less at right angles to the route we were taking. Directly ahead I could see a rise in the ground, fringed here and there with trees. Once we got on to that high ground, I felt sure we would be able to see the road.

Hugging every bit of cover we pushed on towards the high ground, only to find that we were faced by a belt of woods. We had covered the last few miles slowly and cautiously. Now I signalled the jeeps to accelerate. We had to find that road, or at least fix our position, before nightfall.

There was a flash of grey. In that instant I realized we had reached the road. Not only had we reached it, we had roared right across it in daylight and were now heading flat out for a railway level-crossing. To the right I could see the railway station. On the platform a number of people were moving about. Then we were across the railway, past the signal-box, beating it as fast as we could for the cover of the woods.

We stopped only when we had reached the trees. So far there had been no sound of the alarm being raised. From where we were we had a very good view of the road. It was an ideal position for an ambush, but we were on the wrong side of the road. To get back to our base after the strafe we would have to run the gauntlet by crossing it again.

While the rest of the men prepared the jeeps for action, Curly Hall and I crept forward to keep the road under observation, settling ourselves down behind a fern-covered bank. We had a good view for some distance down the road towards Courtenay, though our vision in the other direction was restricted.

Perhaps twenty minutes later a solitary vehicle sped by from the direction of Sens. Curly Hall leaned over to whisper, 'Don't those Volkswagens look like jeeps?' I nodded.

'There may be a convoy somewhere behind. Nip back and warn the others to keep out of sight. We mustn't get tied up before dark or we'll never make it back again across the road.'

He slipped away, to return a minute later. So far there had been no sign of a convoy. Suddenly we froze. Two men in civilian clothes were strolling up the track towards us. They walked slowly past, and stopped about ten yards further down the track. Then they turned and made to walk back again. They had made no sign that they had seen us, but it seemed more than coincidence that they should have chosen to stroll just where we were hiding.

I had no intention of letting them get away. We slipped our carbines over the top of the bank. 'Come here, you two,' I called out in a stage whisper. They turned and came towards us. There was no surprise in their faces and it was obvious they had known we were there. We dragged them down into cover.

The taller of the two looked at us suspiciously. 'Are you with the Americans?'

'Americans? What Americans?' It was my turn to look suspicious.

The tall man jerked his thumb in the direction of Courtenay. 'The Americans at Courtenay, who came this morning.'

This was too much to swallow. I took them along to our

Resistance guides. They questioned the men and said they seemed all right. I put it to the rest of the patrol.

'If these men are right and the Americans are here, then we ought to contact them. But it could be a trap. What do you say? Shall we chance it into Courtenay?'

We drove straight down the wide main road, tensed and ready for instant action. Round a bend a few miles on we ran slap into tanks – five of them. Shermans! The nearest was pulled in alongside a farmhouse. As the gun turret swung round I pulled up with squealing brakes. A head popped out and stared down at us in surprise. It was the tank commander. He hefted himself out and came over to us.

'Say, where've you guys sprung from?' He eyed the Union Jacks curiously. 'Bit off your beat, aren't you? There's no British round here.'

He listened attentively while I explained, asked one or two questions and seemed satisfied. 'Well, if you guys have some information you'd better get on down to Combat B and tell it to them.'

We found Combat B in a field on the other side of the town. There was a colonel shaving in front of his bivouac. I told my story all over again, told him there were no Germans in any force this side of Joigny. He carried on shaving until he had finished the tricky bit around his chin. 'Well, that's not our information. Our reports show that there's a mighty lot of Germans just out there.' He resumed his shaving.

· I was about to make some retort when he pointed to another clump of trees. 'You'd better go and report to Captain Irvine over there. He's our quartermaster. He'll fix you up for the night. The Germans may counter-attack tonight but you get a good night's sleep. You'll be safe enough behind our tanks.'

Speechless, I saluted and walked off. Irvine was a

young chap with an engaging manner and he immediately organized a hot meal for us and produced sleeping-bags. While we ate he asked questions.

'How are you fellows off for food out there?' I told him we had had none dropped for the past week.

'OK. I'll fix you up before you leave tomorrow.' He wandered off, to return a few minutes later with a writing case. 'I guess you'd like to write home, wouldn't you? There's paper and envelopes here. I'll see they get back with our mail.'

I hurriedly scribbled a note to my wife before it got too dark to see, then turned in. It was my first night's sleep since dropping nine days before.

At first light next morning we loaded up with American K rations and set off back to base. The journey was uneventful until we arrived back at the village from which our guides had come. Here we had a terrific welcome. While we drank the wine that was proffered us we were garlanded with flowers by the enthusiastic villagers. When at last we drove away, the jeeps looked more like travelling flower shops than engines of war.

Just outside the village, men of the Resistance were manning a road block. They signalled us to halt. A man had just ridden up on a bicycle. 'Quick,' he called out, 'a German convoy.'

'Where?' I snapped back.

'Passed through the next village half an hour ago.'

'Which direction?'

'Towards Joigny, monsieur. Fifty trucks. A driver and one other man in each . . .'

We shot off down the road at a rate of knots. This was too good to miss. If only we could catch it up.

In the next village another reception committee was waiting for us with flowers and flags, but we had no time to stop. Our well-wishers leaped for their lives as we swept through without slackening pace. But the convoy had vanished.

We reached camp about two o'clock in the afternoon without further incident. The K rations were pounced upon eagerly by the rest of the lads while I reported to Bob what had happened. He was as surprised as I had been at the news.

'Patton's armour at Courtenay? I can't believe it. They must have moved fast.'

'They've been moving fast all right. They were all ticking like clocks about it. Their maintenance officer was crying blue murder. Said he had to use half the tanks as spares to keep the other half going.'

I looked up as I heard the sound of a jeep moving off. It was Stewart. I called him over.

'Where are you off to?'

'One of my gun mountings snapped. I'm going over to Aillant to get the maquis workshops to weld it. Roger and the maquis have all moved over there – to meet the Americans.'

I groaned. 'Don't tell me the perishing idea that the Americans are just round the corner has spread to here now.'

'Apparently. OK if I buzz off now?'

'No, hang on a minute and I'll come with you. Get Curly Hall to bring my jeep round.' He sent one of the chaps off. 'I don't like the idea of one jeep dashing round the countryside by itself.'

We moved off, my own jeep in the lead. As we rolled down the narrow track towards the road I found myself wondering where all these rumours started. Admittedly our French friends were prone to exaggerate, but I could not understand Roger dashing off like this on the strength of a rumour. Still . . .

We were about to turn into the road when I caught

sight of a curl of thick smoke above the trees over to the right. I stopped the jeeps and Stewart came running forward. I pointed. 'See that? What do you make of it?'

'Looks as though it's over towards Les Ormes – something big on fire. What are we going to do?'

'Carry on and keep our eyes open. It may be further than we think.'

At top speed we raced away along the bumpy, dusty road towards the ever-growing column of smoke. Breasting the top of the hill outside Les Ormes I signalled the jeep behind to stop. Together we screamed to a halt. Ahead of us the road forked.

From the left came the crackle of firing. A number of buildings were ablaze. The cross-roads on which we had halted was not more than a hundred yards from the village, but all the noise seemed to be coming from the far end. While I debated what to do a woman on a bicycle came pedalling for dear life down the left-hand fork towards us. Head down, she came quickly on with her grey hair blowing in the wind. Tears streamed down her lined face. With surprising agility she leapt from her bike.

'Quick, messieurs,' she called out, 'save yourselves . . . the Boches . . . there.' She pointed to the burning buildings. 'Now I go to bring the maquis back.'

'Just a moment.' She hesitated as she made to remount her bicycle. 'Quickly, how many Boches are there?'

She shrugged her shoulders. 'Two hundred . . . three hundred,' she hazarded. 'Who knows? A lot. Yes, a lot. Too many for you, monsieur. Now I must go.'

'Wait a minute. We'll go. With our jeeps it will be quicker.' I had made a quick decision. 'Leave it to us.'

Astonishment showed in her face. 'Thank you, monsieur. Thank you, thank you.' She climbed back on to her bike and cycled slowly back into the burning village. The rest of the patrol gathered round.

'Well,' I asked, 'what do you think? Go for the maquis or attack the village ourselves?' It was a hard decision. In my own mind I had made it already, but I wanted the reactions of the others.

We were five in all. Fauchois was the first to speak. 'I say attack.' Fauchois had been sent to us from the French SAS. He carried false papers showing him to be a Canadian to ensure that, should he be captured, his family would not suffer. He was keen, dependable, and ever anxious to get at the '*sales Boches*'.

I turned to ask Curly Hall.

'If we go to Aillant for the maquis I think it will be too late when we get them here.'

'Brearton?'

Brearton was Stewart's driver, and like Stewart, an ex-tank man. His reply was short and to the point. 'Let's have a crack at them.'

'And you, Stewart?'

'I feel like Hall. We haven't time to go for the maquis.'

'Good. That's just what I feel. But we can't make an open attack. I suggest we take this right-hand fork into the part of the village that is quiet. Once in, we can drive through the village at speed with our guns going. We'll have the element of surprise and should be able to shoot our way out of anything we meet. The odds are something like fifty to one, but I hope they'll get such a shock that we'll pull it off.'

Union Jacks fluttering in the wind, we tore down the road, round the bend and into the village. Even as we came into the square I saw him. He was dressed in SS uniform, walking towards us, pistol in hand. He looked up in surprise – and died.

I took in the scene in an instant. The church in the middle of the square . . . a large truck . . . two German staff cars – the crowd of SS men in front of the church . . .

The staff cars and the truck burst into flames as, standing in my seat, I raked the square with fire from my twin machine-guns. The crowd of SS men stampeded for cover. Many of them died in those first few seconds in front of the church, lit by the flickering flames of the burning vehicles.

Even as I fired I shouted to Hall to reverse. The jeep jerked to a halt about thirty yards from the church. The Germans who had escaped the first fury of our assault were now returning our fire. I turned to see why Hall had not got the jeep moving back. He lay slumped over the wheel. The tell-tale gouts of blood told their own story. Curly Hall was dead.

Still firing, I pressed the starter with my foot. The engine was still, hit by the burst of fire that had got Hall. Then my guns jammed. No time to try and put them right. I dashed round to use the rear gun. It fired one burst and stopped.

There was now only the single gun by the driver's seat. I got round to it, managed to fire a couple of short bursts before that, too, jammed. A dud jeep and three jammed guns. Hell, what a mess!

I had forgotten all about the second jeep. Now I could hear its guns hammering away over my shoulder. It was drawn up against the wall of the road leading into the square. There were Germans at the upper windows of the building immediately overlooking us. Stewart's Colt cracked again and again as they tried to fire down on us.

All this I took in in a flash. My own plight was too desperate, standing as I was in the middle of the cross-roads. I reached over and snatched up my carbine. Thank heavens it was semi-automatic. I fired off the fifteen rounds in the magazine . . . changed the magazine. Blast this broken finger. The damned splint gets in the way. Another magazine . . .

I fired wherever I saw movement. A German made a dash for safety. I fired from the hip and he pitched forward on to his face. Now I grabbed Hall, lifting him from the jeep. A sniper stepped from a doorway on my right. I took a quick pot-shot and dropped him. Aim was instinctive.

I managed to get Hall to the centre of the cross-roads. The Germans redoubled their fire. I started shooting again. I could see tracer streaming towards me. I weaved backwards and forwards like a boxer as if to dodge the flying bullets. There came a shout behind me.

'Look out! The orchard on your left!'

There was a low stone wall to the left. I ran to it. On the other side was the orchard. Germans were advancing through it at the double. I fired as fast as I could pull the trigger. They disappeared.

Back to the jeep. Fauchois had run forward and was trying to drag Hall back to the second jeep. 'Get back, you fool! Get back!' I yelled. The Germans were concentrating their fire on him now. No sense in having another man killed.

Standing by the disabled jeep I kept up a rapid rate of fire. How many magazines left? I didn't know. Suddenly I remembered it was my wedding anniversary. With complete inconsequence I found myself thinking: Lord, my wife will be furious if I get myself killed, today of all days.

My right hand jerked and went numb. I looked down. It was smothered in blood. With my finger-tips I fished out another magazine from the pocket of my smock and after much fumbling managed to clip it into the carbine.

With both hands partly out of commission now, my aim was getting erratic. The Germans, who had seen me jump when hit, increased their fire. The sound of firing from the second jeep had stopped. I dared not look round.

Keep on firing, keep on firing . . . the words went round and round in my head.

A German stepped from behind one of the trees to take a more careful aim. I raised my carbine, now slippery with blood, and squeezed the trigger. Nothing happened. I lowered the carbine. My hand jerked again as the marksman's bullet snicked across my knuckles.

I looked down. Two rounds were jammed in the breach. No time to put it right now. I grabbed for my Colt. The holster was empty. I swore. The damn' thing must have jerked loose in the fight. Nothing for it but to get that jammed magazine out. Resting one foot on the jeep I wrestled with it as best I could with my gammy hands. The Germans were still firing, but there was nothing I could do about it until I got that carbine firing again.

The new magazine was in. Miraculously I was still alive. I raised the carbine. From behind came a shout: 'Dash for it!'

I heard the wild revving of an engine. The second jeep had been turned round. Stewart, Brearton and Fauchois were already in it. They shouted again. Firing as I ran, I dashed crabwise towards them. The jeep moved forward even as I leapt for it. Fauchois seized the rear guns and poured a last, long burst into the square. In a cloud of dust we disappeared down the road.

Straight into the nearest woods we drove, down a narrow, almost non-existent ride at break-neck speed. Swinging violently round a bend I was nearly flung from my seat. To save myself I grabbed at the guns. A final burst rent the air, narrowly missing the engine.

Back in camp I broke the news that Hall was dead. It was hard news to tell. He had been with me ever since I joined SAS, always bright, cheery and philosophical. I also knew that, had I not stood up in my seat to fire that first burst, I would have taken the shots that killed him.

At nightfall Stewart Richardson took a patrol back into Les Ormes. The Germans had left. The news he brought back gave us some consolation. No one knew just why the SS men had swooped on the village. Some said they were the advanced guard of a German convoy and they were protecting its passage through the area; others, that it was a reprisal raid for our presence in the area.

However that may be, they had, apart from burning houses, seized twenty men for execution. It was that execution which we had so unexpectedly interrupted outside the church. The first two of the doomed men had been shot as we arrived. The other eighteen escaped in the confusion. Besides the truck and two staff cars destroyed by our fire, the Germans had lost about sixty men dead and wounded. The rest had withdrawn as soon as we broke off the fight.

Details of the skirmish were radioed to London. With my left hand splinted and my right swathed in bandages, I was feeling something less than useless when one of the villagers came running into the camp to say that a large motorized convoy was heading directly for our base.

Mac immediately took out a patrol of two jeeps to ambush it. In camp we waited for the sound of firing. I sat gazing mournfully at my hands, wondering what the blazes I should do if this were an attack on the camp.

There was a sudden shout and Mac's two jeeps came roaring back into camp. I jumped to my feet. Behind his two jeeps came a third one, and another, and another . . . and there was Tony Marsh coming towards me.

'Hello, Harry. Hear you've been getting yourself into a mess.'

'Where on earth have you sprung from?' I still could not grasp this change in events.

Tony beamed. 'When the airborne operation was cancelled we flew into Orléans in Dakotas. Landed on the 19th and came through the lines.'

'Have you got the whole squadron with you?'

'No, just twenty jeeps and Peter's troop. The rest – mainly your chaps – are coming on in a few days' time.'

Over a meal I heard about their trip down. They had found the front line fairly fluid, as I had done on the previous day. However, at Lammerie they had bumped a German column. It was too good a target to miss. Sole 'survivor' was a German staff car which Tony appropriated as his personal transport. The following day they had taken eleven prisoners, and now here they were.

Supplies of much-needed petrol were to be dropped on the next night, the 24th. We signalled a new dropping zone to London, one in the valley just outside Les Ormes. At eight o'clock on the evening of the drop, news was brought that the Germans were once again in Les Ormes, in strength.

It was too late to cancel the drop and we now needed that petrol badly. Tony decided to go ahead and risk it. Luck was with us. The whole operation was carried through without interference. We used a number of the jeeps to collect the containers, sending them charging up and down the road running the length of the DZ. Either the Germans decided to let well alone or, more probably, they mistook the jeeps for one of their own convoys.

The sudden reappearance of these Germans in Les Ormes puzzled us. This was the second time in the last two days. Reports from the Resistance showed that it was happening in other villages in the area. They appeared and vanished again without anyone seeing where they had come from and where they went to. From the 25th to the 29th we sent out patrols daily for a radius of fifty miles round our base. We set road blocks at night. The reports were always the same. There was no sign of German transport on the roads. Yet large bodies of German troops were still reported at places within our ring of patrols. Failing any other satisfactory solution, we were driven to the conclusion that retreating German units were making their way in small parties from one rendezvous to another, keeping clear of the roads.

On the 27th Tony asked me to go back through the lines to contact the rest of the squadron and guide them to our base. As I drove into a nearby village a black Citroën pulled up and from it stepped Colonel Paddy Mayne. Soon after, Tony and David Barnaby turned up. Together we went into one of the houses for a drink and a chat.

This was the first I had seen of Paddy since leaving England. He did not say much about what he had been doing, except that he was not going to let Bill Fraser get away with it. Bill, commanding our 'Houndsworth' base in the Morvan, had signalled back to London for his dress kilt, to impress the local populace. Not to be outdone, Paddy had parachuted down to him resplendent in best Service dress, with highly polished Sam Browne. Since then he had been touring France in his Citroën, visiting the many SAS groups dotted around the country. Urgent signals for him to attend conferences in London followed him around in vain. Paddy was back with his unit.

But I had to push on. We reached Orléans late that afternoon but could find no trace of the SAS column. The following morning we ran them to ground at Ouzouer-sur-Loire, just inside the American lines. From them I learned that there had been a message for me on the early morning broadcast – the only time I had failed to listen. There had also been one for Tony. It sounded as though something was brewing and I decided to push back to camp as fast as possible. We arrived safely there about four o'clock that afternoon.

20
Operation Houndsworth

I gazed round the flat, sun-baked countryside. Beads of sweat trickled down my face, cutting furrows in the white dust that caked my features. I signalled a halt. The six jeeps pulled up beneath the half-dozen or so trees that straggled along the edge of the track. Ahead and to the right were the thickly wooded mountain slopes of the Morvan. That was to be our new operational area. Tony had broken the news to me when I arrived back at 'Kipling' the previous afternoon. A squadron who had been operating down here at the 'Houndsworth' base were due to go home.

We had left 'Kipling' that morning with some two dozen jeeps, in four groups. We had been travelling now for five hours, picking our way along small tracks inches deep in fine white dust. But I had halted not so much for a rest as to check our position. From the valley ahead and just to our left rose the tall spire of a church.

I looked again at the map. I could not be mistaken. That must be Clamecy, and the last broadcast to all patrols had been 'Keep well to the south of Clamecy'. Now it looked as if we were about to drive right into the town. The point was, should I go back and search for another route, or should I carry on? The reports from London had warned that the town was 'heavily occupied' by the Germans.

I talked it over with the other jeep commanders. They were for pushing on and risking it. We climbed back into the jeeps and moved off again slowly. The road dipped and wound down into the valley until, round the last bend, the town came into full view. We were not more than two hundred yards from the outskirts, heading straight for the Route Nationale.

Furtively we nosed out on to the wide tarmac road and swung away from Clamecy. Two miles down the road, according to the map, was a small turning off to the left that we would have to take. Tyres screaming, we raced towards it. If we bumped a German column we would have to shoot it out on the move. There was one very good reason why we wanted to avoid that at this stage. So far, organized jeep patrols had not operated from the 'Houndsworth' base, and we wanted to keep the presence of twenty-four armed jeeps from the Germans as long as we could. We wanted to announce their arrival in our own way and in our own time.

We had travelled about a mile when we first saw them, as yet little more than a blob on the grey ribbon of road. The jeeps were going flat out. The dark blob resolved itself into the distinct shapes of trucks. Anxiously I scanned the road ahead for our turning.

There it was! Scarcely reducing speed we swung the jeeps off the road on to the track that wound its way into the foothills of the Morvan. The Germans must have seen us, but whether they had recognized us for what we were was doubtful. But we could not take the chance of leading them to the 'Houndsworth' base. Out of sight I halted and ran back to where I had a view of the road. The German vehicles were headed for Clamecy.

With a sigh of relief we continued our climb into the heavily-wooded hills. At half past four we caught up with the rest of the column just outside Chalaux. A deep wooded valley fell away sharply to our right. The road curved down along the far side of the valley. We followed it for about a mile, then turned into a large field. Bill Fraser was waiting there to welcome us to 'Houndsworth'.

As soon as the jeeps had been parked under cover we got down to yarning with A Squadron, most of whom had been there since June and who thoroughly deserved their relief.

Alec Muirhead I had not seen since leaving Scotland. Shortly after he had arrived in France he had taken his men out on patrol in the Montsauche area and quickly made contact with a mixed force of Germans and White Russians. As they watched, a staff car arrived from the direction of Nevers. From it stepped a German officer who proceeded to give the class – for that is what it was – a good theoretical grounding in the art of laying ambushes. He then took them off for a practical demonstration that was more successful than he could possibly have imagined. The whole party walked straight into Alec's ambush. The staff officer was killed in the first burst of fire. Thirty of his class were killed with him, four trucks destroyed and one Russian officer captured.

During August Alec tried an experiment and took his mortar section down to Autun. The Germans were operating a synthetic petrol plant there. They kept it under observation during daylight. It was well guarded, with particularly strong anti-aircraft defences. To get into the plant would be a hazardous venture for a doubtful return.

At half past one in the morning, in bright moonlight, the SAS party took up their positions outside the plant and set up the mortars. From where they crouched in a fold in the ground they could hear the sentries being changed. The plant itself stood out in silhouette against the cold night sky. Ranges had been checked from the map during daylight. Alec raised his hand.

'Fire!'

The first bombs sailed away to burst with sharp concussion and flash of flame in the midst of the plant. As fast as they could, now, they slammed bomb after bomb into the barrels of the mortars. In all they loosed off forty, high explosive and incendiary.

The Germans, thinking it was an air raid, sounded the alarm and took to the shelters. By now the storage tanks were well ablaze, the roar of the flames vying with the wail of the siren. The plant superstructure stood out gaunt and grim against the glare. It was still burning three days later.

Ranging over an area of some six thousand square miles, the squadron carried out innumerable ambushes and derailments. During July, Sergeant DuVivier was out on cycle patrol in the area of Entrains when he heard a terrific explosion. From one of the local men he learned that the maquis had blown the line there in order to delay a munitions train. This was too good to be true. DuVivier got word through, by way of the Resistance, to the French workmen who were being made by the Germans to repair the line. These men held up repairs long enough for DuVivier and two men to move up the line towards Cosne, the train's destination.

Carrying thirty pounds of explosives apiece, they cycled up through two medium-sized towns occupied by the Germans. Although they were in battle-dress they were not challenged, and they eventually reached a suitable stretch of line.

Hiding the bikes, they made their way on foot up the track. At a suitable spot they set about laying the charges, three of them, fifty feet apart and all under the same rail. For two hours they scraped away at the ballast with their bare hands and fighting knives, burying the explosives and connecting up the charges. They worked quietly and methodically, aware all the time that they might be surprised by a German patrol alerted by the sound of their exertions, but at last it was finished. Camouflaging the job, they retrieved their bicycles and set off back to base as fast as they could go.

Arriving there, they found that the maquis had already reported the result of the blow to Bill Fraser. Two engines had been completely wrecked, together with a forty-foot wagon loaded with AA guns. Ten other wagons had been derailed.

They also learned that Captain Bradford had been killed. With Sergeant White, Sergeant McGinn, a French mechanic and one of the maquis, they had set out in a jeep to contact DuVivier, deciding on the way to contact Captain Chevalier, *chef de maquis* in the area, who had some information for the SAS. Had it not been for this, things might have turned out differently.

Just after eight in the morning they passed through the village of Lucy, and turned right along a secondary road. They had not gone more than a hundred yards when they came face to face with a German officer and a sergeant. The officer, not realizing they were British, signalled them to halt.

For answer Sergeant White gave them a burst with his guns. Suddenly, round a bend fifteen yards further on, they came on a truck-load of Germans halted at the side of the road. The Germans immediately opened fire. Returning their fire, the jeep swept past only to realize, too late, that they were passing a stationary German convoy of considerable size.

It was too late to turn back. They decided to shoot their way out. They were now coming under heavy fire from the troops in the trucks and in the fields on either side of the road. Raking the trucks with fire, they raced on.

Roy Bradford had been wounded in the left arm and the mechanic killed. The situation was desperate but they could only carry on. They were passing the last truck of the convoy when a heavy burst of machine-gun fire hit the jeep, killing Roy and wounding Sergeant White and the maquisard.

They managed to get out of sight of the convoy before the jeep packed in. Hearing the Germans running down the road the three survivors, two of them wounded, made a dash for the woods, where they threw off their pursuers.

The 'Houndsworth' parties had received first-class co-operation during their operations from Maquis Camille with their headquarters at Chalaux. Although SAS parties made it a general rule not to link themselves too closely with maquis activities, there were times when common danger brought them together.

Such an occasion arose at the beginning of August. Word came that the Germans were planning an attack on the hide-out of Maquis Camille. The 'Houndsworth' base being in the valley just below Chalaux, Bill Fraser went to see Camille to work out a joint plan for the defence of the area. Their trump card was a 6-pounder gun which had been parachuted to the SAS.

On 1 August the gun was hauled into position by four oxen on a forward slope which commanded all the roads leading to Chalaux. With the gun crew went a Bren gun team. The maquisards moved into position at various points round them.

At nine o'clock on the morning of the 3rd, an enemy column was seen approaching along the road from St Martin to Chalaux. It halted, and the Germans, about two hundred of them, started to move up the road from Chalaux to the maquis HQ.

As soon as they deployed, one of the maquis posts opened fire. The main German body halted, but their forward elements carried on until they came under fire from a second maquis post. The first, now reinforced, poured a withering fire into the German ranks.

So far the Germans had not spotted the 6-pounder,

although the SAS Bren team with it was in action. They contented themselves with setting fire to one of the farms and concentrating their fire on the first maquis post.

Two staff cars were now seen approaching along the road to Chalaux. The 6-pounder fired one round at a range of a thousand yards, but missed. The cars, however, withdrew at high speed. Now a German machine-gun, with about fifteen men grouped around it, came into action. Three rounds at seven hundred yards silenced it.

Faced with this unexpected situation the enemy withdrew behind a stone wall for cover. Five shells at five-yard intervals demolished the wall. Two more rounds wiped out a second machine-gun post. The Germans started to retreat, not stopping until they were well out of range. The time was now half past twelve.

At two o'clock an enemy mortar came into position and fired one round. The 6-pounder replied with three rounds, the first one scoring a direct hit.

There was a lull now until five o'clock, when two more mortars took up positions behind a hillock where they could not be engaged by the gun. A machine-gun came into action in the open. The ruse was obvious. They hoped to draw the 6-pounder's fire so that the mortars could engage it. They were disappointed. The SAS Bren team moved downhill and forced them to withdraw.

An infantry attack by the Germans was more successful. The first maquis post was forced to give ground. The SAS gun team, finding themselves threatened by this new attack, removed the firing mechanism from the gun, camouflaged the gun, and withdrew into the maquis HQ at seven-thirty.

At eight-thirty the enemy broke off the attack and withdrew, taking with them their dead and wounded. Two hundred miles behind their own lines, a major German force had been driven off after killing only two maquis and wounding one. SAS casualties were nil.

Trooper Jemson was no different from any other member of the SAS – he was 'good material', and a product of SAS training. He was a member of a small party under Captain Wellstead which went out in the second week in July to blow up the railway line between Digoin and Paray le Monial.

The party reached the railway shortly after midnight and started to lay their charges. To the north they were protected by a wide canal and the river Bourbince. Ian Wellstead left Jemson with a Bren gun to safeguard their line of retreat across the double bridge.

Jemson took up his position in the ditch between the two bridges and to the west of the road. His orders were, if a German patrol should chance by, in no case to fire unless the Germans fired first. He settled down to wait. There was no moon and it was cold. From the direction of the railway he could hear the faint sounds of the rest of the party scraping away the ballast under the line.

Then, from the far side of the road he heard another sound. A platoon of Germans was approaching, one section down each side of the canal and one along the bank of the river. The Germans, too, had heard the sound from the railway. They proceeded to lay an ambush for the SAS saboteurs, taking up positions on both bridges. A Spandau machine-gun was brought into position in the ditch straight across from where Jemson lay, not more than four yards away.

Jemson lay quite quiet, hardly daring to breathe. Around him he could hear the restless movement of the waiting Germans. The long, cold minutes ticked by until, at last, the sounds from the railway track ceased. The SAS party, their job completed, started back towards the rendezvous.

As they approached the first bridge the Spandau opened up on them. Even as they fired, Jemson let fly with his Bren, wiping out the crew at point-blank range.

Rolling from the ditch, down the embankment and into the low ground between river and canal, Jemson now engaged the other German positions so successfully that the SAS party had time to get back to the railway and set off their charges before making good their escape.

For an hour and a half Jemson kept the fight going, moving from one position to another to confuse the enemy, who never for one moment realized that they were opposed by only one man. When he ran out of ammunition for his Bren he continued the fight with his Colt automatic.

Finally, when he considered that the main party had had sufficient time to get well clear, he stripped his Bren gun down into its component parts and threw them away to prevent the gun falling into German hands. A few parting shots from his Colt, and he plunged into the river Bourbince, making good his own escape.

Inevitably much of the work of SAS groups was of an intelligence nature. It was impossible to range so widely behind the German lines without amassing vital information about troop movements and dispositions. Where we were able to take direct offensive action ourselves we did so, and informed London in due course of the results. Where this was impossible we radioed London with the information, for their action. If the target was sufficiently tempting, the weather OK and no better target offered, the RAF obliged. This kind of co-operation never failed to impress our friends of the maquis.

It was often the 'routine' patrol that paid off in unexpectedness, as on the day when one of the 'Houndsworth' parties hit what was obviously an outer ring defence. The question that intrigued them was, what was being defended? Moving with great caution, they penetrated the outer ring successfully. The heavy inner defences clearly indicated a target of some importance, but they were not prepared for what they found – Rommel's headquarters! A message was flashed to London on the emergency schedule. From an airfield in southern England the RAF planes took off. Headquarters and defences were destroyed. Rommel escaped: he was not at home when the RAF called.

An important part of the Allied beach-head strategy had been the cutting of the bridges across the Seine. That this had been effectively done was in no doubt, yet large forces of Germans were getting across. It was an SAS group which solved the mystery. The Germans had built temporary bridges with their decks below the surface of the water, thus escaping the attention of Allied bombers. A short signal to London soon rectified this.

The movement of troops and munitions was vital to the German forces battling to hold the advancing Allies. They went to extraordinary lengths to hide these movements from the air, but they could not escape the eyes on the ground. John Tonkin, operating in the 'Loire bend' in the area of Poitiers, had blown each of the railway lines there several times. It was getting increasingly difficult for the Germans to keep up with the work of repairing them.

John tapped his map. 'We'll cut the line here, tonight.' He and his party arrived in the vicinity of the target in the late afternoon. They had decided to lie-up till dark in a nearby wood. Entering it cautiously they nearly ran full tilt into a German sentry. Going to ground they waited till he had passed, then crawled forward slowly to investigate. The Germans had run a spur line from the railway into the wood. John counted. In the clearing were eleven railway tankers – petrol! Or were they empty?

There was only one way to find out. They waited in

hiding until it was dark; then, quietly and painstakingly, John crawled down into the clearing until he reached the first tanker. So far so good. The sentry moved further away down the track. Cautiously John pulled himself beneath the tanker, and tapped. It was full. The sentry stopped. Had he heard? John kept quite still until he heard the man continue his pacing. Quickly he pulled himself from tanker to tanker. They were all full.

He waited until the sentry passed the end of his beat, returned and moved away again. Then he crawled quickly to where the rest of the party were lying ready to cover his withdrawal if necessary. As soon as they had put sufficient distance between them and the clearing a message flashed to London – target, map co-ordinates. They settled down to wait for dawn.

The skies lightened. Flying low out of the north-east came the RAF rocket-firing Typhoons – straight for the hidden petrol train. A roar and a sheet of flame. In minutes it was all over.

But things did not always go our way. Information could be wrong – and often was – and it could be too late. On 22 August the chance of a lifetime was missed. The Germans, their hold on France loosening, were smuggling Marshal Pétain out of the country. Overnight he stayed in Saulieu, not more than half an hour's drive away from the SAS base. But Pétain was one of the aces in the German pack. They had no intention of letting anyone trump that ace. The security black-out clamped down on Saulieu was so tight that it was twelve hours before the news could be smuggled out. When it did reach the SAS base, Bren groups were rushed at once in an effort to wrest him from the Germans, but he had gone.

21
Claudine

The sound of a jeep roaring into camp woke me with a start. Tony stirred.

'That you, Sergeant-Major Lilley?'

'Yes, sir . . . Lieutenant Goddard's dead.'

We both leapt to our feet. The sergeant-major lit a cigarette and puffed it slowly. With 'Monty' Goddard he had gone out that morning to pick up a jeep trailer that had been ditched the previous day. Everything had gone smoothly until they neared Tannay. There, coming round a bend at speed, they had run into a group of maquisards preparing an ambush.

'I don't know whether you remember, as we came down to "Houndsworth", a big white house on the side of a hill this side of Tannay – with trees round it?' The cigarette glowed brighter. 'That was their headquarters.'

They had had news that two truck-loads of Germans were on their way to attack them, and their eyes lit up when they saw the jeeps with their machine-guns. It did not take them long to see that the situation had miraculously changed in their favour.

Monty agreed to help. The jeeps would ambush the trucks from cover at the nearby cross-roads. The men of the maquis would take up positions on the hillside from where they could fire down on the Germans.

The plan settled, the two jeeps continued up the road to the bend before the cross-roads. There Monty halted them and went forward to reconnoitre on foot. He had hardly stepped out of view when he came running back at the double. He yanked the rear Vickers off one of the jeeps and disappeared again without a word. The sergeant-major went after him. At the bend he slowed, and worked his way forward till he could see round the curve in the road.

Sitting in the middle of the cross-roads was a German mobile 36-millimetre quick-firer. Monty was walking steadily towards it down the centre of the road, his Vickers at the ready. The Germans just stared, seemingly too surprised to do anything. Monty continued walking.

Ten yards separated him from the German gun crew. He opened up, firing from the hip. The Germans collapsed over their gun, wiped out by his first burst.

With the same deliberate calm he took a hand grenade from his belt and tossed it into the truck. He must have spotted the second quick-firer as he turned to walk away from the first, because he suddenly jerked up his Vickers just as it opened up on him.

He dived for the ditch and lay there while shells tore into the banking above, sending spurts of brown earth kicking into the air. The sergeant-major thought he had been hit but, a minute later, he jumped up and started to run back to the jeeps. The Germans opened up again, and got him before he could get to safety.

We had not interrupted while the sergeant-major was talking, but now Tony asked what had been in my own mind.

'What about the maquis?'

'Not a sign of them. Went off and left us to get on with it, the lousy so-and-sos. One of our jeeps was hit and we had to leave it behind.'

We sat there in silence for a while, the tips of our cigarettes glowing in the darkness. Monty had come to us with the reputation for being a first-class administrative officer. He joined the SAS to get away from that reputation. He wanted action. Now, in his first major action with us, he had been killed. Tony broke the silence.

'You had better take a patrol out again tomorrow, Sergeant-Major.'

'Yes, sir.'

'See what you can find out . . . the usual.'

'Yes, sir.'

He returned about noon. The maquis headquarters had been burnt out. Monty had been buried by the Resistance in Tannay cemetery alongside three men of the Resistance who had been shot by the Germans.

The following day Tony and I lunched with Camille at his maquis HQ above Chalaux. A Squadron were going home. They had found Camille's co-operation invaluable during their stay. We felt we could profitably continue that association. Camille was a short, stocky man with crisp, dark hair and horn-rimmed glasses, and with a fund of good humour. He also had things organized. He offered to run a telephone line from our camp to the 'underground' exchange, an offer we readily accepted.

However, the camp we were in was far from ideal. We were only two kilometres from Brassy. There were only two exits – one on to the Lormes–Brassy road and the other on to the Brassy–Chalaux road. The wood we were in was too small to manoeuvre in, should we be attacked. Its only advantage was the stream running through it.

Our uneasiness about the site of our camp was unexpectedly brought to a head by a message brought by one of the villagers. A force of three hundred Germans, at Molfrey, wanted to surrender. They had refused to surrender to the maquis, no doubt guessing what their fate would be. They would, however, surrender to the British. Tony sent Ted Badger off with two jeeps to see what he could do.

Ted shared the views of Tony and myself – that it was another wild-goose chase. Heaven knows, we went off on enough of them. Imagine his surprise, therefore, on arriving in Molfrey to find . . . three hundred Germans, more or less. Leaving the jeeps to cover him, Ted went forward slowly to parley with them under the protection of a near-white handkerchief tied to a stick. But the Germans, it seemed, had changed their minds. They didn't want to surrender. They wanted to fight.

Ted dropped to the ground as they opened fire. The jeeps returned it while he scrambled back to them. Six men against three hundred. They would be lucky to get out alive. He had a quick look round. Reasonable room to manoeuvre, that was something. A bullet ricocheted angrily off the forward gun mounting, to whine past his head. 'Back to cover.' He waved towards the trees behind and to the left. The jeeps went into reverse, guns hammering away.

Despite the odds, the volume of fire put up by the two jeeps was disconcerting the Germans. Under the withering hail of bullets their aim became erratic. Ted looked at the remaining magazines. If they could hold out until dark they would have a chance of breaking off the engagement.

'OK. Short bursts, and only when you see a worthwhile target. Otherwise, carbines.'

For over an hour they skirmished round, moving to new positions as the Germans threatened to encircle them and all the while watching anxiously the dwindling ammunition. It still wanted half an hour to dark when the firing stopped. Hands above their heads the Germans came forward – seventy-six in all. They were quickly disarmed and handed over to the local maquis with strict instructions that they were to be treated as prisoners of war.

Tony was well pleased with the night's work, but he voiced my own doubts. 'You know, I'm not at all happy about this camp, Harry. We're too near Brassy – and has it struck you, those Germans obviously knew we were here.'

We arranged our operations so that while half the patrols were out the remainder were available for the defence of the base. The following morning one of the out-patrols wirelessed back that a large German force had occupied Corbigny, not many miles away. Tony brought me the news.

'That settles it, Harry. We'll have to find another base. It looks as if the Germans are going to use the road through Brassy as an escape route, and we can't attack them from here. We're too near the road. If they do come through Brassy the odds are they'll push a flank guard up the road here. Then we've had it. I think you and I ought to make a recce for a new base tomorrow.'

That afternoon I went up to the A Squadron camp to get my hand dressed by Mike McCready, the MO. I also wanted to see Alec before he left to ask him to give my wife a message when he got back. It was dark when I returned. Through the trees I could see the red glow of the fire, with the HQ lads clustered round it. Tony looked up as I approached, and hurried over.

'We've got a visitor, Harry – an English girl. Says she's a British agent. Her name's Claudine.'

'Claudine?' I experienced a sudden shock of surprise. 'That's the girl Bob and I came across up at "Kipling" – Roger's courier.'

'You know her, then?'

'Know of her. What's she doing here?'

'Apparently she helped one of the A Squadron patrols and they brought her back.'

She was sitting on a fallen tree by the fire. Tony beckoned her over.

'I wonder if you'd mind going over the information you gave me earlier?'

'Not at all.' She fished a map out of the pocket of the battle-dress someone had lent her, and spread it out on the bonnet of the jeep.

'These and these' – she pointed with her finger – 'are the areas where the Resistance are now in control.' She traced a line across the map. 'This is the general line . . .'

The line ran north of our area. Tony asked a question.

'I wonder if you'd do something for us?'

'Certainly, if I can. What is it?'

'A German column is supposed to have halted at Corbigny. We'd like to know how long it is staying there, and which way it's headed.'

'Yes, I can do that for you. I'll have to get out of this battle-dress, though, and you'll have to lend me a bicycle.'

'A bicycle?' Tony thought for a moment. 'I think I can get you one from A Squadron.'

We were up at first light. Claudine had already left for Corbigny. We grabbed some breakfast before setting off to look for our new base. All morning and most of the afternoon we wandered through the woods between Brassy and Chalaux until at last we came upon a veritable network of hidden tracks overgrown with thickets and brambles. One of them led across a small stream. On the far side we found what we were looking for. Stopping only to make a quick allocation of areas to the various patrols, we headed back to camp. One thing was obvious. No one had been this way for years. We bulldozed our own tracks through the thick undergrowth, coming out shortly, much to our surprise, on A Squadron's dropping zone. Things could hardly have turned out better – a well-hidden base, plenty of fresh water and a good DZ close at hand.

We struck the valley road just below Chalaux and set off at speed for the camp.

Approaching the fork road just above the camp we

suddenly spotted one of the jeeps among the trees, guns trained on the road. We pulled up.

'What's wrong?'

'The Germans are in Brassy.'

Tony put his foot down hard. Two jeeps were covering the Brassy entrance to the base. Two more were at the Lormes entrance. The sergeant-major had made all the necessary preparations to blow up petrol and explosives dumps in case we had to pull out in a hurry. There was no question of moving before morning. Equipment would have to be loaded and ammunition and petrol ferried across to the new site. It would be the best part of a day's job.

Although we felt certain that the Germans were preparing a sweep of the area, we had no real evidence that they knew of our whereabouts. It seemed more likely that they were again after Camille. Tony ordered an all-night stand-to, although we were more worried about a dawn attack.

Cold and fatigue ate into us. Our eyes smarted with staring into the darkness. Minutes crept like leaden hours and dawn seemed an eternity away, but at last a slight breeze ruffled the topmost leaves of the trees about us. A pale flush spread across the sky from the east. A distant cock crowed shrilly. The flush of dawn merged into full daylight – and still no attack.

We began to move to our new base. As soon as the jeeps were loaded I took the first patrol over. From then on it was a shuttle service all morning with men and stores.

About two o'clock we got an urgent message from a Bren gun post covering the road from Brassy. Down in the village tanks were on the move. In less time than it takes to tell we had manhandled the 6-pounder, which A Squadron had handed over to us, into position pointing down the road. Tony and I stood by it until the last load of stores had gone. Then, hitching it to the jeep, we withdrew the Bren post and set off for our new base.

As we jolted through the forest there came the sound of firing behind us. The Germans, advancing up the road to the old camp, had run into one of Camille's ambushes. After half an hour they withdrew, taking their dead and wounded with them.

We had a parachutage that night. Besides the usual petrol, food and ammunition, we were expecting another officer – John Scott. We were a bit worried with the Germans so close but it was too late to cancel the drop. The first plane arrived over the DZ at 0200 hours. We lit the fires. Like a huge black bird the plane flew up the valley towards us. There was a sudden yell as a container came hurtling earthwards with its 'chute still closed. It hit the ground with a reverberating thud, and burst into flames not more than thirty yards from where Tony and I were standing. That was one lot of petrol we would not get.

The plane circled round and came in again. A lone figure floated away behind it, away towards the trees. Two or three of the men dashed over to where he had landed. They were searching around when a head popped up from a ditch.

'You on my side?' queried a voice hastily. It was John Scott.

A Squadron left for home next day. When John Tonkin's party had been repatriated during the first week in August, an SAS officer specially briefed in airfield preparation was dropped to them. Under his direction, and with the help of the local inhabitants, they got busy with jeeps and farm tackle levelling off a large field. Then a signal was sent to London. The following night two Hudsons landed on the airstrip they had built in German-occupied France. They were back in England for breakfast.

Now, however, the front was so fluid that it was decided to send A Squadron through to the American lines. They left in a fleet of civilian cars with two of our jeep patrols as escort.

Mike McCready, the medical officer, and Fraser McGlusky, the padre, stayed behind to carry on their work with us.

The padre's work was particularly noteworthy, being almost undoubtedly the first time a chaplain had carried on his ministry so far behind enemy lines. Services were held at each camp, at the men's request. Nearly everyone attended, gathering round the altar cloth with its Cross and embroidered regimental badge. The enemy were never too near to keep us from singing the familiar hymns, though their distance from camp limited the strength of the singing. In one camp a Confirmation class was held.

It suddenly occurred to me that we had had no news from Claudine. I mentioned it to Tony.

'Claudine? Sorry, Harry, I forgot to tell you. I checked up on her with London.'

'What on earth for?'

'Remember the Germans attacked our old camp just after we left? I thought it a bit suspicious, so soon after she had left us. London say they know of no British agent of that name.'

'You think she was working for the Gestapo?'

'Looks like it, doesn't it?'

Shortly after leaving us, the bicycle we had lent Claudine broke down. She finished the journey to Corbigny on foot, with no stockings and in wooden sandals. There she found three road blocks manned by Germans. She talked her way past the first two, but at the third she was pulled up by a German sergeant who asked her her business in Corbigny.

'My teeth hurt. I want to see a dentist,' she replied,

dreading lest she should be taken to a German army dentist who would soon find out that there was nothing wrong with her teeth.

'Wait there.' The sergeant disappeared into a nearby house. She wondered if she should make a dash for it. She had no papers of any description on her but, before she could make up her mind, he reappeared with something in his hand.

'Here you are. Take this. It'll help the pain.'

She took the proffered aspirins and thankfully made her way into Corbigny to get the information we wanted. She soon realized the information would be of no use to us and she dared not risk the journey back through the road blocks. So Tony and I were left to draw our wrong conclusions because someone in London had bungled.

Our operations from the new base were highly successful. Ambushes were laid. Troop movements and other intelligence were radioed back to London. We ranged further and further afield. Patrols were absent from base for days at a time. Had we had more powerful radios on the jeeps, we could have kept road-watching parties out all the time. As it was they had to return to base to report, wasting time and petrol, and letting other targets slip through their fingers.

We thought of using maquis road-watching parties but had had one or two unfortunate experiences with their 'information'. They sent us a report that some two hundred German tanks near Lormes, out of petrol and ammunition, wanted to surrender. We sent out a patrol at once. After Ted Badger's experience at Molfrey they proceeded with the utmost caution, which was as well. They found no tanks, but they did find Germans – waiting in ambush. A tree had been dragged across the road behind a bend and the SAS party came under heavy fire from automatic weapons. The leading jeep was hit and put out of action, its crew baling out and making good their escape, unharmed, in the second jeep.

We lost one other jeep, from Roy Close's patrol. Hearing that a German convoy was heading his way he at once put his two jeeps in ambush positions. He had not long to wait. Down the road came a line of trucks. As they came under his sights he gave the signal to fire. Several trucks were knocked out by the first few bursts, some fifteen Germans being caught in the cross-fire from the jeeps as they dashed for cover from the trucks.

Then, from a truck further down the road, came a veritable hail of fire as covers were ripped back to reveal machine-guns and a quick-firer. A direct hit on one of the jeeps by this 'Q-truck' convinced Roy that the time had come to be somewhere else. With no casualties, he returned to base.

We hit the Germans wherever we found them, but at this stage, the difficulty quite often was to find them. About the middle of September, Ted Badger and I took the HQ patrol out to Eschampes, overlooking the road leading to Saulieu. Seeing no sign of life, we went into the village where we were given a right royal welcome. We thought it kinder not to tell the villagers that we expected a convoy of four thousand SS troops to pass through that night. We had the information from another SAS area that they were headed our way.

Before dark we got the jeeps in position on the far side of the village where they could fire over a low stone wall at a range of about two hundred yards. But, with the exception of one false alarm when four stray horses came galloping down the road in the misty dawn, the night passed without incident.

We waited in our ambush positions all next morning till our SQMS, 'Grazzi' Shaw, developed a raging toothache. We called a halt to the war and decided we had to get him to a dentist. The nearest one was in Saulieu, we learned. Not knowing whether the Germans were there or not, we set out intending to smuggle him into a dentist's if necessary.

We approached the town with proper caution, nosing our way down the hill past the first few houses. Then Ted Badger let out a yell.

'Jeepers creepers, look at that!'

People were pouring out of the houses in their hundreds.

'This laddie here' – Ted jerked his head at the Frenchman sitting proudly on the bonnet of his jeep – 'says the Germans have just driven out of the other end of the town. They think we're chasing them.'

'Ask him if he knows a dentist.'

He gave the thumbs-up sign and, edging our way carefully through the jostling, cheering crowds, we pushed into the centre of town to pull up before the dentist's. 'Grazzi' dashed inside to renewed cheers. The dentist took one look and got to work.

It seemed that the whole town was crowded round our jeeps. The little street was packed tight with struggling, cheering humanity. The more adventurous climbed on to the jeeps to stand there swaying dangerously. Champagne appeared as if by magic. One man, waving a bottle high above his head, dashed into the dentist's surgery where 'Grazzi' had just spat out the offending tooth, and insisted that he wash his mouth out with champagne.

The whole town was crazy. We drove slowly round the streets thronged with cheering crowds and into the square where the tricolour was hoisted. Extremists in the crowd dragged out a number of girls accused of 'collaborating' with the Germans, intending to degrade them by shaving their heads, but we did not wait. With a last wave we left Saulieu and returned to base. When the French army

from the south arrived two days later they found the town
already liberated.

Unknown to us, Lieutenant Mycock's patrol had
already been in touch with this French army. Following a
successful attack on a convoy of four hundred Germans
in the Autun area, he got the shock of his life when he
ran slap into the French tanks. Happily, the mutual
surprise was such that there were no casualties on either
side, and he led the army in triumph into Autun.

That night he slept in a civilized bed. When he awoke
next morning it was to learn that a large German column
was advancing to re-take the town. He at once set off to
meet it, apparently with some idea of persuading its
commander to surrender.

He returned in triumph with three thousand prisoners,
his only casualty being one man shot through the thigh.
How he did it he would never divulge.

Lieutenant Oates, operating not far away in the Châtil-
lon area, had sat overlooking the road from Nevers to
Autun all night without seeing any movement and was
about to pull out when, at first light, a horse-drawn
column came down the road and halted right opposite his
ambush position. He waited patiently while the horses
were unhitched for watering, chuckling with malicious
glee at the antics of a portly German officer trying to
catch a horse that had broken away. He caught it at last.

The jeeps opened up, raking the column with tracer
and incendiaries. Fourteen of the wagons burst into
flames. Suddenly, to their surprise, the sides of two of the
wagons dropped down with a crash and concealed cannon-
guns came into action against them. From the rear of the
column German infantry skirmished up the hill towards
them. Oates decided to call it a day.

Flying weather in the Morvan was now rapidly deteriorating. Night after night we waited for a parachutage, but

no planes came. Short of petrol, patrols were forced to operate over an ever dwindling area. Except for small parties of up to a dozen men making their way across country, hiding in woods, there seemed to be no Germans within a radius of fifty miles of our base.

Then came a signal from London to contact General de Lattre de Tassigny, who was with the French army coming up from the south. I decided to take Roy and his patrol. We scrounged round and got enough petrol to take us on the first stage of our journey. Then started a wild chase across France, searching for the elusive general.

'He is in Autun.' We get there. 'He is not here. No, he is in Mâcon.' We try Mâcon. 'The general? No, no. He is in Dijon.'

It was in Dijon that we eventually ran him to earth. Scruffy and covered in dust, we marched up to the hotel that he had made his headquarters; Roy, myself and Corporal Barongelle of the French SAS. Barongelle acted as spokesman. To a French officer he explained: 'We have a mission to contact the general. Our instructions are from London, by radio.'

The officer led us up the wide curving staircase, along thickly carpeted corridors and into a waiting-room. He excused himself and in a few minutes returned with another officer.

'I am sorry but the general is busy in conference, but this officer will take you to our intelligence room.'

To him we explained that we had been ordered to co-ordinate our activities with the general's plan. He nodded. In the intelligence room all the maps and traces were put at our disposal. French and American troop dispositions were explained to us and the plan of campaign, including details of the imminent switch round of French and American troops in front of Belfort.

It did not take long to convince me that to operate in

the Belfort Gap would be a quick form of suicide. Whoever in London had dreamed up this crazy idea either had a touching faith in the invincibility of the SAS, or an abysmal ignorance of the progress of the fighting. I politely took my leave and counted myself well out of an impossible situation. Even had there been any opportunity of operating with this army I would not have risked a single life to do so. From beginning to end not one person asked us for any identification. For all they knew, we might have been German agents. The Germans were certainly nearer than the nearest British troops.

We arrived back at 'Houndsworth' to find that orders had been received not to chase the Germans any further afield – though how we could do that without any petrol was not explained – but we were to pull out to Cosne-sur-Loire to refit. We had not enough petrol even for that.

We did leave our forest hide-out, and camped on the DZ. I was sunning myself when Corporal Danger looked up from his radio.

'Message just through, sir. Would you mind helping me decode it?'

I started to read back the groups from the pad. Suddenly he interrupted. 'This is about a drop . . .' He had not got the words out before we heard the sound of approaching planes. Together we dashed on to the DZ with yellow smoke signals. The thick yellow smoke drifted across the DZ as the first plane flew in, dropping its containers. Eight of them, one after the other dropped their precious loads. When the last had gone I looked round at the gallons of petrol littered over the dropping zone, and nearly cried with frustration.

22

Odds Against

'Do you see what I see?' Ted Badger was staring incredulously over my shoulder.

I glanced round. An armoured car – an American one – was just driving into the garage yard. As it pulled up alongside the jeep we were working on a lieutenant stuck his head out of the turret. He had about a week's growth of straggly beard and his eyes were red and sore from lack of sleep.

'Say, captain, can you tell me where the Germans are around here?'

I stared back at him blankly. He gave a low, apologetic laugh. 'Sorry. Probably I should introduce myself. We're an advanced patrol of an American combat team. We were told there's a lot of Jerries round here.'

'Can I see your identification?'

'Sure.'

It seemed all right. I handed it back.

'Well, there's some the other side of the Loire, here – about thirty thousand of them.'

The lieutenant whistled. 'Thirty thousand! That's a lot of Germans. But you guys aren't even carrying pistols. How come?'

'They don't worry us. All they want to do is get back to the Fatherland. Of course, if they came over in a bunch we'd have had it. But they come over in dribs and drabs hoping we won't see them.' I grinned. 'If you'd come half an hour earlier you could have got some cigarettes from the YMCA van.'

This time he grinned.

'OK captain. Quit kidding. My leg don't stretch that far.'

'I'm not kidding. It gets through to us once a week. We generally give it an escort this side of Briare.'

He scratched his beard thoughtfully.

'OK, I'll give you best on that. Well, thanks for the information. Be seeing you.'

We had been in Cosne for two weeks now. It was a pleasant little town on the east bank of the Loire, and we had straightway moved in to a couple of hotels. Now, in the large garage we had requisitioned, we were busy overhauling the jeeps. They needed it after their months of jolting over forest tracks with two and three times their normal load. B Squadron, who had been operating inside the Loire bend, were concentrated at Briare a few miles to the north. The only people who had not moved into civilized surroundings were the patrols who had remained with Peter Davis when the rest of us had moved to 'Houndsworth'. They seemed quite happy in their forest camp outside St Amand.

They were only six miles away and, since I had had very little news of Peter, I went along to see him one evening for a yarn. I found the camp inches deep in mud.

'What on earth do you want to stick out here for, Pete?' I asked as I walked with him to his area. 'I'd have thought you would have had enough of the forest. And this mud!'

'The mud is a bit of a bind, but apart from that, we're very comfortable. Anyway we don't have to live on tinned rations like you. We get fresh meat and vegetables every day, with plenty of eggs and milk.'

'I see what you mean.' We walked over to his tent. The floor was covered with bracken. I squatted on the bottom of his sleeping-bag.

'What have you been doing since we pushed off to "Houndsworth"?'

'Well, we moved the "Kipling" base down here so that we could operate against the Loire bridges.'

'Any luck?'

'Oh, the usual. Ambushes, reporting troop movements. Our best do, though, was immediately after you left for "Houndsworth". I took three patrols out to operate against the La Charité–Clamecy road. One of the jeeps turned over on the way down and I left another with it for protection. That left me with only seven.

'We got into position about six o'clock that evening. I had five of the jeeps with me in a small wood about four kilometres west of Nannay. The other two, with the 3-inch mortars, I left in position about two miles away.

'We waited all night but nothing turned up. The mortar jeeps joined us about nine o'clock next morning and, as there was still no sign of Jerry, I decided to have a look at another road.

'We had just got the jeeps down on to the road when the head of a German convoy appeared round a bend about three hundred yards away. The leading vehicle was a saloon car with, immediately behind it, a section of infantry.

'Only two of the jeeps were in a position to fire, and they opened up. Jerry started firing back but couldn't hit us. I sent Sergeant Mitchell round the right flank with six men and I took six round the left. I got within thirty yards or so of the enemy section lying in the ditch. We were banging away at each other for five minutes or more, tossing grenades at each other like toffee apples.

'It didn't seem to be getting us anywhere, so I called up one of the jeeps to dash down the road spraying the ditches. Then we rushed them. Three of the Jerries were dead and three of them wounded. The rest of the column had withdrawn. They were still sniping but we searched the car and found a map case with orders in it.'

'Anything important?'

'According to these orders, the column was about three hundred and fifty strong, consisting of two infantry companies supported by a machine-gun section, an anti-tank section and a light ack-ack section.

'I told the wounded we were British and that we were the advanced guard of a large force. Then we left them and got into position again about two miles down the road, on a hill about three hundred yards from the road. I got the mortars sighted on to the road, left one jeep to cover our rear and the other four firing down the road.

'About midday we heard firing again and, shortly after, two Frenchmen cycled up and told us the Germans had fired on them. We waited there till a quarter past seven that evening, when a very big convoy came in sight. There were about thirty vehicles including five-ton lorries, civilian cars and scout cars. Three of the lorries were towing 20-millimetre cannon guns.'

'Just the job.'

'I didn't think so at the time. Anyway, they halted just below us, presumably to clear Nannay. That was just what I wanted. We knocked hell out of them for five minutes, firing about four thousand rounds of tracer and incendiary.

'But they were ready for us. They were firing back within fifteen seconds of our opening fire. Then three of the trucks dropped their sides and 20-millimetres came into action. They also started putting down a heavy concentration of light mortar fire. Things were humming, all right. They were out to make a job of it – or of us. German infantry were coming up the hill and I could see scout cars working round our flanks. I decided it was time I wasn't there, so we pulled back into the Forêt de Donzy.

'One scout car followed, but it didn't seem too anxious to come to grips and we lost it. The battle raged for an hour and a half after we'd left. They must have got through a devil of a lot of ammunition firing at nothing at all.'

'Any casualties?'

'Two jeeps knocked out. Corporal Connor was missing but he turned up two days later. The Germans had taken him prisoner. Fortunately a German mortar bomb landed near him and his two captors, and he took advantage of the confusion. He gave the chap who was holding him a hefty kick in the stomach and made a break for it.'

Peter stubbed out his cigarette and lit another.

'We got the full story later from the maquis and the FFI. Two hours after the Germans had withdrawn in the morning attack, they returned to the same spot and took up a defensive position with seven anti-tank guns. They also shot two civilians.

'After the evening attack two lorries and a car were burnt out, and fifteen vehicles had to be towed away. Three ambulances had to make several trips from La Charité for the dead and wounded.

'This second attack must have convinced them that the story we had told the wounded men in the morning was true, and that there really was a big British force approaching. They scrambled back to La Charité and started putting the town in a state of defence ready for the big attack, erecting barricades, setting up gun positions and siting anti-tank guns. But, by that time, we were back in camp having a late supper.'

It was only now that I heard the full story of what had happened to Captain Pat Garstin and his party.

There were twelve of them altogether due to drop near La Ferté-Alais. Arrangements were made with Special Forces to receive them. A message was sent out from the BBC, warning the reception committee to stand by for the night of 3–4 July. At the last minute the drop had to be cancelled, but it was then too late to warn the committee, who waited all night on the DZ. While they were there they heard the sound of automatic fire in the neighbourhood.

In response to another BBC message they returned to the dropping zone the next night. The first two men to arrive were fired upon and killed by the Germans who were waiting for them. The rest, realizing that something had gone wrong, returned home. What they did not know was that the Germans were in possession of the night's recognition letter.

At 0153 hours the plane arrived over the DZ, the recognition letter was flashed and the men began to drop. As they touched down the Germans, who had surrounded the DZ, opened fire with light automatic weapons. Of the twelve men, nine were taken prisoner and of these four were wounded. One man, realizing the Germans were there, and having been dropped wide of the DZ, managed to get away and contact the FFI.

The other two men landed in the trees close to the DZ. Together they made their way to the dropping zone, not realizing anything was amiss. As they reached the edge of the trees they heard Lieutenant Wiehe call out: 'Who's there?'

'Norman and Morrison.'

'Stay where you are. I've caught a packet . . . can't walk . . . can't even crawl.'

'Hold on a minute, we'll get you in.'

'No, you don't. Keep in those trees. They'd spot you straight away in this moonlight.' He paused for breath. 'Make for the beach-head . . . tell them what's happened . . . good luck.'

'OK, sir.' They gave the thumbs-up sign and disappeared into the wood. For twelve days they pushed on in a north-westerly direction, dodging German patrols and

convoys, occasionally getting food from friendly Frenchmen and women until they arrived one night at a farm
near St Chéron.

Here they were told that the Allies were near and they
were advised to remain in hiding in a nearby wood. A
couple of nights later the son of the house came to them.
He had promised to try and put them in contact with the
maquis, but instead, he had come to tell them that the
maquis were on the run. However, he promised to try
and put them in touch with 'someone else'.

The someone else proved to be the headmaster of one
of the schools in the district, who said he would do his
best to get them through the lines. Later he returned to
say he had got a message through to London by way of
Paris and that plans were almost complete to get them out
by air.

Norman and Morrison waited on tenterhooks for his
next visit, but days passed without any sign of him. Then
the son arrived with two young women who said they
were school-teachers. They spoke fluent English. The
headmaster, they explained, had made a foolish mistake.
The Gestapo had arrested him and he had been shot.

The people at the farm had supplied them with civilian
clothes as soon as they arrived there. Their uniforms they
had buried in the woods. The two school-teachers brought
them English books to read. They were reasonably safe,
they were assured.

They had been up to the farm for a meal and were
leaving to go back to their hide-out when in walked a
German officer. There was no escape. Morrison walked
right past him. Norman hurried across the farmyard and
industriously shooed the ducks away from the pond. The
officer ignored them, and they breathed again.

The next time they saw the two school-teachers was on
15 August when they turned up in a jeep. The Americans

had arrived. They dug up their uniforms and were back in England by 19 August.

The men who had been taken prisoner on the DZ were less fortunate. They were taken to Gestapo headquarters in Paris for 'forcible interrogation'. The Germans, apparently, were convinced that the party was the forerunner of a full-scale airborne landing. The interrogation having produced no results, the Germans kept them under lock and key in a converted Paris hotel. Then, on 8 August they were given civilian clothes and told they were going to be exchanged for some German agents detained by the British in London. The clothes were necessary for them to pass through neutral territory.

At one o'clock on the morning of the 9th they were bundled into a lorry and taken north to a wood near Beauvais. At six o'clock they were ordered out of the lorry and made to walk up a narrow path to a clearing in the wood. Suspecting the truth, Corporal Vaculik of the French SAS asked their escort if they were to be shot, and was told they were.

Pat Garstin managed to give them some last-minute whispered instructions. Then they were lined up. Facing them were two officers of the Gestapo with sub-machine-pistols at the ready. A third man, a Gestapo agent in plain clothes, read out the sentence. A sergeant translated into English.

'For having wished to work in collaboration with the French terrorists and thus to endanger the security of the German army, you are condemned to the penalty of death and will be shot.'

On hearing the word 'shot', the SAS men made a concerted dash for the woods. Corporal Vaculik managed to get clear, followed by the Gestapo, firing as they ran. Corporal Jones tripped and fell but the Gestapo men ran past him, probably taking him for dead. When he got to his feet again he saw four bodies lying on the ground, but had to get at once into the woods before the Germans returned.

Vaculik and Jones were put in touch with each other by the maquis some ten days later and made their way back to England.

At the end of the week Paddy Mayne arrived by air from England where he had been discussing our future plans. I had last seen him at 'Houndsworth' when he had asked us whether we wished to go home or take on a new job. We had unanimously plumped for a new job. And now here he was with our orders.

We were to spend the winter in Holland with the Second Army, each patrol being attached to a field security section. Our job was to do their 'strong arm' work, routing out wanted Nazis. In conception the job was an ideal one. As the army moved forward into the attack, our patrols were to dash forward ahead of the leading elements to seize wanted men or prevent important papers from being destroyed.

Passing through Brussels on the way to Holland, we had numerous requests from young Belgians who wanted to join us. We took on two of them. One blew himself up with a petrol cooker and promptly went to hospital. The other was named Martell and belonged to the famous wine and spirits firm of that name. As a result, we were very well off for brandy, and had so much champagne that, one morning, we opened a dozen bottles and shaved in it.

The Second Army spent the winter on the line of the Maas carrying out only local actions, and after the first fortnight we had little to do. During February we were moved to Antwerp to counter an expected German airborne attack on the port, which did not materialize.

In the first week in March we were ordered home.

23

In at the Death

'Telegram for you.' My wife looked hopeful. 'What is it – extension of leave?'

I handed it to her. 'No. Report back at once.'

It was dark when I reached Chelmsford camp. Tony was there. Peter had not yet arrived.

'What's it all about, Tony?'

'We're off to Germany.'

'When?'

'Day after tomorrow.'

'Jumping?'

'No, going by sea with the jeeps. And we've a lot of work to do before then, drawing kit, getting the jeeps ready. We'll probably be working most of tomorrow night.'

The MT section had been working at full pressure all through our leave, overhauling the jeeps, modifying armour and gun mountings. They worked all through the night to get them ready, and by the following evening the last one was finished.

We were organized into patrols of three jeeps, with one change in armament. Two of the jeeps, as usual, were armed with the twin Vickers K. But now the third mounted in front a big 'point five'. We worked late into the night by the lights of the jeeps, fixing the guns and filling the magazines.

So far, all we knew was that we were going to Germany. A and D Squadrons were already over there but we had no news of them. We were still in the dark when we left Chelmsford next morning for Tilbury. We sailed on the night tide for Ostend. On 7 April we set out in the jeeps for Germany. Through Holland, threading our way past columns of tanks, through Cleves and Emmerich, devastated and laid waste, along streets that picked their way through heaps of rubble and crumbling grey masonry, until on the afternoon of the 9th we arrived south of Meppen in north-west Germany.

We pulled off the road into a large wood and prepared to camp for the night. In a hollow in the centre of the wood we tried out the guns. We were to relieve an armoured car regiment, we heard. Paddy was to speak to us at five o'clock.

We squatted in a semi-circle round him, maps on our knees.

'We're just outside Meppen, as you know. The Canadians took the bridge there this morning. Tomorrow the Canadian 4th Armoured Division is going to push on to Oldenburg – that's about sixty miles away. We are to operate on its left flank. After we have reached Oldenburg, we will push up north to the Wilhelmshaven area and make a nuisance of ourselves. Now, is that clear?'

We nodded and he went on.

'As to details. We will operate in two columns – Tony's squadron across the bridge here, and Dick Bond's just to the south.' He gave us map references. 'The columns will converge and rendezvous at certain points before setting off again. Map references of these points . . .'

In the misty morning light of 10 April the long column of heavily-armed jeeps snaked out of the wood on to the road. Heavy-eyed tankmen of the Canadian 4th Armoured Division blinked incredulously as the tiny vehicles roared past the huge Shermans and across the bridge at Meppen.

This was not SAS work as we knew it, but it was a job of work. We were satisfied, if a little perturbed. Our 'mechanized mess tins' were poor substitutes for the armoured cars we were relieving.

My own troop headed the column with Stewart's patrol leading. As we approached the bridge over the first canal, Stewart signalled a halt. There was a sudden crackle of fire from the far side. The leading jeep replied, then came racing back. 'No use, Harry: the bridge is down. We'll have to try somewhere else.'

We turned round, found the road again and headed towards the next bridge. Same story. The bridge was down and the enemy had it covered. Before the morning mists had cleared we had probed again and again at the German defences, looking for a weak spot, but everywhere we turned we were faced by the Kusten canal – and our route lay on the far side.

As the sun came up above the trees, Paddy drove up.

'Tony, Dick Bond's got through further down the road. I'm going to put both squadrons through there.'

Within half an hour we had caught up with the other column. Together, blasting away at road blocks, we tore into the heart of German territory towards Borgerwald, across quickly improvised bridges, along the narrow dusty lanes. From Borgerwald down in the valley came the heavy and sustained fire of machine-guns. The radio crackled.

'We've hit trouble. Squadron commander killed. Leading section pinned down. Trying to get them out, but it looks sticky.'

My jeeps were pulled up at the side of the road, looking down on Borgerwald. The firing from the town increased as other B Squadron patrols, trying to outflank the German strongpoint, opened fire. The radio came to life again.

'Another man killed. Two wounded. Still trying to extricate.'

Down the road from the rear of the column came Paddy's jeep in a swirl of dust. Flat out, he flashed past and headed downhill straight for the heart of the trouble. Alone, sweeping past the strongpoint, he raked it with fire, turned and with guns still blazing swept back again, stopping only to lift the wounded men into his jeep.

A second and a third time he returned, unscathed in the face of withering fire, to rescue the survivors of the trapped section, and to recover the two bodies.

After a brief engagement at the next village sixty Germans, including young paratroopers, surrendered. We found a large dump of weapons, ammunition and explosives in a barn. Tony asked me to stay behind to clear the village and blow the dump. While two of the patrols cleared out the civilians and shooed away the cows, I searched in the back of my jeep for a Lewes bomb. I found one, but the coloured band which showed the length of the time delay had rubbed off. Placing it deep down in the dump I broke the pencil. I had hoped it was a ten minute delay but after ten minutes nothing happened so I pushed on. About twenty minutes later, as we were approaching Esterwegen, there came the sound of a heavy explosion, and a column of smoke and flame appeared above the trees behind us.

At Esterwegen we halted for a meal. There was a certain amount of sniping from the woods and Peter suddenly caught sight of one of the snipers round the corner of a building close by. Running forward with Sergeant Mitchell, he called on the German to come out. Both held their carbines at the ready. The German did come out, but not with his hands up. While they watched him he raised his pistol slowly and fired twice, hitting Peter in the shoulder before making his escape.

After travelling all afternoon across country, Paddy decided to halt for the night and sent me on ahead to find a suitable laager for the vehicles. The jeeps were moving into position when one of them went tearing down the road, its 'point five' thumping away. It was Paddy. He had spotted movement in the ditches about two hundred yards away and went bald-headed for the Germans lurking there. They were a cycle patrol armed with anti-tank bazookas. Two of them were dying, two escaped and the rest were taken prisoner.

As the sun went down on our first day in Germany, pillars of smoke from burning houses rose into the still air, while, all along the axis of our advance, the white flags of surrender drooped from windows and trees. Over to the right thundered the guns of the Canadian armour, and answering pillars of smoke darkened the sky.

All next morning we pushed on, clearing villages and taking more prisoners, not without a good deal of determined opposition from youngsters of fifteen and sixteen, hurriedly drafted into the army to die for their Führer.

Shortly after noon Tony sent for me. 'Look, Harry. B Squadron is in this village here, and they're having some trouble. They've got part way into the village but there the Germans are holding them. It seems to be deadlock.

'Now if you look here,' – he indicated the map – 'you'll see a small track leading down parallel to the main road of the village and just east of it. I want you to take your troop down there and engage the village from the flank. Is that quite clear?'

'Quite.'

'OK, then. Keep in touch by radio. I'll be listening out.'

The track was about three hundred yards from the village and completely open. There was the sound of desultory firing from the village. Cautiously I led my twelve jeeps down the track. The firing stopped. I halted and had a good look at the village through my glasses.

There was nothing to tell me where B Squadron finished and the Germans began. I called Tony and reported.

'You had better come back, Harry, and discuss it. Leave the jeeps there.'

When I got back I explained the situation as well as I could and Tony decided to come back with me. We pulled up at the rear of the troop. As we did there came the crash of an exploding mortar bomb. I jerked round. The earth mushroomed up not forty yards away. With a yell of warning to the rest of the troop we dived for the cover of the ditch. There was two to three feet of dirty water in it, but it was cover and with machine-guns there was nothing we could do against mortars.

The men of the other patrols had followed us into the ditch. Only the first two jeeps had had time to get away round a bend in the road. As we crouched there a heavy concentration of bombs plastered the track, deafening us with the concussion. Had we stayed on the jeeps our casualties must have been nearly a hundred per cent.

I glanced at Tony. 'We can't stay here,' I whispered. 'They're going to follow this up with an infantry attack.'

'You're right. See if you can get a pair of guns down off one of the jeeps.'

I waited for the next salvo of bombs to fall, then scrambled up the bank of the ditch. I was reaching for the guns when I heard the plop, plop, plop of the mortars in the distance. I slid back again. With the help of one of the lads I got a pair of guns at the second attempt. I propped them up on top of the ditch and glanced down the sights.

'No good, Tony,' I called out. 'We've no field of fire. They'd be on us before we could do anything. I think we'd better work our way up the ditch and cover the jeeps from a flank with our carbines.'

'OK. Pass the word down.'

Heads down, in single file we started to make our laborious way up the ditch. The water was filling my parachute jacket, threatening to drag me down. We wormed our way through culverts, our noses barely above the filthy water. The dead weight of our clothes made it tiring work. The man ahead of me stopped and sank back into the water. Two of us got him up again.

The mortar bombs were still falling but they were behind us now. The man who had gone under earlier stopped again. 'It's no use. I can't go any further,' he panted.

We were all whacked. Tony called a halt. I crawled over to him. 'I'm going to push on, Tony, and try and get Peter's troop up to us. It's about our only chance of getting out.'

How far I crawled after that I do not know, nor how long it took me, but I was suddenly faced with a blocked culvert. There was nothing for it but to wriggle over the top. A machine-gun chattered into life somewhere, but nothing came my way. I flopped down into the ditch on the other side and lay there getting back my breath. A sniper's bullet smacked into the mud inches from my head, and from behind. I wasted no more time in resting.

Where the devil was I? I raised my head cautiously to peer out of the ditch. What I saw sent me ducking back quickly. Peter's jeeps were coming down the track, and I had no desire to be shot by them. I snatched off my beret, put it on the end of my carbine, and waved it frantically above my head. The jeeps stopped. I heard Peter call out. I crawled from the ditch and ran towards him.

He had summed up the situation, and spotted the Germans. With his 'point fives' he started to blast hell out of the village while his other jeeps moved forward under cover from their fire to pick up the rest of the men. The

Germans were now returning the fire. With men clinging to the jeeps like limpets we pulled out.

It was Oates who had got clear with the two leading jeeps when the mortars first opened up. He now turned up at the cross-roads with news of a concealed approach to the abandoned jeeps. I went back with him to see how many we could retrieve. We found them pitted with mortar fragments. Of the twelve, two had been taken away by the Germans and seven knocked out by the mortars, but our casualties were nil.

Towing the damaged jeeps we carried on to the first rendezvous with B Squadron. There, in a large wood, we prepared to laager for the night. We had advanced about thirty miles since leaving Meppen the previous morning, but apart from the sound of the guns, there was no sign of the Canadian armour.

We started to brew up when, out of the gloom, came two jeeps flying large white flags. Captain Iredale had been badly wounded and the RE officer, Edwards, had taken him to the nearest hospital, which happened to be German. Now they brought disturbing news. They thought they had been followed back. Immediately Paddy gave orders to move deeper into the woods. We quickly packed up the jeeps again and moved off. As the last jeep left the clearing the first mortar bomb fell with a crash.

We knew from what Edwards had said that there were tanks and German 'eighty-eights' in the area. Petrol was low, many of the jeeps had been hit and were on tow, and we were carrying more than a hundred prisoners. In complete darkness now, we pushed deeper into the woods to spend an uneasy night waiting for the dawn. The prisoners, who outnumbered us, were put in the centre of the clearing round which we were laagered, covered by two Brens. All through the night we could hear the thunder of guns and the whine and crash of mortar bombs.

The Germans were searching the forest. How long before they found us?

At first light, a patrol of three jeeps under Lieutenant Surrey-Dane was sent out to try to contact the Canadians. The rest of us waited. I got busy bringing my diary up to date.

German machine-guns opened up even as the sentry shouted his warning. Bullets ripped through the trees and whined angrily across the clearing. The battle was on. All the firing was coming from the far side where Peter's jeeps were. He at once returned the fire, blazing away into the woods at the unseen enemy. We on our side were unable to fire for fear of hitting our own men.

Without waiting for orders, five Bren gunners got up and walked slowly into the woods to search out the hidden Germans. With them, armed only with a camera, went Paddy Mayne. Hidden in the undergrowth, the Germans had all the advantages. Slowly the Bren gunners were forced to give ground.

During this time the German prisoners had been lying out in the open. Now the senior German officer asked if they might be allowed to withdraw into the low ground behind us. Receiving an assurance that no one would attempt to escape, Paddy agreed.

They wormed their way back and began to dig fox-holes with hands and feet as they lay there. One of them took a book from his pack and began to read. He looked up from his book once only – to warn us to watch our right flank.

A tracked vehicle came crashing through the trees. The firing faltered and stopped. Down the ride and into the clearing raced a flame-throwing tank with an escort of carriers. The Canadians had arrived. As we left the forest, a long line of Shermans advanced in line abreast across the fields in pursuit of the German Army. The end was near.

We returned to Lorup, with casualties in men and jeeps. We reorganized and refitted. It was here that we first heard of the other two squadrons operating further to the east. Working closely with tanks and armoured cars they had been in nine actions, killing just under two hundred, capturing two hundred and thirty-three.

In our own sector it was evident from the nature of the country, the stubborn resistance of the German para-troops, and the cratering of roads and bridges, that no great penetration was possible. It was decided to move over to the right flank of the Canadians and work with their armoured reconnaissance.

For ten days we fought our way forward with them from Vrees towards Garrel, probing defences, mopping up strongpoints. On 23 April we were placed under command of an independent armoured brigade which was to try again to break through in the vicinity of Oldenburg.

We were still operating in this way when, on 4 May, came news of the end of hostilities in Europe. But it was left to Tony to play the trump card. He interrupted the celebrations to read out a signal he had received from London.

'All squadrons will concentrate at Poperinghe for return to England.'

Appendices

A
Summary of Operational Results of 1st SAS; France, June to September 1944

Personnel

Enemy killed	330
Enemy killed or wounded	430
Enemy POW	232
Enemy POW negotiated and later captured	3,000

Communications

Trains derailed or destroyed	17
Railway trucks destroyed	40
Railway lines cut	43
Important telephone lines cut	8
Power lines damaged	1
Bridges blown	5
Roads blocked	2

Military Vehicles

Staff cars destroyed	5
Armoured cars knocked out	3
Lorries destroyed	84
Motor cycles knocked out	2
Motor transport captured	12
Horse transport knocked out	14
Guns destroyed	1
Aircraft shot down	1 and 1 probable

Miscellaneous

Synthetic refinery mortared twice
Goods yard destroyed
Railway turntable destroyed
Gasoline factory demolished
2,000–3,000 maquis armed
16 Allied aircrew rescued
12 enemy airfields reconnoitred
Field-Marshal Rommel's Tactical HQ twice located

Targets given to RAF and bombed

11 petrol trains
12 ammunition dumps
1 flying-bomb site
1 enemy division on move
2 enemy aerodromes
1 SS barracks (300 SS killed)
1 radio station

B
Order of the Day

Letter from General Eisenhower to
Brigadier McLeod, SAS Brigade

Dear McLeod,

I wish to send my congratulations to all ranks of the Special Air Service Brigade on the contribution which they have made to the success of the Allied Expeditionary Force.

The ruthlessness with which the enemy have attacked Special Air Service troops has been an indication of the injury which you were able to cause to the German armed forces both by your own efforts and by the information which you gave of German dispositions and movements.

Many Special Air Service troops are still behind enemy lines; others are being reformed for new tasks. To all of them I say, 'Well done, and good luck.'

Yours sincerely,

(signed) Dwight D. Eisenhower

8 October, 1944

C

Broadcast by Lieutenant-General F. A. M. Browning, CB, DSO, to SAS Troops Behind the German Lines, 1900 Hours, 8 September 1944

Now that the story of your operations and exploits since D-day is becoming known and confirmed, I am speaking to you this evening in order to tell you what Field Marshal Montgomery and the commanders in the field feel about your activities.

I saw the Commander-in-Chief yesterday and told him I would be speaking to you today. He proposes to send you a personal message, and in the meantime, I am going to tell you what views are held about your efforts.

It is considered that the operations you have carried out have had more effect in hastening the disintegration of the German Seventh and Fifth Armies than any other single effort in the Army. Considering the numbers involved, you have done a job of work which has had a most telling effect on the enemy and which, I fully believe, no other troops in the world could have done.

I know the strain has been great because operating as you do entails the most constant vigilance and cunning which no other troops are called upon to display.

I personally have kept in the closest touch with all your activities and have attempted to direct them as a result of the information the Armies and you have supplied so that, firstly, you were given fair, reasonable, but vital tasks, and at the same time those tasks were designed to have the most effect against the German Armies as a whole.

To say that you have done your job well is to put it mildly. You have done magnificently. There is still a lot of clearing up to be done, and in this you are pulling more than your full weight.

You will get Field Marshal Montgomery's message shortly, but in the meantime I want you to know how we and the rest of the Army feel about you. In this short talk I hope I have made that abundantly clear to you all.

Good fortune and good hunting.

Index